Research Methods for Cultural Studies

RESEARCH METHODS FOR THE ARTS AND HUMANITIES

Published Titles

Research Methods for English Studies
Edited by Gabrielle Griffin

Research Methods for Law
Edited by Mike McConville and Wing Hong Chui

Forthcoming Titles

Textual Editing in English Studies
Research Methods for History
Research Methods for Practice-based Research
Research Methods for Film Studies
Research Methods for Linguistics
Research Methods in Theatre Studies
Research Methods for Geography
Resarch Methods for Education

Advisory Board

Professor Geoffrey Crossick, Chief Executive, AHRB

Professor Warwick Gould, Director, Institute of English Studies, London

Professor David Bradby, Theatre Studies, Royal Holloway, London

Professor Angela McRobbie, Media and Communication Studies, Goldsmith's College, London

Professor Robert Morris, History, Edinburgh University

Professor Harold Short, Director of the Centre for Computing in the Humanities (CCH) at King's College London

Research Methods for Cultural Studies

Edited by Michael Pickering

Edinburgh University Press

© in this edition, Edinburgh University Press, 2008
© in the individual contributions is retained by the authors
Reprinted 2009

Edinburgh University Press Ltd
22 George Square, Edinburgh

Typeset in 11/13 Ehrhardt by
Servis Filmsetting Ltd, Manchester, and
printed and bound in Great Britain by
Cromwell Press Group, Trowbridge, Wilts

A CIP record for this book is available from the British Library

ISBN 978 0 7486 2577 2 (hardback)
ISBN 978 0 7486 2578 9 (paperback)

The right of the contributors
to be identified as authors of this work
has been asserted in accordance with
the Copyright, Designs and Patents Act 1988.

Contents

List of Figures

Introduction

Michael Pickering

BRINGING METHODS INTO THE MIX

There has long been a reluctance to bring any explicit discussion of methods and methodology into cultural studies. This can be explained in various ways. We can see it first of all as connected with the field's renegade character, and its conscious dissociation from established academic disciplines. Developing and adhering to a particular set of methods was considered to be characteristic of those disciplines and somehow compromised by an unexamined notion of empirical enquiry. Cultural studies has preferred to borrow techniques and methods from established disciplines without subscribing to any disciplinary credentials itself. Empirical enquiry has been treated with suspicion or regarded as woefully insufficient in itself, primarily because of the emphasis in cultural studies on fully conceptualising a topic of enquiry and locating it within a more general theoretical problematic. Along with a heavy reliance on textual analysis of one kind or another, applying techniques of close reading to a broad range of cultural phenomena, cultural studies has been distinguished as a field of study by the ways it has engaged with theory and sought to apply it, rather than by its adoption or development of practical methods.

The influence of theoretical issues and preoccupations has gone hand in hand with an inclination to ask critical questions about the rules of asking questions, with codified procedures and the prescription of set methods seeming to inhibit the free play of critique. By defining its practice as operating in opposition to disciplinary boundaries and controls, such procedures and methods have been regarded as imposing constraints on intellectual enquiry, particularly where this is dealing with the politics of culture or with the reproduction of relations of power in particular cultural texts or practices. Academic boundaries and prescribed methods have at times been associated with such reproduction, perhaps especially in relation to male control of intellectual agendas and priorities. There has even been a suspicion that particular methods inevitably impart legitimacy to the interpretations made of what is studied, or determine assessment of the truth or falsity of statements.

There is nothing inevitable about this. It depends on who is handling and applying them, as does what is accomplished more broadly in particular academic disciplines. Rigid adherence to the regulative proprieties of academic disciplines can of course lead to intellectually hide-bound ways of thinking, but this is not in itself an argument against disciplines as relatively autonomous domains of enquiry and practice. Particular established disciplines like sociology or anthropology provide generative frameworks for gathering data or conducting analysis, but this does not mean that relevant ideas and approaches from elsewhere are intellectually out of bounds. There have in any case been various developments in established disciplines that bring them relatively close to the interdisciplinary field of cultural studies. Key examples are cultural history, the sociology of culture, cultural geography, symbolic anthropology and the new historicism in literary studies. In the light of such developments, associating disciplinarity with being necessarily agnostic in relation to questions of power, even as being intellectually authoritarian, carries little credibility. Following certain methodological rules or procedures is obviously not incompatible with searching analysis or critique.

For one reason or another, cultural studies has been lax in thinking about methods, and so failed to engage in any breadth with questions of methodological limit, effectiveness and scope in cultural enquiry and analysis. In teaching within the field over the past twenty-five years and more, I have often been asked by students where they can go to learn about how to do cultural studies. I have explained in various ways why it is not possible to locate such a source and why thinking of cultural studies as driven by a definite series of methods and techniques is inappropriate. I have also grown increasingly dissatisfied with my own answers to this question. It has seemed to me to involve collusion with, even endorsement of, the lack of formal discussion and awareness of methods and methodological issues and problems. For this reason, the question of methods has risen on my own agenda as an external examiner in cultural studies in various UK universities. I have become increasingly convinced of the need for course teams in cultural studies teaching to begin addressing this question in a formal and full-blooded way. Methods are undoubtedly a missing dimension in cultural studies.

Even a cursory glance at the many cultural studies textbooks available shows that few cover research methods, certainly not in any depth. Of course, a few chapters or books that have recently appeared are exceptions proving the rule, but the bias is still to cultural theory, with methodological issues only dealt with from a critical theoretical perspective, if at all. It is one thing to engage in methodological debates, but quite another to offer sustained reflection, example and guidance on the actual practice of research in cultural studies. This is what is missing from cultural studies, regardless of where it is practised. The question of methods is largely neglected, with research on audiences and fans being the only area of cultural studies work where they may surface. Against the emphasis placed on textual analysis, the dearth of fieldwork-based empirical research and the lack of methodological development and discussion are clearly apparent. These biases and areas of neglect are partly to do with underfunding in higher education, at least in the UK, and partly to do with the derivation of the field of cultural studies from the humanities, particularly literary studies. Yet cultural studies has also drawn on the social sciences and has clear affinities with social science disciplines, particularly sociology. The neglect of methods in cultural studies seems more and more to be surrounded by evasion and excuses. It is now clear that the field can no longer continue with an ad hoc approach to the techniques and strategies of actually doing cultural analysis. It can no longer avoid the question of methods.

Failure to address methods as a core concern not only prevents the field from becoming more clearly defined. There are also practical reasons why this omission must be redressed. It is increasingly a pedagogical requirement of funding bodies around the world that postgraduate students are offered training in research methods. Any new Masters programme in cultural analysis would now look odd if it did not build such training into its curriculum. The importance of this is not confined to students on such programmes, for increasingly students are moving on from taught Masters programmes to doctoral research. Very few students today embark on MPhil/PhD research without some prior knowledge and expertise in research methods. The need for such knowledge and expertise is not confined to postgraduate level; many undergraduate courses in cultural as well as media and communication studies require students to undertake a research project, usually in their third year, as a culminating point of their work in these fields. It is no longer sufficient to fall back on some generalised notion of 'ways of reading' as the means for undertaking the sustained enquiry and analysis that such projects involve. The same applies to loose sets of procedures for doing ethnography. Cultural studies must now develop research training and start thinking about research methods in a more sustained manner. That is the purpose of this book. The intention is to help facilitate this process and establish methods training as an integral component of the field.

The methods presented and the methodological discussions dealt with in this book are meant to enable research work within cultural studies by providing helpful frameworks and clear outlines of practice. They are transferable to similar work elsewhere and are designed to help break down further the false dichotomy between humanities and social science disciplines. These disciplines obviously have distinct and circumscribed concerns as specific domains of critical enquiry and investigation, but are now characterised just as much by the degree to which they draw on their neighbours and are informed by a range of different perspectives. Academic disciplines in the humanities and social sciences have, in other words, become increasingly interdisciplinary. For this reason the relevance of this book across the humanities and social sciences is very broad indeed, even if the principal intended readership remains those working in cultural studies or immediately adjacent and overlapping fields.

The general purpose of this book is twofold. The first is to offer a set of explanations, frameworks and guidelines for doing research in cultural studies. The book covers various research methods and techniques, and discusses various sources and resources upon which students may draw. Its general philosophy is pluralist in that it advocates using mixed methods, taking an eclectic approach to research topics rather than confining research activity to any single avenue of investigation. The virtue of this is that the strengths of one method may help overcome the limitations of another, while using two or more methods in any specific research project will help to build up a richer data set. The second purpose of the book is to offer an intervention in the field of cultural studies, addressing both students *and* researchers within the field more generally. The intention here is to move beyond the limited position of carping and cavilling at the methodological weaknesses of other disciplines, and to help avoid the situation when work is regarded as adequate if it simply extrapolates from a given body of theory and chooses its evidence where this becomes appropriate. We need instead to begin setting out a specific methods stall in cultural studies itself. In this respect it is hoped that the book will help to define the methodological characteristics and approaches to doing cultural studies research that are relatively distinct to the field, or at least contribute as an ensemble to giving a clearer sense of definition and direction to what the field is about as a specific area of interdisciplinary research. It is this twofold purpose of the book that makes it special and significant as a contribution to the field.

The book can be seen as a response to Angela McRobbie's call for a return to sociological questions in cultural studies, and more specifically to what she calls the three Es: the empirical, the ethnographic and the experiential. While ethnographic methods are included in the book, figuring centrally in two of the chapters, it also covers other methods of empirical investigation, such as qualitative in-depth interviews and focus groups. The emphasis placed by McRobbie on lived experience is also present, with the opening chapter of the book endorsing her identification of this as a form of investigation as well as a range of resources for, firstly, charting 'empirical changes in culture and society on living human subjects' and, secondly, inviting 'these same human subjects . . . to reflect on how they live through and make sense of such changes' (McRobbie 1997: 170). Despite the intervening ten years, the response to McRobbie's call for work in the three Es has been very meagre. It is time to make amends for this.

This book does not set out to do that by prescribing a fixed list of methods that should be rigidly followed. Methods are guidelines for practice, and researchers should feel free to adopt them to suit their purposes. The editorial line I have tried to establish is for putting imagination into practice via a set of identifiable procedures and reliable methods and, where investigation demands, re-imagining methods in the interests of modes of research and analysis which are at once more challenging and more nuanced. If, at the same time, we can move to research and analysis in cultural studies that grows more evidence-sensitive and less theoretically presumptuous, more participant-oriented and less neurotic about its own epistemological standing, then we shall have helped the field to progress. Cultural theory is important for a whole host of reasons, but the purpose of research is not confined to constructing and refining theoretical models and templates. And while theory may shape conceptions and direct us to some key questions, analysis should not be driven by it. None of this is meant to detract from continuing to see culture acting as the symbolic sites of social power. Culture is of course more than this, but the key emphasis on power remains distinctive to cultural studies. The point of the book is quite different. It is based on the clear need to develop cultural studies, much more than has been the case so far, as a field of empirical enquiry that draws on a distinct set of investigative procedures. The book defines and outlines these procedures, though without claiming to be comprehensive or all-embracing. The aim is to shift the balance in cultural studies from the epistemological to the empirical, not in order to curtail the former, but rather to make the field more practically based in the generation, presentation and analysis of its always vital evidence.

OUTLINE OF THE BOOK

The book is divided into five distinct sections. We start with an application of culture in the widest sense as referring to how we experience and make sense of the particular social worlds in which we participate and are integrally a part of at any specific stage in our lives. There is of course no single, absolute definition of cultural studies that covers all aspects of its research practice and theoretical orientation, but attending to experience via the social relations in which it occurs and the cultural forms through which these are understood is of major importance to what is investigated within the field. That is why the book begins with a section focusing on the lived experience of individuals and social groups, and the centrality of narrative in making sense and meaning of this experience.

Experience has always been a key term in cultural studies. It has informed research practice, data generation and modes of analysis within the field. It has been considered a primary resource, providing evidence of and giving insight into everyday cultures, past and present. At the same time, as a cultural category and a critical tool, it has been subject to trenchant criticism, particularly at the hands of poststructuralists and those writing from related theoretical positions. In the first chapter, I argue for the continuing importance of the concept of experience in cultural studies. This arises out of the tensions and conflicts over what is made of experience in our understanding of the social world. The concept is approached through its dual qualities, such as those of proximity and distance, and situated and mediated participation. Various examples of these are discussed throughout the chapter. For me, the greatest significance of experience in cultural analysis is as an intermediary category coming between ways of being and ways of knowing. This connects with how it is discussed methodologically. Experience is the ground on which researcher and researched come together in some way across the rifts and gulfs between their life histories. The chapter discusses how this ground may be approached and how it affects the research relation. It is a recurrent theme throughout the book.

Stories are central to the ways in which people make sense of their experience and interpret the social world. In everyday life and popular culture, we are continually engaged in narratives of one kind or another. They fill our days and form our lives. They link us together socially and allow us to bring past and present into relative coherence. In the second chapter, Steph Lawler examines the importance of narrative for cultural studies research. Her concern is twofold. Firstly, she addresses the ways in which stories circulate socially as cultural resources, how they operate in our everyday lives as organising devices through which we interpret and constitute the world. Secondly, she is concerned with how researchers can approach and themselves interpret these narratives. Beginning with a definition of narrative as consisting of the three elements of characters, action and plot, she builds up a general case that shows the major strengths of narrative as a critical tool and analytical method. She then turns to consideration of a particularly tricky problem – the truth status of narratives. Does it matter whether narratives about the social world are true in the sense that they refer, in however mediated a manner, to an empirical world 'out there'? Are narrative truths local and contingent, rather than universal and absolute? In what ways are truth claims politically significant? To engage with some of the complexities of these questions, Lawler uses the example of *Fragments*, a narrative account of Holocaust survival, written by Binjamin Wilkormirski, which was subsequently revealed as a false memoir. The extent to which it matters that *Fragments* is false depends on a central question of narrative research – what can narratives do? The chapter concludes by outlining different ways of reading narratives, and different stages in the production of narrative and the meanings that can be made of it.

The second section of the book deals with research into two major, interdependent dimensions of contemporary cultural life. These cover the processes of making cultural products in the cultural industries, and of consuming and assimilating these products by audiences and fans. In the third chapter, Aeron Davis looks at three methodological approaches to researching cultural production, which he categorises as political economy, textual analysis and sociological/ethnographic work. The last of these is given greatest consideration, focusing particularly on the practical issues it raises. Davis regards the sociological investigation of cultural production as perhaps the most difficult, but also the most rewarding, not least because it involves looking first-hand at the practices and conventions that are involved in cultural production. The three approaches outlined are not of course mutually exclusive, but can be used in combination. Where this is possible, it would obviously be preferable to adopting only one specific line of methods, for the three approaches have different strengths and together can compensate for each others' weaknesses. Throughout the chapter, Davis draws on his own experience, particularly in researching news production as a social and cultural process. He focuses on such practical issues as research aims and objectives in interviewing, interviewee selection, making contact, preparation for interviews, conducting interviews, and post-interview activities and relations.

In the fourth chapter, Anneke Meyer examines ways of investigating consumption and cultural consumers. Culture and consumption are so deeply intertwined that consumption has to be seen as a form of culture, a cultural practice. It includes media consumption but also exceeds it, as for instance in the more general relation of consumption to everyday life and lifestyles. In her chapter, Meyer takes two case studies as illustrative of ways of investigating cultural consumers. The first of these involves her own research on readers' consumption of newspaper discourses on paedophilia and the ways this affects their understandings of the issue (see Meyer 2007). The second is Wendy Simonds's research on female consumers of self-help literature and how this literature is bound up with gender identity. The chapter outlines two research methods which can be used to design and carry out research on cultural consumption. These are face-to-face interviews and focus groups. Both research methods are qualitative and promise to produce in-depth understanding of the processes of consumption and their consequences by directly involving and listening to research subjects. Meyer discusses their respective advantages and difficulties, practical as well as theoretical, and locates these in the dynamics between research contexts and methods. Particular challenges and problems are framed within the relationships between media and consumer discourses, and the overall complexities reflected in the terminological shift from 'audience' to 'cultural consumer'. Cultural consumption is diffuse and involves multiple practices and sites, discourses move and intersect across cultural sites, and the lines between production and consumption are increasingly blurred as everyday cultural consumers may also be cultural producers of one kind or another. Meyer examines what these complexities mean for researching cultural consumers, and offers practical guidance in conducting interviews and focus groups by breaking these research processes down into a set of clearly delineated key stages.

The third section of the book extends concern with qualitative methods to methods concerned with quantification. The section considers quantitative and qualitative approaches together, not as paradigmatic methodological alternatives but as approaches to empirical research that mutually enhance each other. Their value for each other lies precisely in their differences. Quantitative analysis has long had an uncertain status within cultural studies. For many years, its main significance seemed to reside in its ritual evocation as a risibly simplistic method of data generation and investigation. It has been used as a rhetorical foil in order to valorise the qualitative and humanistic modes of analysis that have dominated the field, and has often been regarded, in an unexamined way, either as epistemologically flawed or ideologically contaminated. David Deacon's chapter mounts a major challenge to this conception of quantification. He begins his chapter with the results of a content analysis of a large sample of refereed articles published in recent issues of three internationally read cultural studies journals. These show that many people writing within the field cite numerical data in the most uncritical way. The data are taken on trust. Deacon also shows how these articles frequently (the word is used advisedly) make quasi-quantitative statements in the most unreflexive way, seeming to show that despite the usual rhetoric, counting does count, and does so even when it is not actually counted.

All this seems indicative of a general indifference to, and disinterest in, quantified forms of knowledge among cultural studies researchers. Deacon explores why this has been the case, and what consequences it has for the field. Among other things, cultural studies is closing itself off from various political options. By regarding its main intellectual concerns as engaging with theory and exploring the intricate textures of qualitative data, it runs the risk of not being capable of contesting the validity of numerical evidence when this is used for quite reactionary purposes. Such evidence can marshal considerable rhetorical power, and critical analysts should have at their disposal the ability to critique and challenge this if they want to intervene in political issues or participate in debates about cultural and public policy. Various other limitations attendant on avoiding quantification are discussed in the chapter, along with examples of research that have successfully combined both qualitative and quantitative methods. Quantitative approaches cannot simply be dismissed as belonging to the social sciences and so not part of cultural studies. To the contrary: cultural studies should be part of the social sciences, or rather, should be conceived as achieving more and proving more effective when it works across a broad range of interfaces between disciplines in both the humanities and the social sciences. Deacon's chapter delivers a highly convincing argument. It makes clear that cultural studies should overcome its prejudice against numbers in the interests of strengthening and refining its methodological credentials.

Having shown why counting counts, we move to a chapter which discusses why observation matters. Close observation remains a key method of investigation in cultural studies and related fields. In her chapter, Virginia Nightingale explores emerging developments in qualitative research and in particular a conception of observation as reliant on cooperative interaction and communicative exchange between researcher and research participants. In observation-based fieldwork, such exchange is the medium through which research data is produced. It is a guard against projection, since analysis of the data must occur in a place where the experience of researcher and researched meet up. Fieldwork of this kind must be as self-reflexive as possible, as must the subsequent analysis. While she addresses various characteristic weaknesses associated with participant observation and ethnography, Nightingale shows that observation matters for cultural research because it brings researchers and research subjects into direct and immediate contact, and provides opportunities for addressing and adjusting their asymmetrical relation to authorial power. These opportunities have considerable potential for producing new kinds of knowledge based on the recognition and management of differences in power. The challenge lies in how to transform what they produce into recorded forms available for analysis while also thinking about how observation is being conducted, what it means for the participants and where the presence and position of the researcher may influence the research process. Observation matters because it brings the participants' worlds of experience into closely considered view. The communicative exchange on which it is based means that neither side's version can any longer be considered paramount or as necessarily carrying greater authority than the other.

The fourth section brings together two chapters that focus on ways of analysing the visual image, and ways of analysing spoken and written discourse. Living in contemporary media cultures, in which visual signification and natural language are continually intersecting, should make obvious the need to consider images and texts alongside each other, yet this is honoured more in the breach than the observance. Media and cultural studies have been to the fore in helping overcome this tendency, and have done so because of their awareness of the need to negotiate the limitations of academic specialisms when investigating the multiple convergences and flows in cultures of modernity. In her chapter, Sarah Pink seeks to advance the interdisciplinary nature of this work even further. Visual cultural analysis has become an established method in cultural studies, drawing largely on art history and media studies approaches. While it focuses on notions of the visual, as well as the analysis of the image itself, there has been surprisingly little connection between these attempts to understand the visual and the ethnographic approaches that have become increasingly popular amongst cultural studies scholars. In her approach to the project of a visual cultural studies, Pink draws particularly on methods in visual anthropology and visual sociology as a way of linking up with the enthusiasm for ethnography that has developed in cultural studies.

Pink's chapter is based on the recognition that the uses of visual media and visual methods, among both researchers and research participants, are located in particular social relationships and cultural practices. Institutional and contextual meanings are in turn embedded in visual images, in the conventions that inform their production, and in the role of situated human agents as viewers and interpreters of images. While her preoccupation in the chapter is with the experience of visual images, Pink recognises that no experience is ever purely visual. In both everyday life and popular culture we are dealing, often enough, with combinations of visual and written texts, so it would now be quite untenable for any of the visual sub-disciplines to operate only with the visual. Pink conceives of ethnographic research as consisting of visual and sensory embodied experience and knowledge, and this can best be communicated by combining images and words. The emphasis she places on experience links back to the initial chapter in the book, but takes this forward into her own set of concerns by dwelling particularly on the multi-sensorial nature of human experience. This provides the basis for her discussion of appropriate methods for investigating people's experience via an approach which views this as being sensorily embodied as well as socially embedded. The aspiration is to cover as much as possible of the entire range of participants' experience from its pre-reflective to its closely interpreted incarnations. The chapter provides illustration of what is involved with two case studies: Pink's own research into a community garden project connected with the Slow City (Cittàslow) movement in the UK, and a research project in which she is a co-participant, based on the visual representations found on a Spanish website, which has involved a close examination of Spanish social relations and cultural values. The chapter offers a valuable contribution to developing a visual methodology in cultural studies research.

As Pink makes clear, she shares Virginia Nightingale's ethnographic concern to develop collaborative, non-hierarchical methods in cultural studies research. Their chapters show in various ways why this concern is important, but among the most significant of these is that it may serve to bring into the light the question of whose 'voice' is being heard, and possibly privileged, in any specific research project or sample of cultural analysis. It is desperately easy to assume what is involved in the experience of research participants, and perhaps as well feel one has the intellectual authority to configure this on their behalf. The whole emphasis on experience as set out at the start of the book is designed as a counter to these tendencies.

In his chapter, Martin Barker picks up on a similar danger that is latent in much of the work in cultural studies conducted under the catch-all label of discourse analysis. While this involves a wide variety of approaches, theoretically as well as methodologically, it has had a tremendous impact on cultural analysis in the most general sense. The benefits are many, but Barker is concerned with the way they have come at a price. His chapter explores a set of methodological problems in analysing discourse that have gone largely unnoticed. They involve assumptions about the cultural power of discourses, and that easy slide that can occur from the analysis of meanings in a cultural text to the impact it has on its recipients. This is not the only problem. There are also those of the convenient sample, where evidence is matched up to a pre-given theoretical position, and, if predominant theories of discourse are correct, the compromising position in which they place studies of reception. For Barker, the claims often made about those on the receiving end of discourses are not only untested, but also thoroughly disabling for other areas of research. They amount to rendering audience studies untenable.

Barker's chapter begins by tracing the ways in which 'discourse' came into theoretical and analytical prominence in cultural studies. In what is an especially helpful exercise in clarification, he identifies seven main tendencies in discourse theory, and on the basis of this is able to show that the majority of these tend to treat 'power' as the central given of discourse. Using an investigation of two key texts on critical discourse analysis and cultural studies as the basis of his argument, Barker goes on to unpack a key set of assumptions about the alleged power of discourses. The point of this is to establish the basis on which discourse analysis, or any other form of qualitative research, can be said to be trustworthy. The question of trust is, for Barker, the qualitative researcher's equivalent of the touchstones of validity, reliability and generalisability in quantitative research. How is this to be gained? Barker proposes a set of methodological principles for ensuring trustworthiness. These involve a defensible corpus of material for use in discourse analysis; defensible methods as we move from text to context or tack back and forth between them; and taking responsibility for implied claims, particularly about reception. Barker uses his own experience of participating in the international *Lord of the Rings* audience project to illustrate the practical strategies and methodological steps which these principles can entail.

These principles are of course not confined to discourse analysis, but can be applied to cultural analysis more generally. It may not be possible or desirable, in every item of work we engage in, to take the full circuit of culture into consideration, but we should be wary of specialising in one component of the circuit and on the basis of this alone, making assumptions or suppositions about what happens elsewhere in the circuit. What Barker is calling for is greater honesty about the limits of any specific method and how other methods may take us beyond them. His chapter offers a timely remedy for the overreaching presumptions of discourse theory and discourse analysis.

In news studies, the focus of Aeron Davis's case study in Chapter 3, discourse analysis provides a now established set of techniques and procedures for studying news texts and their journalistic construction. Such analysis has been confined to the narrative structure and rhetorical devices of contemporary news content. This is all on a par with the relentless present-centredness of so much work in media and cultural studies. The concluding section of the book is designed as a counterbalance to the historical myopia that besets many areas of cultural studies scholarship. It is concerned with both memory and history.

In focusing on memory in her chapter, Emily Keightley discusses this both as a method of investigation and as a topic for cultural studies work. She is concerned to establish its importance in both these respects. Individually and collectively, memory is the key register of our temporalised experience. It acts as the central modality of our relation to the past in the present, rather than a transparent lens through which all the past remains visible. For Keightley, this means that in taking memory as both topic and tool, we have to move out from under the shadow of professional historiography with its own definite set of epistemological criteria, and refuse to be hidebound by any of the generalised empirical requirements in the social sciences. Memory studies require their own methods.

Keightley explores memory as a site of struggle, pleasure and agency in relation to the broader interests of cultural studies. She forges the link between cultural memory as research topic and research tool in the distinction between public and private modes of memory. Methodologically, research on cultural memory has to take account of this differentiation but also attend to the ways in which they interact with and inform each other. As her succinct account makes clear, cultural studies research on memory attends to the social relations of the interaction between individual and public forms of memory, whether these involve family photograph albums, commemoration practices or popular festivals. The chapter takes Frigga Haug's method of memory work as it was developed in studying female sexualisation as one example of how memory can be used as a research technique, while an account of Keightley's own work on women's forms of remembering in everyday life illustrates how memory can be such a productive site for investigating vernacular engagements with the past in day-to-day social relations.

As a technique for investigating uses of the past in the present, memory is not of course infallible. It may provide stunningly vivid detail not available anywhere else, but its validity cannot simply be taken on trust. The cultural evidence provided by memory, in interviews with different individuals and groups, needs always to be checked, as far as this is possible, against other documentary sources, such as newspapers, and other informants, whether in the same social category or one deliberately contrasting with it. Keightley insists on the methodological importance of triangulation with other forms of evidence and accounts in order to ensure the value and determine the status of what memory work provides. This does not compromise vernacular accounts as a legitimate source of knowledge about the past, as professional historiographical principles have in the past. Rather, it recognises more fairly what distinguishes memory in cultural practices and processes, and why the popular stake in mundane forms of memory is important.

Somewhat paradoxically, this stake becomes more important as changes in our social and cultural experience seem increasingly to accelerate. It is not altogether clear whether this is a 'despite' or 'because of' relation, but it is clearly related as well to the popular experience of history and the huge upsurge of interest in everything from family histories to the history of wars and empires. This is my starting point in the final chapter of the book, which seeks a much closer working relationship between history and cultural studies. The differences between history and cultural studies are easy to spot. History tends to become bogged down in the past, is meticulous with empirical details and lax in conceptualisation. Cultural studies tends to become bogged down in the present, is selective with empirical details, and strenuous in conceptualisation. Maybe if the two forms of study attended to each other more, these tendencies would become less strained, and more balanced out. Cultural studies does of course refer to the past, but almost ritualistically, as if to ward off some unwanted spirit. History is evoked, but not engaged with. It is the ghost at the cultural studies banquet.

For me, cultural studies without a historical dimension is weak, but I also want to push historians towards greater recognition of what strengths they may derive from attending to work in cultural studies. The fuller dialogue I seek has by definition to be two-way. As with the other chapter in this final section, I approach history as both topic and tool: a broad set of resources for studying everyday cultures in the past and a broad set of techniques for thinking about historical experience and representation in the present. This is closely related to the dual approach taken in the chapter of canvassing for forms of cultural history informed by the theoretical and hermeneutical concerns of cultural studies, and forms of contemporary cultural analysis that take cultural history as one of their key bearings, and interrogate media representations of the past in a variety of different genres ranging from historical news studies (the need for which was hinted at above) to costume dramas and romance fiction based in past periods.

The chapter discusses two methodological pitfalls in any historical work: relativist particularism and absolutist presentism. What these involve both conceptually and in their analytical fallout is presented in detail at various points in the chapter. I also address two contrasting but inter-reliant modes of research experience which can be roughly characterised as studiousness and illumination. The second may be what we strive for most but, in a methodological version of the 'no gain without pain' adage, it is not possible without the first. I begin the chapter by addressing why, in contrast to the field in its early formation, history and cultural studies have become divergent. I then discuss examples from a broad range of recent work which show how cultural studies and history can inform and enhance each other. I conclude the chapter by discussing some of the methodological difficulties I faced in recently completed work on historical racism in British popular entertainment.

The overall methodological message of the final section as a whole is straightforward. Attend to contemporary issues by all means, and insist on the impossibility of understanding the past except within the present, but do not imagine you can think about the present or the past wholly on contemporary grounds, only on what seems urgently relevant now, and finally, always, always, historicise.

Lives and Lived Experiences

CHAPTER 1

Experience and the Social World

Michael Pickering

Experience is central to cultural studies. It is a key category of analysis within the field, and has been drawn on as concrete material for many of the issues which cultural studies has pursued. It has also become a recognised dimension of research practice itself. Its value has nevertheless been contested, both as a form of research data and as an analytical concept. This was particularly the case during the ascendancy of poststructuralism in cultural studies, but more broadly how it should be used as a resource and what place it has as evidence are questions that have generated considerable debate. The purpose of this chapter is not to retrace the various perspectives on such debate or deal generally with the history of ideas about the category of experience.[1] Although experience is generally accorded a positive value, the senses it has and the perspectives applied to it are multiple, so much so that any rehearsal of its general range and of attacks upon its conceptual credentials, even within cultural studies, would require extensive discussion and elaboration.[2] My intention here is more modest in scope, and this is to add further impetus to the renewal of interest in the category of experience that has arisen over the past ten years or so, both within cultural studies and across adjacent fields of study.

The chapter has three main aims. First, it tries to explain why attending to experience remains an important task for cultural studies. This certainly involves grappling with the problems and difficulties it raises, and while some of these will be covered, the primary emphasis in what follows is on re-establishing the methodological significance of attending to experience for the general project of cultural studies. Second, it examines the implications for research methodology of the fact that while experience is common to both researcher and researched, the specific experiences we have are always in some degree different and individual to us, as are the ways we derive meaning and significance from experience or draw on our experience to contest other cultural definitions put upon experience, particularly by those in positions of power, authority and control. The tensions and conflicts over what is made of experience in our understandings of the social world are what make it an important category for cultural studies. Third, the chapter tries to clear the ground for deploying various methods in researching people's experience of the social world. It does this by mapping the conceptual properties of experience in terms of various dualities operative within the category, such as proximity and distance, cultural process and outcome, situated and mediated participation, and the balance between speaking and listening. While these are all significant, above all else I approach experience as an intermediary category coming between ways of being and ways of knowing. Examining experience in these ways is not simply an exercise in theorisation, though it is partly that. More importantly, it is a matter of setting out certain mutually constitutive relations within the category so that the research methods discussed later in the book can be more effectively put into use and managed. I hope in doing this to show why, as a protean, refractory phenomenon, experience is so culturally multifarious and, as an analytical category, so wonderfully awkward.

One of the distinguishing features of cultural studies is its focus on the subjective dimension of social relations, on how particular social arrangements and configurations are lived and made sense of, so highlighting the complex intersections between public culture and private subjectivity and the transformative potentials that may arise there. These are crucial for our sense of who we are or might become, and experience – not only what is undergone but also how this is articulated, understood, drawn on and shared with others – is, or so I shall claim, vital to our changing identities and changing conceptions of the social worlds we live in. Chris Kearney (2003: 42) has recently observed that 'any consideration of the way individuals engage in the process of recreating their identities by continually reflecting upon their lived experience, is largely missing from current research'. To regard this process as learning directly about self and the social world through experience is clearly superficial and inadequate, suggesting a unilinear movement and unitary subject, and allowing little scope for dealing with contradictions between experiences, between experience and cultural forms, or between experience and identity. This conception of experience is the result of the underlying humanist model of explanation on which it is based. It does not mean that experience itself has thereby to be dismissed, but it does mean it should be reconceived. My argument is that, subject to such reconception, engaging in the kind of consideration Kearney refers to should remain a major component of cultural studies research, and should be more in evidence than is currently the case. That is why this book begins with a chapter on experience.

DISTANCE AND PROXIMITY

The first point to make is that experience is never pure or transparent. If experience is to be used to provide evidence and gain insight into everyday cultures, and if ideas about it are to inform research practice and modes of analysis within cultural studies, what is gathered in the name of experience cannot simply be presented as raw data, or regarded as offering a direct expression of people's participation in different cultural fields. We talk of 'lived' experience, but experience always involves interpretation of what happens in life, of what makes our perceptions, feelings, and actions meaningful. This depends on how they come into expression and are conceptualised, organised and given temporal identity, or, in other words, how experience is given the quality of narrative.

There have been times in the development of the field when it has seemed appropriate to make space for otherwise silent or marginalised voices to be heard, and to present the narratives of their experience directly in their own words. This has accompanied greater recognition of the need to deploy research methods in a more participant-centred way, and to develop relations between researchers and researched on a subject/subject basis rather than attempting to adopt a position of spurious detachment from an isolated object of research, as with the natural science model of research. Such an approach raises the question of the researcher's involvement, for this is obviously directed in certain ways and depends on some degree of theoretical understanding of whatever is being researched, whether this is experience of gender, social class, ethnicity or whatever. What counts is awareness of how this understanding shapes the research and how it should be open to being reshaped by the findings of the research.

The process of research is one of dialogue, but this does not mean that cultural studies researchers should assume that knowledge simply derives from experience (the position of empiricism) or that experience simply validates what is said (the position of self-authenticating standpoint theories).[3] Respecting what is said by research subjects is one side of the deal. The other is balancing this with a critical regard for what any kind of evidence might mean and how this evidence relates to the structural location of the research subject. Experience can certainly be regarded as evidence of distinctive forms of social life and integral to everyday encounters and relations, but understanding how it is so is never straightforward.

Experience is always to be interrogated. It has to be approached carefully and critically because it is not simply equivalent to what happens to us. Experience is just as much about what we make out of what happens to us, and for many that is where its value really lies. There are of course experiences we choose to have, for whatever reason, and experiences that are imposed on us, sometimes against our will or because they are or seem unavoidable. There are also experiences on which we have reflected deeply and which we have absorbed into our self-knowledge, and others we hardly think about at all, of which we are only tacitly aware as we go about our day-to-day lives. Our lives are a peculiar compound of various forms of experience, which is partly why defining experience is so difficult. Experience seems to embrace so much while also providing basic material for the examined life. There can be no absolute definition of the category, which means we have to think of it in both general and specific terms as we use it to develop knowledge about our lives and the lives of other people, in other places and circumstances, other periods and historical formations. We may be glad that we have not shared some of the experiences of other people – the experience of endemic poverty, forced migration or racist oppression, for example – but we can learn from how they have been endured, handled, assimilated, resisted. It is not just a question of trying to relate the experience of others to what we may distill from our own, but also of recognising how self-legitimating narrative schemas are vital in the formation of social and cultural identities, enabling the process of discriminating and evaluating across experiences, and providing a means of countering being spoken for or stereotypically 'othered'.

Cultural analysis adds to this the difficult task of bringing what the anthropologist Clifford Geertz (1983: 58) calls experience-near concepts into illuminating connection with the experience–distant concepts which 'theorists have fashioned in order to capture the general features of social life'. He counsels against trying 'to get yourself into some inner correspondence of spirit with your informants', for you cannot magically assume the position and perspective from within which their own lives are lived. Rather, the trick 'is to figure out what the devil they think they are up to'.

Geertz's distinction between what is experientially proximate and distant is an extension of the distinction between first-hand and second-hand experience, and the different kinds of concept and account accompanying them, with 'fear' and 'phobia' being examples of concepts that are relatively experience-near and experience-far. This is another way of talking about the two-sides-to-a-deal issue, for cultural analysis needs to move back and forth between what informants say and do and what can be made of all that, for otherwise you stand in danger of becoming either 'awash in immediacies, as well as entangled in vernacular', or 'stranded in abstractions and smothered in jargon' (Geertz 1983: 57).

Ann Gray (1997: 95) has characterised the problem of failing to move between these two sides in cultural studies as exaggerating either 'the ideologically constructed subject' or 'the active and creative human agent'. The ethnographer who has spent too long on the street of corner may emphasise the latter, whereas the theorist who has spent too long blinking under a desklamp may emphasise the former. Both have need of another kind of trick, which is to bring both agency and ideology into continual view of each other rather than swinging between the two poles they represent. That is no easy task, but if acted-upon experience is never brought to bear on ideological structures, or long-term structural determinants are never seen in terms of everyday social practices, we end up in the dead-end canyon of impossible dualisms. Structures determine what we do but are also inhabited and ways are chosen among them. Agency should be emphasised but not exaggerated, which means that we should weigh studies of active audiences, reflexive consumers and everyday creativity against questions of control over the resources and operations involved in cultural production and access to different cultural practices and different forms of cultural consumption.

Attending to experience is necessary but never enough in itself, whether this is our own experience or those of others, or whether the experience is relatively contemporary or (involving another kind of distance) related to previous historical formations. Each of these bring their own difficulties, and while we may personally value our own experiences most, attending to them is neither easier nor of a higher order than engaging with experience beyond the ambit of our own lives and circumstances.

ESSENTIALISM AND EXPERIENCE

By implication at least, first-hand experience is elevated above others when it is viewed in an essentialist way and taken to be unimpeachably self-validating. Essentialism conveys the sense that for any particular social category, for example that of gender or ethnicity, there is an underlying essence defining the 'real' or 'true' nature of the category's experience. This is the case for Robert Bly (1991) who has argued that men possess a naturally wild, but now denied or repressed, masculine essence, but most instances of essentialist thinking are nothing like as notable. Generally less strenuously and extensively discussed, everyday manifestations of racial or gender essentialism are legion, whether it is black people being referred to as 'naturally' rhythmical, or women as 'naturally' nurturing, caring and cooperative. Such claims take us close to stereotyping since for any specific group they identify a set of fixed, unchanging characteristics that define the group and therefore the core or essential experience of the group. For women, the counter-case is summarised in Simone de Beauvoir's famous adage that 'one is not born, but becomes a woman' (1984: 295). There is in other words nothing 'natural' about womanhood or manhood, and becoming a man or woman is always a cultural process, historically specific and historically variant.

That is perhaps the position you would expect to be taken in cultural studies, but for feminists working in the field it is not necessarily so straightforward. How do you argue against, say, violent pornography or the stereotypical positioning of women in popular music without invoking men, women and women's collective experience in essentialist terms? This difficulty has led some to pursue a case for 'strategic essentialism' as a way of avoiding the essentialist/anti-essentialist dichotomy, but the grounds for its superiority over other forms of essentialism remain contested. There are a number of different critical positions within feminism on questions of experience and essentialism, as there are on the category of experience itself, especially in relation to such key variables as gender and sexual orientation, or others which intersect with gender, such as ethnicity, social class and age group. These differences are indicative of the problems involved in representation, which arise because of the gap between knowledge and experience. Essentialism offers the false hope of reconciling them. So when problems of representation relate to the absence or marginalisation of a particular group's experience in representation, either historically or in contemporary forms of popular culture, there is a strong temptation to present the 'voices' of that experience as if what is said is self-evidently 'true' or 'authentic'. This is understandable as a means of warding off the threat of being spoken of by others or of others speaking on behalf of you when this is accomplished in ways detrimental to your own values and interests, whether these are to do with sexuality, the experience of being racialised or whatever. Yet to think of experience as necessarily providing an alibi for knowledge is one of the illusions of relativism.

Cultural studies has proved appealing to some members of oppressed or marginalised groups because it allows a space for the articulation of their experience where this is not available in more conventional or established academic disciplines. This can seem empowering, but its value does not cancel out the need to be self-reflexive about that experience, or to automatically act as a guard against reifying 'self' above the struggle for reflexivity. Nor does it mean that questions about the historical specificity and cultural representativeness of experience do not need addressing. The historical recovery of previously neglected experience or the assertive differentiation of experience between distinct social groups and categories carries the danger of historical and cultural populism and can lead researchers back into the snare of essentialism, strategic or otherwise. This tendency in cultural studies and related fields, especially when directed against the 'distortions and occlusions' in the representation of marginalised or oppressed groups, has been polemically dismissed by Stefan Collini (1999: 259–60) as vote-catching 'grievance studies'. This ignores the real grievances and the gains that are involved in opening up subaltern experiences to analysis and scholarship, but it does point up certain weaknesses. Privileging category-based experience may not only lead back into essentialism but also neglect the intersections of gender, ethnicity and social class, and so confine questions of identity and representation to whatever is held to be specific to the self-legitimated experience. It also begs the question of how we can understand each other's experience, regardless of how 'we' is defined in any cross-category situation.

SITUATED AND MEDIATED EXPERIENCE

This question will always be present. Though it needs to be properly addressed in any investigation and analysis of the experiences of particular social groups, the difficulties it creates do not negate the value of attending to the experience of hitherto neglected, concealed, or misrepresented groups outside of the social mainstream. The main reason for this is the contribution it can make to cultural democratisation.[4] One example of this is working-class writing. Historically, the endeavours of working-class people to engage in literary forms of writing were in stark contrast to those from privileged class backgrounds. They had to overcome rudimentary levels of schooling and seek to educate themselves, wrenching whatever little spare time for study or writing they could from long hours at workbench or sink, coalface or loom, clerical office or cash-till. They drew directly from the reservoir of their own experience, for it was commonly felt that this was where the wellsprings of their creative art would lie, with form and technique being secondary considerations. They had intimate experience of their social world of everyday life and labour, inhabiting it with an insider's web of intricate knowledge. Through writing they were trying to make their world more widely known as well as making more sense of it for themselves. The significance of such writing is to be found not only in what was written but also in the act of writing, for that is where their effort to democratise the arts lay, in their 'shared sense of entitlement to participate in cultural activities' (Hilliard 2006: 6). In any example like this, there may be a temptation to idealise their battle against prejudice, condescension or snobbery, to romanticise the struggle of those striving against the odds to give expression to their experience, or to essentalise such experience. We should be alert to these pitfalls, but they only arise in the first place out of sympathy with subaltern experiences, and concern to engage with and articulate them. This concern cannot simply be dismissed as the populist amplification of grievance, for what is at stake is aligning the study of culture with the cause of cultural democratisation.

This impulse remains all-important in differentiating cultural studies from disciplines attending only to officially accredited artforms. In this respect experience acts as a methodological touchstone in sounding an insistence on the significance of listening to others and attending to what is relatively distinctive in their way of knowing their immediate social world, for it is only by doing this that we can glean any sense of what is involved in their subjectivities, self-formation, life histories and participation in social and cultural identities.

There is of course nothing preventing cultural studies from studying forms of 'high' culture as well as popular culture, but what is crucial is how we understand the bearings which any expressive cultural form has on socially and historically specific experience and how this articulates with broader determinate structures of social life. While cultural studies is in some respects close to other forms of social enquiry, its special point of interest is with how particular social worlds are experienced, and how the diverse stuff of that experience is subjectively felt and articulated by those who live it, and not by any others, neither sociologists nor historians nor whoever else may be involved in the enquiry in any particular case. It is the subjective dimension of lived social worlds that experience occupies, and it is this which is central to the concerns of cultural studies. Theory provides us with a map to help us understand how social worlds are configured, but unless we attend to experience we will not be able to follow the map into the living landscape to which it relates.

Considering the diverse stuff of experience brings us back to the distinction between first-hand and second-hand experience, involving that which occurs to us in an immediate and relatively direct way and that which occurs at a distance, in some unfamiliar elsewhere. It is not a hard-and-fast distinction. In our increasingly mediated world much of what we experience comes to us from a source that is not local or proximate to our material existence or particular cultural corpus of knowledge. Such media as cinema, radio, television and the internet involve contact with far-off peoples and places. There may be moments when such contact affects us in an immediate and direct way, making it difficult to dissociate from events that are tangible and here-and-now. While we do draw lines between situated and mediated experience, our lives are a complex mixture of both, as we watch the evening news on TV and talk to our children, or visit an online interactive website before strolling down to our local pub. It is easy to exaggerate modernity's usurpation of place by space and more particularly the dissolution of locally based experience by communication technologies, so overlooking how people have long travelled imaginatively to other times and places via biblical tales, folk songs and stories, or more recently via novels, verse and various theatrical entertainments. Staying at home and going places is not exclusive to the experience of television. The mixture of situated and mediated experience today is a matter of scale as well as diversity, and for many this has steadily grown in both respects throughout the past century, with what is experienced symbolically becoming increasingly entwined with what is experienced through our own sensory perception. New communications technologies do not suddenly burst on the scene and alter our spatial and temporal modalities of experience overnight. Even virtual reality was prefigured in the mid-nineteenth century by early visual media like the stereoscope, the experience of which was described by Oliver Wendell Holmes (1861: 14–15) as creating 'a dream-like exaltation of the faculties, a kind of clairvoyance, in which we seem to leave the body behind us and sail away into one strange scene after another like disembodied spirits'.

The relationship between situated and mediated experience is interactive. This means that in making experience a focus of enquiry and attending to how the social world is experienced on its everyday ground, we have to recognise that the media are an intrinsic, regularly experienced feature of that ground, influencing how people see the local world around them and interpret events on their own doorstep, as well as their views of cultural difference and their sense of global interconnectedness. The disembedding processes associated with communications technologies are also subject to processes of situated assimilation, and we need to attend to the ways in which various groups and communities relate what they consume to the contexts of their ongoing day-to-day lives, entwining symbolic encounters with face-to-face interactions and re-embedding mediated experiences in mundane affairs. How these processes work in relation to each other is always contingent upon the particular social worlds in which people live, both materially and symbolically. This is not simply to be celebrated as cultural pluralism, for it involves the politics of location and how location produces conflicting versions of experience. Certain definitions of experience have power over other definitions, as for instance in the way they may universalise what is socially and historically particular to, say, the self-presentation of white men or Western women. Dealing critically with the discursive construction of experience has then to counter the tendency in cross-cultural analysis towards a homogenising 'psychologization of complex and contradictory historical and cultural realities' which flattens difference into some putative sameness of experience, a move challenged by Chandra Talpade Mohanty (1987: 39) in relation to first-world feminism: 'The experience of being a woman can create an illusory unity, for it is not the experience of being woman, but the meanings attached to gender, race, class, and age at various historical moments that is of strategic significance'.

POSITION AND PERSPECTIVE

Adopting the emphasis Mohanty places on historical moments seems to me one of the best ways of avoiding the trap of speaking for others in the guise of bland sociological universals, for it creates the need to build up a thickly textured account of how social structures and processes are lived through the welter of everyday experience at a particular historical juncture. The analytical focus in such work can range from autobiographical self-reflection to ethnographic-style accounts of the lived cultural participation of particular groups or categories of people. Both can involve questions about personal and collective experience, and the relations between researcher and researched, but whatever the focus we need always to distinguish between speaking for others and making space for heterogeneous 'voices' which, among other things, ask the questions: whose accounts count, and why? The broad seas of experience continually lay siege to island fortresses guarding exclusive claims as to what is sociologically, historically, and politically significant.

Attending to experience in cultural studies research, as in any other field of the human sciences, involves gathering material about other social lives and other cultural mappings of the social world. Any speaking of self or from the perspective given to us by our own locations and cultural mappings has to be balanced by listening to others and investigating the matrix of experience from which they speak of themselves. While it is important to remember that as a researcher you are an experiencing subject yourself, research is not simply about the validation of your own experience and what you may have drawn from it. Here Ann Gray (1997: 99) is right to argue that 'the extent to which the intellectual is prepared to investigate his/her positionality is what is at stake for a genuinely reflexive and radical use of the category of "experience"', but also right immediately to go on from this to argue for the need to explore struggles for meaning (not just our own) in the construction of social and cultural identities (not just our own), whether this is through listening to people in conversational interviews, building up life stories though oral history techniques or drawing on existing biographical writings. Attending to experience then involves gathering and interrogating representations and expressions of 'direct personal participation in or observation of events; accumulated knowledge of the world in particular sets of circumstances; what it is like to live in these circumstances and the personal feelings and emotions which are engendered' (ibid.). To this we need to add that closely examining the narrative accounts people give of their on-the-ground experience does not mean that these have to accepted wholesale, or regarded as self-evidently authentic, but it does mean working with the recognition that our lives are storied, that we impose a narrative structure on the disparate and contingent features of our experience in order to make its scenes and figures acquire coherence, and that experience is only understood in the discursive forms in which it achieves expression. Experience is not opposed to those forms but realised within them, while practical knowledge of language and discourse comes from experiencing how they can be used to achieve expression in concrete situations.

Echoing an earlier point, how experience is expressed has always to be questioned, but questioning experience is different from using our positionality and way of knowing about the world to displace other people's accounts of their experience, or from misusing an assumed intellectual authority to dismiss such accounts as falsely conscious and politically compromised, seeking certainty in theory instead. Theory without reference to experience may appear cogent and comprehensive, but experience always has the potential to offer empirical exceptions that do not fit the theoretical rule, to disrupt intellectual exposition, to contradict ideas. This is because experience constitutes the meeting-place of individual perception and cultural meaning, self and symbolic forms, life-story and social conditions of existence. Experience occupies the contested territory between ways of being and ways of knowing.

EXPERIENCE AS PROCESS AND PRODUCT

Occupying that territory leads us to another duality of structure inherent in experience. It is manifest in the continual unfolding of experience in time while also acting back on that ongoing development across time. The relevant distinction here is between experience as process and experience as product. These are far from exclusive. Both are set in play at once, and operate with mutual reference to each other.

With this in mind, we can speak on the one hand of a subject's immersion in a flow of action, observation or feeling where the meanings of events, encounters, episodes or states of being are relatively inchoate, and not as yet realised in any developed manner that can be carried forwards into the future. On the other hand, we can refer to what is derived by the subject from the everyday reality of the social world they inhabit where the meanings of what has happened are more fully interpreted and assimilated, as the accepted products of experience, against which change and development, or disruption and loss, can be assessed, now and in the future. Both of these dimensions of experience can be referred to as lived in that they cover what has been moved through, and learned from, in a vast array of possibilities and consequences.

The qualities and values of different forms and modalities of experience are articulated, weighed and arranged, in the contingent and always provisional art of understanding, only on the basis of the transactional relationship between these two dimensions of experience. It is particularly at the point of experience as process that definite, and at times quite subtle, qualitative features of social and cultural life are felt, sometimes intensely, regardless of whether they have achieved any conventional cultural expression. It is also at this point that the tension arises between what is felt and what is known, and between what is established and what is changing.[5] Creative cultural practices work with this tension, but if they are to have a fruitful outcome they first need to know thoroughly what it is they have to go beyond. That is why we should understand experience in this specific manifestation of its dualities as it occurs in the intermediate spaces between the established structures of social worlds and the dynamic processes through which they are lived.

The focus of cultural analysis is then on how this duality is represented and given expression, or when it is distorted and occluded, on the task of explaining this and bringing it into play, not in ways that disregard people's own accounts but in ways that cross-refer different accounts and remain alert to contradictions, ambivalences and silences across different narratives. What is not said in recounting experience may be just as important as what is said.

Two brief points follow from this. First, an informing premise of all cultural studies research should be that people are self-interpreting, and how they understand their experience of and in the social world is fundamental to cultural analysis. Even if the subjects' self-definition of an experience is limited or heavily skewed, it is central to what we study and cannot be bracketed out of the equation as it is in positivist, naturalist and behaviourist approaches. Second, while it is always important to attend to others' experience in the various accounts given of it, experience is neither sufficient in itself nor sufficient for analysis. Attending to experience is to utilise an analytical resource. Analytically it requires the tools for interrogation which we can bring from cultural theory, but as a resource it can also be used to interrogate the abstract formulations of theory. It is a two-way process.

QUALITIES OF EXPERIENCE

We cannot make sense of any experience, our own or those of other people, without reference to conceptual and theoretical ideas of one kind or another, or without carefully applying the methods we bring to bear on eliciting and helping bring into being stories of the experience of social worlds. Experience is not the high road to the palace of wisdom. We utilise methods because they supply us with procedures and principles for generating data about social and cultural experience, how it is configured and articulated, and we draw on theories because they supply us with frameworks for analysing that experience and the forms in which it is expressed. It is a mistake to assume that such expression simply bears the experience we seek to uncover or recover, that it brings to us pearls of evidence already formed before the application of method or analytical examination. You cannot explore experience in the hope of discovering a set of methods, but you can apply a set of methods to the narration of experience, both in generating it and analysing it.

Attending to experience as process and product is nevertheless of enormous importance in telling us about how social worlds are inhabited and understood, in a forwards and backwards motion between what has happened and what is made of it, in the continual, reflexive, interpretive accounts of which any individual is in some way an author. This is not to say that narrative articulations of experience provide us with direct, unmediated access to experience, but to emphasise that experience only attains meaning when it is framed within communicative form. It is only in such form that it enters into social exchange and cultural circulation, whether this is a letter from a soldier abroad to a loved one back home, a sardonic comment on the gap between social experience and political rhetoric whispered in someone's ear at an electoral rally, a television drama about bullying at school, or an old blues record that is reinterpreted across several generations. Experience does not attain meaning once and for all. Some stories are told and retold, and often honed and polished in the retelling, and how they are heard and understood depends on the social location and historicity of their auditors. Even in the first move to communicative form, there is a crucial distinction between experience and how it becomes framed in words, images, music or gestures. Once again this mutable category generates rule and deviance at one and the same time, for we also have to acknowledge that experience and the subjectivities through which it is lived and narrated are not simply determined by the language and discourse in which they achieve expression. One of the reasons why experience is always worth attending to as a category is that it is not wholly encompassed by language and narration: 'any attempt to transmute the tingle and smack of lived experience into language loses something essential to it' (Magee 2003: 286). This may lead at times to metaphysical vapourings or the false elevation of experience over understanding, but that does not demean the category itself.

We should always see experience and expression as transactional, for if they were not, experience would become endlessly repetitive and expression would become irredeemably stale. Experience is not a category that is fixed or given but a modality of human existence that is contingent and changeable, moving between what is familiar and unfamiliar, and registering the incessant tension between who we are and what we know. Experience seems at some points to confirm what we know, and at others to pull us up short, surprise us into rethinking, make us reassess what we have previously accepted or taken for granted. It is because experience can operate in both these ways that we need to build it into our research practice. We should expect research to act in both these ways, to proceed in certain ways as we would expect, but also from time to time to subvert those expectations and challenge our assumptions about the evidence we confront. This brings me to the final quality of duality in experience which I want to discuss.

As a category, experience embraces routine activities and mundane occurrences, and events, encounters, responses to what happens to us which somehow stand out, which act as the culmination of a certain process or the precipitation of certain feelings, perceptions or thoughts. In attaining prominence in this way, these extraordinary experiences shed light backwards and forwards in our lives, giving new meaning to what we have experienced or will experience in a more habitual manner, perhaps making us realise that this is what such-and-such a poet or novelist meant in a particular passage which we had not fully grasped at all. The distinction here is between experience in its quotidian usualness and *an* experience that creates a heightened perceptual or intellectual arousal and seems to impart to us a vital quality of experience that henceforth remains key to the way we conceive of ourselves and the shifting pattern of our lives.[6]

Experience is thus structured around expectations and breaks with those expectations in ways directly relevant to what we want to derive from research. If research and the methods we employ only confirm our expectations, little is achieved. While we do not anticipate our findings being totally contrary to our initiating assumptions or hypotheses, research would be a dull and relatively valueless affair if these were never challenged or upset by the evidence that is produced. Just as with our day-to-day experience, much of what we do in the course of researching is a matter of routine. The elements of surprise in research are inseparable from the more common passages that lead up to and away from them, but they are central to making research in itself a rewarding experience.

SUMMARY: KEY POINTS

- The chapter explains why experience is a question of critical importance for cultural studies. Most of all, this importance arises out of the tensions and conflicts over what is made of experience in our understandings of the social world.
- The methodological significance of experience as a category is addressed in terms of (1) the politics of culture and the work of cultural studies in promoting cultural democratisation; and (2) the relations of researcher and researched, and between evidence and analysis.
- Experience is approached as a vital analytical resource which is always in need of interrogation.
- Experience is conceptually outlined in the chapter via examples of its dual qualities. In particular, it is conceived as an intermediary category coming between ways of being and ways of knowing.

FURTHER READING

Although experience is a key category in the social sciences and humanities, it has not received much critical attention as a concept. This has recently been rectified by Martin Jay (2005) for uses of the concept in philosophy and social theory, historiography and aesthetics. I have responded to the poststructuralist rejection of the concept in Pickering (1997), while also dealing with its uses in social history and cultural theory, feminism and critical hermeneutics. See ch. 6 in particular for my assessment of the use of the term experience in the work of Raymond Williams and E. P. Thompson. Keith Negus and I approach artistic and cultural practices in terms of the communication of experience in *Creativity, Communication and Cultural Value* (2004). Among other writers, we draw there on the American pragmatist philosopher, John Dewey, particularly in *Art as Experience* (1980); Richard Shusterman (1992) also builds on Dewey in developing a philosophical aesthetics for the late-modern period. Turner and Bruner (1986) is a stimulating collection of essays on the anthropological uses of the concept. Engagement with the alleged loss of integrated experience in capitalist modernity, by intellectuals including Adorno, Benjamin and Kracauer, is covered in most of the commentary associated with them and with critical theory more generally; see, for example, Cesar (1992), and Caygill (1998). A stimulating theoretical engagement with experience, gender and personal identity is Probyn (1993), while Kruks (2001) offers an interesting phenomenological treatment of experience. Finally, for the life history approach in sociology, see, for example, Bertaux (1981), Plummer (2001), and Roberts (2001).

NOTES

1. For a wide-ranging survey of such ideas, see Jay (2005).
2. For its use in cultural studies, including discussion of its methodological and analytical value, see Pickering (1997).
3. An example of a self-authenticating standpoint claim is Alison Jagger's (1983: 384) assertion that because of their subordinate status, 'women do not have a clear interest in mystifying reality and so are likely to develop a clearer and more trustworthy understanding of the world'. For further discussion, see Harding (1993); McLennan (1995); Skeggs (1995); also Segal (1987).
4. The phrase 'democratization of culture' comes from Karl Mannheim's 1933 essay on this topic, which he described as involving a broadening out of those 'actively participating in cultural life, either as creators or as recipients' (Mannheim 1956).
5. This relates to Raymond Williams's concept of structure of feeling, the real strength of which lies in its application to liminal forms of experience in the process of coming into expressive form (see Pickering 1997: ch. 2).
6. Keith Negus and I have discussed this aspect of duality in experience in greater detail in our discussion of the relation between experience, creativity and cultural value (Negus and Pickering 2004: ch. 2).

CHAPTER 2

Stories and the Social World

Steph Lawler

It is hard to take more than a step without narrating . . . The stories of our days and the stories in our days are joined in that autobiography we are all engaged in making and remaking, as long as we live, which we never complete, though we all know how it is going to end. (Barbara Hardy, *Tellers and Listeners*, p. 4)

INTRODUCTION: THE STORIES OF OUR DAYS AND THE STORIES IN OUR DAYS

As Barbara Hardy, among others, has noted, narratives are integral to social life (1975). People continually tell stories to themselves and to others, gathering up fragments of the day to make a coherent whole, or fragments of occurrences in a life to make a coherent life story. Even though most people will not write autobiographies, all of us are engaged in the projects of our own autobiography, which we manifest every time we tell others about our lives, attend an interview, or simply engage in processes of thinking about and understanding the world and our place within it. In all of these processes, we are telling stories to ourselves and to others. These stories are not simple reflections of a set of 'facts': rather, they are organising devices through which we interpret and constitute the world. And indeed how could we not do this, since the social world is itself, as Somers and Gibson put it, 'storied'? That is, stories surround us, not only in novels, films, memoirs and other cultural forms which *explicitly* present themselves in terms of stories, but also in therapeutic encounters, newspaper articles, social theories and just the everyday ways in which people make sense of all of the discrete and diverse elements of a life.

This chapter is concerned with the ways in which stories – or narratives[1] – become social and cultural resources through which people engage in this sense-making. Specifically, it is concerned with how researchers can address and interpret those narratives. It will consider the question of what narratives can do, and it will do this through considering some of the ways in which they embed us within a historically and socially constituted world. I consider stories here as both resources that are drawn on and as social and cultural productions used by people in their everyday lives to make sense of those lives. Such stories are bound up with people's everyday worlds. Unlike the traditional 'Once upon a time' story, which, as Asa Berger notes, 'situates the story in the past and suggests that it takes place in a different world, one far removed from that of the teller, listener, or reader' (Berger 1997: 84), the kinds of stories I am considering here are precisely within the worlds of tellers, listeners and readers. In fairy stories, normal rules do not apply (Lacey 2000) but in life stories and similar narratives, rules are precisely the point: I cannot tell a life story that does not adhere to local (in time and space) 'intelligibility norms' (Gergen and Gergen 1986). So, a story of a childhood blighted by parental neglect tends to earn readers' sympathy because it is (in the twenty-first century) intelligible. A story of a childhood blighted by witchcraft (intelligible in, say, sixteenth-century England) seems likely today to be met with some scepticism.

While, conventionally, the study of narratives has centred on narratology – that is on the technical components of narratives themselves – I am more concerned here with the ways in which narratives circulate socially as cultural and social resources. These are stories through which social actors make sense of the world, of their place within it, and of their own identities. Paul Ricoeur (1991) usefully distinguishes between narratology and *emplotment*, or the creative work of reading and producing narratives. While narratology remains 'within' the narrative, examining the structure of the narrative itself, the kind of narrative analysis advocated by Ricoeur (and which I will discuss here) considers the narrative in its social context: stories completed, not in the components of the story itself, but in the circulation of relations between story, the producer of the story, and the audience for the story, in the context of local rules for what constitutes a *meaningful* story.

Instead of interrogating the deep structures of narrative, Ricoeur is more concerned with the question of what narrative *does*. For him, narrative is a key means through which people understand and make sense of the social world, and of their place within it. The world is intelligible because we can situate it within a story. We are intelligible because we can turn the multiple events of our lives into stories. In this respect, existing stories, whether in literary or cultural forms, or underwriting social and scientific theories, become resources to use for social actors in constructing their *own* stories. We may see ourselves, for example, as heroically overcoming obstacles and setbacks in our lives; or romantically driven by forces outside our control; or stoically enduring ill-treatment. In any case, we are using existing narratives to make sense of, and ultimately to construct, our own lives and worlds. In this sense, we become the heroes of our own lives. That we are unable to be the authors of our own lives is an effect of the fact that no plot ever originates with us. To be sure, we may re-work and change all the plots, but we are using them as resources nevertheless.

At this point – and especially because narrative is frequently left ill-defined – it is worth providing a definition of what a narrative is. I will, however, develop this definition throughout the chapter since it is integral to how narratives can be researched and analysed. At its most basic, narrative, in this schema, refers to an account which has three elements: characters (human or non-human), action (movement through time) and plot (Somers and Gibson 1994). The plot is key. Plots are not selected a priori but are *produced* through processes of emplotment in which events are linked to other events, in causal relationships. Earlier events are understood as causing later events, but of course not all earlier events are told. There is no narrative which can tell *everything*. What is told is selected because it is understood as having a meaningful place in the narrative. But it is then *given* meaning through its very inclusion in the narrative. As the readers or hearers of (the audience to) a narrative, people expect a narrated event to have a significance – to cause, and to be caused by, other events.

Here is an example:

> **Gina:** My mother was very much one of those working-class mothers, where you don't play in the house. You know, the house has got to be kept clean. You play outside. Your friends don't come into the house and mess the house up. Er, you don't have people round for tea, unless it's something special, or they're your relations . . . She would always get very nervous if visitors came, you know. Everything would have to be just so . . . So I had it in my head, when I decided that I wanted children, that . . . I wanted to have people in and out all the time. Lots of life, lots of different kinds of people, lots of different influences, different ages. You know, *life* in the house . . . I wanted to live in a big rambly house. I wanted a big garden, you know. I wanted there to be trees, somewhere the kids could play. I suppose I had middle-class aspirations for my kids. I wanted them to be a bit like the Famous Five[2] [laughs]. I wanted them to have sort of adventures, and dogs, and, you know, erm, sort of paddle in streams . . . I wanted the skies always to be blue, and the sun to shine, and I wanted to make jam and cakes and bread and do all those things. And then I did sort of try to do that when I came to live [here] (*Emphasis hers*).

This fragment of a larger narrative is taken from research I did on the mother-daughter relationship (Lawler 2000). This particular extract is taken from one of four interviews with Gina,[3] a woman in her forties, recounting here the difference between her own style of mothering, and that of her mother. Although brief, and apparently straightforward, it is rich with meaning, as Gina uses a range of cultural symbols to tell her story. I will return, by way of illustration, to this narrative, but for now I simply want to note the ways in which disparate components are brought together. This brief narrative includes the characters of Gina and her mother, as well as Gina's fantasy children, and the children she actually went on to have. There is movement through time as disparate elements of the narrative – the tidy house, Gina's desires for (and achievement of) a different kind of life, the rambly house, the Famous Five, jam-making – all of these disparate things are brought together, through the plot itself, into a coherent overall story. These occurrences are made into events by the very fact of being included in the narrative. The events themselves are brought together within an overall plot in which they are linked, the end seemingly *inevitably* linked to the beginning in a causal relationship. Within this narrative, Gina's later life is presented and understood as being an outcome of her earlier life: the respectable working-class childhood leading to a desire for a kind of bourgeois-bohemian existence, later achieved and realised. The later events are understood as being caused by earlier ones.

Within narratives, and through processes of emplotment, prior events seem inevitably to lead to later ones, and the end of the story is understood as the culmination and actualisation of prior events. Significance is conferred in earlier events by what comes later. In this sense, narratives become naturalised as the episodes which make up the 'plot' appear inevitable, and even universal. The end of a story does not have to be predictable, but it must be meaningful. In short, a narrative must have a *point*: the question every narrator tries to fend off is, 'So what?' (Ricoeur 1980; Steedman 1989). And for narratives to have a point, they must incorporate this important element of bringing together disparate elements into a single plot:

> The connectivity of parts is precisely why narrativity turns 'events' into episodes, whether the sequence of episodes is presented or experienced in anything resembling chronological or categorical order. And it is emplotment which translates events into episodes. As a mode of explanation, causal emplotment is an accounting (however fantastic or implicit) of why a narrative has the story line it does. (Somers and Gibson 1994: 58)

The plot is a central feature of narrative: it is, fundamentally, what *makes* the narrative, in that it brings together different events and episodes into a meaningful whole: events or episodes are not thrown together at random, but are linked together. We 'read the end into the beginning and the beginning into the end', as Ricoeur puts it (Ricoeur 1980: 183), interpreting later events in the light of earlier ones, so that the end of the story seems to inevitably follow from the beginning. Both the narrator and the audience will participate in these processes of linking – which Ricoeur calls 'emplotment' – through a shared cultural understanding that *these* events have a place in *this* narrative. Emplotment is the 'creative centre of narrative' (Ricoeur 1991: 24).

SOME BACKGROUND

Although attention to narrative emplotment in social and cultural research is relatively recent, concern with the social uses and dynamics of narratives has a much longer history. Ricoeur, for example, takes his notion of emplotment from Aristotle, whose concept of plot was that of an integrating structure (Ricoeur 1991). However, attention to narratives has been vivified from the twentieth century as a result of a number of intellectual developments. These developments have included, crucially, what has come to be called 'the linguistic turn', in which language came to be seen, not as a simple and transparent carrier of 'facts', but as integral to the making of meaning. One outcome of this has been a conceptualising of research, and indeed of social action itself, in terms of 'texts', so that an attention to the 'how?' as well as the 'what?' becomes crucial.

More broadly, however, narrative theory, in the sense in which I use it here, has to be understood as embedded within a hermeneutic tradition. Hermeneutics has its roots in biblical scholarship, though it is now more commonly associated with philosophical enquiry associated with phenomenology. It takes as its focus ways of understanding. Its concern is less 'what happened?' than 'what is the significance of this event?' (White 1996). This is about more than simply understanding the stories themselves: it incorporates, rather, a view of the social world as always interpreted, and of interpretation as central to people's social existence. Hermeneutic inquiry focuses centrally on investigations of meaning and interpretation, and locates interpretation within the specifics of a history and a culture (Crotty 1998).

This focus on the centrality of meaning and understanding is vital to an understanding of narratives, since, I would argue, narratives *always and necessarily* build in attempts at understanding. We can perhaps see this most clearly in its negative – in the ways in which a refusal to be an audience to a narrative entails a refusal to understand. There may be good reasons to refuse to hear someone's story but such a refusal is always a violent act in that it stands as a refusal to offer the person any understanding.[4] Of course, this does not mean that hearing someone's story entails an automatic understanding: my point is, rather, that narrative is a necessary (though not a sufficient) mode of understanding of the world.

WHY STUDY NARRATIVE? OPPORTUNITIES AND PROBLEMS

If, as I have argued, stories run through social life such that the social world is itself storied, then it is not enough to simply look for narratives and then show that they are there. Barbara Czarniawska, after Solow (1988), characterises this as a 'Look, Ma, there is a narrative!' approach (Czarniawska 2004: 41). This, as she points out, is inadequate. The point, rather, is consider 'the consequences of storytelling – for those who tell the stories and for those who study them' (2004: 41) and, I would add, for broader social and cultural relations.

In this spirit, I want, in this section, to consider what studying narratives can achieve. In my consideration of what narratives can do, I will highlight two features: narratives as bridging the divide between self and other, individual and 'society'; and as bridging the gap between past and present.

Self and Other

Narratives plunge us into a sociality. Whatever stories we tell must challenge the myth of the atomised individual, for two principal reasons: firstly, because there is always more than one story to tell about any event, or any life; and secondly, because we cannot produce stories out of nothing, and must instead draw on the narrative resources available to us. The multiplicity of narratives springs, no doubt, from a multiplicity of perspectives. Taking Gina's narrative (above), it is easy to consider the ways in which her mother might produce a different narrative, perhaps one that explains her own approach to domestic life, or even one that refutes Gina's own. Or, Gina's children might have a different story to tell about their mother, or about their own childhood. Furthermore, others' stories sometimes provide the basis for our own, as intimates furnish parts of stories that have been forgotten, or (as in the case of early childhood) furnish the stories themselves. Even memory itself – which is conventionally understood as being 'owned' by the individual – can be seen as being produced in complex, intersubjective relationships. Jeffrey Prager, for example, writes of 'the ways in which the cultural and the interpersonal interpenetrate in memory, a process generally thought to be purely individual' and argues that memories are 'the result of an individual's relation to both self and the outside world' (2000: 59–60).

In general, people have quite high levels of tolerance for a diversity of interpretations and hence of narratives, although, as I will discuss below, this variety is not endless. The point I want to make here, however, is that this very diversity indicates the ways in which people exist in what we might see as interpretive collectivities. An attention to narrative reminds us of this.

However, it is perhaps in considering the second point – the ways in which individual social actors draw on wider cultural resources in producing narratives – that a challenge to the self-other binary is most clearly seen. I have already suggested that individual narratives must conform to intelligibility rules which are socially and historically specific. More than this, however, for several authors, the social world is filled with stories: it comes to us already 'storied'. Somers and Gibson argue:

> [S]tories guide action; . . . people construct identities (however multiple and changing) by locating themselves or being located within a repertoire of emplotted stories; . . . 'experience' is constituted through narratives; . . .people make sense of what has happened and is happening to them by attempting to assemble or in some way to integrate these happenings within one or more narratives; and . . . people are guided to act in certain ways, and not others, on the basis of the projections, expectations, and memories derived from a multiplicity but ultimately linked repertoire of available social, public and cultural narratives. (Somers and Gibson 1994: 38–9)

If the social world is always-already storied, it puts constraints on the stories we produce. Gina's narrative, for example, only makes sense in a time and place in which we understand mothering as significant, if not decisive, for how the child (and especially the daughter) turns out; in which we associate certain ways of living with certain class milieus, and so on. Our social milieu also provides a set of *resources* on which we can draw to produce our own stories. There are, for example, the plots provided by the literary tradition, but narratives are also provided by soap operas, 'expert' advice, talk shows and so on. Through using existing narratives we create our own.

If this is so, then narrative provides us with means of contextualising people's individual narratives, so that they are always embedded within publicly-circulating narratives that are specific to times and places.

Past and Present

> Memories are their own descendants, masquerading as the ancestors of the past. (David Mitchell, *Ghostwritten*, p. 326)

Any research which aims to understand how people themselves live and understand their everyday lives must consider the past as well as the present. No-one lives in an eternal present and the past – both individually and socially – informs and impacts on people's presents. As John Berger has observed, ' "I am" includes all that has made me so . . . It is already biographical' (Berger 1992: 370–1).

However, the past, being the past, is no longer with us. It lives on only in representations of itself – in dreams, memories, images, and, above all, in the stories or narratives which work as means of bringing together these mediated fragments into another representation – a narrative in which events bring about other events: a narrative with a beginning, a middle, and (however deferred) an end. There is, in other words, no unmediated access to the past and, indeed, the very act of recalling and telling the past is an exercise in interpretation.

To make this point is not simply to notice that memory is unreliable, although it is. It is to consider, firstly, the significance of memory for narratives – and especially for life narratives; and, secondly, to foreground the role of interpretation. Memory is reconstructive (Misztal 2003): what is remembered depends on what 'makes sense' in the context. To remember is not like watching a video (Hacking 1995). As Carolyn Steedman comments:

> We all return to memories and dreams . . . again and again; the story we tell of our life is reshaped around them. But the point doesn't lie there, back in the past, back in the lost time at which they happened; the only point lies in interpretation. The past is re-used through the agency of social information, and that interpretation of it can only be made with what people know of a social world and their place within it. (Steedman 1989: 5)

Steedman herself develops this point in her own exploration of narrative in *Landscape for a Good Woman*. Subtitled *A story of two lives*, this book contains the story of Steedman's own life together with that of her mother. These life narratives are interwoven with social history, fragments of fairy stories, and a psychoanalytic case study (Freud's 'Dora'). The text as a whole is framed by Steedman's own analysis of the various narratives contained in the text, as well as a meta-commentary on narrative itself. Steedman's text considers individual biographies in the context of social relations. Indeed, by considering social relations in their historical and political specificity, she is able to consider why events become 'episodes' at all.

It is difficult to summarise this complex text, but one of its striking features is the ways in which Steedman embeds her own autobiography within the lives of others, and within the historical contexts of her parents' and grandparents' worlds. She embeds it, too, within a political analysis which highlights the peculiar marginality and estrangement of the 'clever' working-class girl growing up in the mid-twentieth century. Thus, *Landscape* illustrates the two features of narrative's bridging work that I am highlighting here (self/other; past/present) and also demonstrates the broader point that all stories are told from a particular point of view. The following passage gives a sense of this embeddedness and these interconnections:

> Upstairs, a long time ago, [my mother] had cried, standing on the bare
> floorboards in the front bedroom, just after we moved to this house in
> Streatham Hill in 1951, my baby sister in her carry-cot. We both watched
> the dumpy retreating figure of the health-visitor through the curtainless
> windows. The woman had said, 'This house isn't fit for a baby' . . .
>
> And I? I will do everything and anything until the end of my days to
> stop anyone ever talking to me like that woman talked to my mother. It
> is in this place, this bare, curtainless bedroom that lies my secret
> and shameful defiance. I read a women's book, meet such a woman at a
> party . . . and think quite deliberately as we talk: we are divided: a
> hundred years ago I'd have been cleaning your shoes. I know this and
> you don't. (Steedman 1989: 1–2)

Here, emplotment takes place around Steedman's 'secret and shameful
defiance', instilled out of watching her mother's humiliation at the hands of the
health visitor. Out of the curtainless bedroom, the baby in the cot and the
woman at the party, Steedman weaves a story of classed identity, class envy and
class politics. As she writes, all stories are 'the same story in the end: the story
of how the individual came to be the way she is' (Steedman 1989: 132), and this
is the story of how Steedman came to be the way she is.

Steedman's text, however, takes us both into and out of this story. By considering the context (the history, the politics) and the inter-textuality of her
story, she is able to offer her own interpretations – interpretations, in part, of
her own memories – which make the narrative more than the sum of its parts.

THE THORNY ISSUE OF 'TRUTH'

The issue of whether or not a narrative is 'true' is usually bracketed within contemporary analyses. Czarniawska, for example, while acknowledging that analysts do not have to accept 'tall tales', suggests that questions of fact or fiction
are of little concern, especially when considering not *what* a text says, but *how*
it says it. While sociologists from the Chicago School, working in the mid-
twentieth century, often went to great lengths to determine whether their
respondents' narratives were factually correct or not, few researchers now
trouble themselves with the problem.

In fact I think there are good reasons for this, not least a perception of the
inadequacy of the correspondence theory of truth, in which (narrative and
other) texts refer to an unproblematic world of facts 'out there'. If everything
is symbolically mediated (and from a narrative perspective, it is) then to
propose that there is a world of things that escape this mediation is illogical. So,
for example, Donna Haraway argues:

Stories are not 'fictions' in the sense of being 'made up'. Rather, narratives are devices to produce certain kinds of meaning. I try to use stories to tell what I think is the truth – a located, embodied, contingent and *therefore* real truth. (Haraway 1997: 230; emphasis added)

Haraway, then, seems to be suggesting that 'truth' is to be found in location, embodiment, contingency. I think what lies behind this comment is Haraway's refusal to claim authority for her stories – a refusal to claim that any one account is the 'god's eye view' (Haraway 1991). This is part of her critique of a spurious objectivity that claims to be able to see the world 'as it is', while really being the subjective position of those with the power to claim objectivity. In terms of Haraway's analysis of knowledge-production, this has been an important critique. But to see 'truth' as inhering in located-ness may lead us into difficulties. Don't narratives make some moral claim for recognition?

There are certainly times when people demand a recognition that some things happened while other things definitely did not. For example, Lundy and McGovern's (2006) study of a participatory action research project in Ardoyne, Northern Ireland, was concerned with precisely the importance, to participants of different religious communities, of having specific truth claims validated. In this example, truth claims are politically important. While the difficulties of establishing them cannot be underestimated, it is clear that they cannot simply be dispensed with.

I would also argue, however, that contested claims to truth can tell us something interesting about narrative itself. That is, they can tell us something about the importance of an *interpretive community*. To illustrate my argument here, I will discuss the complex narrative of Binjamin Wilkormiski.[5]

Wilkormiski is a Swiss musician and instrument-maker who, in 1995, published a memoir, *Bruchstücke*, in Germany. Several translations quickly followed, including the English version, *Fragments: Memories of a Childhood, 1939–1948*. The book was a memoir of a Jewish child's experiences in a Latvian ghetto and in Nazi death camps, and, after the war, in a Swiss orphanage. It received tremendous critical acclaim and won a number of prestigious awards.

The publication of the memoir brought Wilkormiski to public attention and there were numerous lecture tours and invitations to speak. It seemed clear that his apparent psychological distress was an outcome of his traumatised childhood. In other words, in the narrative of Wilkormiski's life, the story of 'how he came to be the way he is', to paraphrase Steedman, is a story of extraordinary suffering. His adult life is made explicable through a plot that is familiar – the obscene plot of Nazi genocide.

It quickly become clear, however, that, according to all the available evidence, *Fragments* was fraudulent. Investigative work by a Swiss journalist, Daniel Ganzfield, and later by a Swiss historian, Stefan Maechler, revealed

Binjamin Wilkormiski to have been born Bruno Grosjean, a Swiss Gentile, born to a single mother and subsequently adopted by a wealthy Swiss couple. He was not Jewish, not Latvian, and had never been in a camp. This revelation brought public outcry and the withdrawal of prizes and awards. Wilkormiski/Grosjean, however, refutes this evidence and refuses to accept that the memoir is in any way fraudulent. Indeed, he has indicated that he regards any failure to believe his story as a form of holocaust-denial.

I certainly do not want to offer any kind of psychological or other analysis of Wilkormiski himself. I am, rather, interested in two different issues: firstly, the appropriation of other stories as the raw materials from which to make one's own, and secondly, the reception to this narrative. Does it matter that it was false? Indeed, how can one know whether it is or not?

Gross and Hoffman suggest that Wilkormiski's identification with the Holocaust – even to the degree of inserting himself into a story that was not his – is perfectly coherent in a contemporary 'victim culture'. They write:

> It is easy to dismiss Wilkomirski as someone whose personal suffering has led him to over-identify with victims of the Holocaust, but in [a contemporary] victim culture . . . this is just what he is supposed to do. Institutions as influential as the US Holocaust Memorial Museum teach the Holocaust through transference and identification. (2004: 34)[6]

In other words, Wilkormiski has successfully achieved identification with what Lauren Berlant has called 'the subject of pain' (Berlant 2000), and it is hardly surprising that he has done so, especially in 'an age of identity politics, when being a victim is a mark of distinction' (Gross and Hoffman 2004: 32). He has taken existing narratives – apparently as diverse as Holocaust memoirs and the children's story *Heidi* (Maechler 2001) – to produce his own story and his own identity. Analysts' accounts point to the likelihood that he himself is invested in this identity and in some sense believes it to be his own. Isn't this what we all do? I have argued, following Ricoeur and others, that we draw on the narratives of our time and place to creatively assemble a life narrative of our own.

But Wilkormiski's is a narrative identity cast adrift from the facts of the case as embodied in official documents, and in the memories and life histories of others. Any one of these can be faulty, of course, but the weight of evidence would seem, on every count, to bear against the Wilkormiski story. So we are returned to the question, does it matter?

Audiences tend to expect claims which are passed off as true (as in written memoirs or even spoken accounts) to accord with the 'facts'. Otherwise, some breach of sociality is seen to have occurred: the perpetrator of the lie has broken a set of social rules. While most people are probably comfortable with the notion that all facts are interpreted, there does seem to be an expectation of a relationship between fact and interpretation, in lay accounts as much as in academic analyses. Non-fiction narratives, it is expected, must accord *in some way*, not only with sets of intelligibility rules, but with the accounts and memories and recordings of others. When they do not, a sense of betrayal – a breach of a social contract or social promise – frequently occurs. This is because, as I noted above, life narratives can never be individualised, atomised accounts, but must include some account of the lives of others. The ethical imperative seems to lie in a demand that narratives ought to be rendered sufficiently faithfully that others can recognise the story and, if they are sufficiently close to the storyteller, should be able to recognise themselves within it. This must go beyond an emotional identification ('yes, it was like that for me') to a more 'objective' identification ('yes, it was like that').

Of course there are numerous difficulties here since memory, as I noted above, is notoriously unreliable and, clearly, people often remember the same event entirely differently – the source of many familial disputes. Wilkormiski's narrative, however, was not only false but could not be attributed to an idiosyncrasy of interpretation – after all, he was either in the camps or he was not. But, crucially, his story laid claim to a 'privileged' suffering identity – that of Holocaust survivor. It may be, as Gross and Hoffman argue, that he was only obeying the demands of a culture that encourages identification with a suffering other – and indeed encourages the forging of an identity on that basis. But the public *response* to his life narrative would suggest that, however strong the tendency to value pain as a means of identification, this is not considered to be sufficient to guarantee the truth of an account. It would suggest, further, that some form of social contract is seen to be broken when people overtly fabricate an identity that does not accord with the narratives and lives of others (though again, I must add, there are certain levels of tolerance in some circumstances, and not in others).

The main point I want to make here is that the breach of sociality that is seen to occur when people take on a fraudulent identity is another indication of the inherently social character of narrative identity. Narratives are collective in the sense that no narrative belongs to the teller alone: they also incorporate the narratives of others. They must, as Hacking puts it, 'mesh with the rest of the world and with other people's stories, at least in externals' (Hacking 1995: 251). As such, they must contribute to a form of sociality in which (within certain limits) they are seen as more or less according with the knowledge and experience and indeed the narratives of others.

The Wilkormiski case raises some important issues. It illustrates the ways in which people draw on a repertoire of existing narratives to produce their own narrative, the significance of an audience in receiving, understanding and interpreting a narrative, and the central importance of the time and space within which personal narratives are embedded. It also tells us something important about the collective, deeply social character of narrative. The contract between ourselves and others demands some minimal level of agreement, so that people cannot simply claim to be whatever and whoever they want; or, at least, such a move will not work without the consent and agreement of others.

USING NARRATIVE IN CULTURAL ANALYSIS: INTERPRETING THE INTERPRETERS

So far, I have suggested that an examination of narratives enables a greater focus on the collective, social character of the world and enables, too, a contextualising of the subject of narrative within time and space. Personal narratives do not exist in a vacuum but draw from a range of available cultural narratives. And then, of course, having gone into social circulation, they too become resources on which to draw, whether on a small or a grand scale.

Narratives as used by people in their everyday lives can take a number of forms. They can be 'found' as in, for example, urban myths (see Moriarty 2005) or in published accounts like that of Wilkormiski; they can be elicited, as Gina's was, in interviews – in her case, over the course of four interviews; they can be produced by the analyst her/himself, as Steedman's *Landscape* is. How, then, can the researcher approach the task of exploring and analysing narratives?

Clearly, when reading and analysing narratives, it is important to be conscious of the multiple levels of interpretation – and multiple narratives – at work. There is the interpretation offered by the 'author' of the narrative, and the interpretation of that interpretation undertaken by the researcher. The finished product – another narrative – will then be subject to the interpretations of readers, who may then engage in writing with the text . . . and so on.

How, then, can the researcher approach narratives? I do not think it is possible to lay down rules, but Michael Crotty gives a useful schema in his suggestion of three ways to read texts: empathic, interactive, and transactional.

The empathic mode represents an attempt to understand (though not necessarily to agree with) the author's standpoint. 'The author is speaking to us, and we are listening. We try to enter into the mind and personage of the author, seeking to see things from the author's perspective' (Crotty 1998: 109). *The interactive approach* goes beyond this to a dialogue with the author (I assume that Crotty does not have in mind a literal dialogue, as one might have, say, in an interview, but rather an internal dialogue with the author as we read the text). In this mode, reading can become more critical and the text can be read 'against the grain': that is, against the apparent or manifest intentions of its author.

In the third, *transactional mode*, there is a more active engagement with the text:

Out of the engagement comes something quite new. The insights that
emerge were never in the mind of the author. They are not in the
author's text. They were not with us as we picked up the text to read it.
They have come into being in and out of our engagement with it.
(Crotty 1998: 109–10)

In all of these approaches, it is clear that the power to make meaning resides
neither entirely with the 'author' of the narrative, nor with the researcher (the
'audience'). Where this meaning is made shifts between the different positions,
with the empathic mode privileging the author, the interactive mode privileging
the reader, and the transactional mode setting up a dialectic between both parties.

In practice, I think most researchers would be inclined to combine these
approaches but Crotty's schema is a useful starting point for thinking about
analysing narratives. It also raises an interesting point that he himself does not
pursue. Crotty seems here to be concerned with how researchers can approach
the 'finished' text, but in some cases (such as Gina's narrative, above) the text
is not finished by the time the researcher gets to it, but co-produced within the
research setting. Clearly, if a researcher is interested in producing research
texts (for example, interview transcripts) that contain narratives, then s/he
must enable and encourage research participants to produce those narratives.
But in important respects, such narratives are always co-productions. Even if
the researcher's intervention is minimal, the prompts used and questions asked
will guide research participants in certain directions.

Indeed, we are never dealing with one narrative but several, or, at least, with
several stages in the production of a narrative. It is worth outlining these stages.

The production of a narrative. In the case of 'found narratives', the researcher
may not know about the conditions or circumstances in which the narrative
was produced, but if narratives are produced within the research setting,
the researcher not only knows about the narrative's production, but is a co-
producer. That is, the kinds of questions asked, the framing of the research, the
researcher's own intervention, and so on, will all inform the narratives produced
by research participants. It is important to note, however, that the narrative is
unlikely to have been produced *ab initio* within the research. Rather, research
participants bring to the research their own interpretations of, and stories about,
their worlds – 'the stories of their days and the stories in their days'.

The analysis of a narrative. Here, the researcher/analyst seems to have free rein
in taking and analysing a complete (if not a final) narrative. Indeed, this notion
of 'free rein' chimes with a contemporary emphasis which privileges the reader,
rather than the author, of a text (in this case, a narrative text). Clearly, to say
that a text means whatever the author intends (Knapp and Michaels 1985)

assumes a fixity of meaning and subverts any notion of multiple meanings. It also assumes that the reader could *know* what the author intends, and, indeed, it would do away with any need for analysis since the narrative would simply 'speak for itself'. That it cannot indicates the ways in which readers will bring their own interpretations to the text – a staple insight of hermeneutic theory.

For example, Gina's narrative is (in my interpretation) 'about' more than a tidy house, dreams of jam-making and children like the Famous Five. It is also 'about' authoritative discourses of motherhood in which 'free expression' in children is valued (and tidy houses are not!); about class relations in which it is better to have a 'big rambly house'; about Gina's relationships with her mother and with her children. None of these things is directly referenced in the text. My referencing them as part of my interpretation is a result of my own focus as researcher, my reading of her narrative in a context, and against a backdrop of other texts. It is, of course, open to different, oppositional interpretations in its turn. Paul Ricoeur argues:

> [E]very reading of a text always takes place within a community, a tradition or a living current of thought, all of which display presuppositions and exigencies, regardless of how closely a reading may be tied to the *quid*, to 'that in view of which' the text was written. (Ricoeur 2004a: 3)

On the other hand, can a text mean anything at all? Can it be entirely set free of its author? In some ways it can, but there are some things that it would seem perverse to claim a text is about. There is, as Umberto Eco (1992) argues, an 'aboutness' to a text that sets limits on interpretations. Texts are not necessarily internally consistent or coherent, but they are rarely completely incoherent either. The point I want to make here, however, is that there is a range of interpretations to be made, but that range is not infinite. Nevertheless, an important insight of hermeneutic approaches is that the interpretation can go beyond the initial interpretation of the author. Crotty argues:

> Included in much hermeneutic theory is the prospect of gaining an understanding of the text that is deeper or goes further than the author's own understandings. This aim derives from the view that in large measure authors' meanings and intentions remain implicit and go unrecognised by the authors themselves. Because in the writing of the text so much is simply taken for granted, skilled hermeneutic inquiry has the potential to uncover meanings and intentions that are, in this sense, hidden in the text. Interpreters may end up with an explicit awareness of meanings, and especially assumptions, that the authors themselves would have been unable to articulate. (Crotty 1998: 91)[7]

But how is that interpretation to be made at all? What checks exist on the researcher's interpretation? In much research, measures of validity would serve as such checks, but Barbara Czarniawska argues that conventional notions of validity – which she defines here as the (research) text's correspondence to the world – do not work when considering narratives. This, she argues, is because the correspondence theory of truth – in which texts ('words') correspond with things 'out there' ('worlds') – does not work. We cannot compare 'words' with 'worlds': worlds are always interpreted and symbolised within words (or in other forms). In the end we can only compare texts with other texts.

This is an important point when thinking of what narratives can do. Comparing 'words with worlds' is a hopeless mission when everything comes to us culturally mediated. However, the definition of validity outlined by Czarniawska – correspondence with an unmediated idea of 'the real world' – is only one definition of validity. A broader, more encompassing definition concerns whether the completed research does what it claims to do and shows what it claims to show. Here again, however, such validity criteria are not necessarily straightforward when considering research based on narrative analysis, because such work tends to be – and can only be – more concerned with exploration than with showing 'results'. If narratives are concerned with understanding and meaning, and if meanings are indeterminate, then pinning down precise criteria for validity is going to be difficult.

Does this mean, then, that 'anything goes'? I think this is far from the case and that an attention to how the narrative is produced, analysed and presented is crucial. Above all, I would argue the notion that the research must show and say what it claims is crucial. In the end, however, the analysis of narratives is an interpretive exercise for which the analyst must take responsibility; about which s/he must be reflexive; and which s/he must open to as much scrutiny as possible. This is why the third stage in narrative research – *the production of a research narrative* – is also important. In this, the researcher's own account of how the analysis 'came to be the way it is', clarity, reflexivity and openness are crucial.

In sum, the study of narrative can offer researchers and analysts important insights into the social world. Narratives, considered as cultural resources which people use creatively to situate themselves within worlds, show the complex ways in which people interpret the social world, and the ways in which they position themselves enmeshed in links of self and other, past and present.

SUMMARY: KEY POINTS

- Narratives are always bound up with processes of interpretation and understanding.

- Narratives link together self and other, past and present, thus exploding the myth of the atomised individual, existing in an eternal present.
- Narratives link together events and the interpretation of those events.
- Narratives always have a (real or imagined) audience with whom a social contract or social promise exists.
- The analysis of narratives is multi-layered and requires sensitivity and reflexivity on the part of the researcher.

FURTHER READING

Much work on narrative emplotment tends to deal with narrative at a conceptual level, rather than with the analysis of narratives in various kinds of texts. Nevertheless, this work is important, especially since, as I noted above, the question of what narrative *is* is often left vaguely or un-defined. Somers and Gibson (1994) give a clear exposition, as do Ewick and Silbey (1995) while also discussing some examples of narratives in legal settings. Richard Kearney (2002) considers both fictional and non-fictional narratives and deals with the distinction between truth and falsehood. Kearney's work on Paul Ricoeur (2004) is an excellent introduction to Ricoeur's work. There is some interesting life history work which considers (albeit often rather obliquely) issues of narrative. Some good examples include the work of Prue Chamberlayne and collaborators – see, for example, Chamberlayne et al. (2000), Miller (1999) and Stanley (1992). My own work on the mother-daughter relationship (Lawler 1999, 2000) uses narrative to explore life trajectories, especially through classed movement. Barbara Czaniawska (2004) offers an interesting look at the uses and applications of narrative research, and provides an excellent resource for anyone embarking on this form of work.

NOTES

1. Even though there is some debate about whether stories and narratives are identical, I will use both terms more or less interchangeably throughout this chapter since, for the purposes of my argument here, they do the same work.
2. The Famous Five are a group of four white, middle-class children and a dog who feature in a series of books written between the 1940s and the 1960s by the English children's author Enid Blyton.
3. A pseudonym.
4. In 1990, Claude Lanzmann, maker of the film *Shoah*, refused to be present at a screening of a Dutch film about Edward Wirths, a camp doctor in

Auschwitz. For Lanzmann, the screening of the film (the telling of Wirth's story) and he suggests, any form of narrative about the perpetrators of the Holocaust, necessarily entails an attempt at understanding: asking the question 'why?' which, he argues, should not be asked about the Holocaust. The point here is not whether or not Lanzmann is right, but that, both for him and for those who disagreed with him, the question 'why?' – the impulse to understanding – is an intrinsic part of narrative. See Lanzmann (1995).

5. I take my account of Wilkormiski's life from Lappin (1999) and Maechler (2001). I discuss this case in more detail in Lawler (2008).

6. The Holocaust Memorial Museum in Washington DC does this through, for example, assigning visitors identity cards with the names of victims on them. Visitors do not know at this point whether or not they will 'survive'. In this way, as Gross and Hoffman point out, 'The emphasis is on the visceral, the emotive and the artifatual: the museum personalizes history, encouraging visitors to identify with and put themselves in the place of the victims. This is precisely what Wilkormiski has done' (2004: 34).

7. This is similar to Michael Pickering's observation, in Chapter 1 of this volume, that researchers need to take account not only of what research subjects say, but also of the social location of the research subject. As he suggests, respect for the accounts of research subjects does not necessarily mean that their accounts are the last word on the subject.

Production and Consumption

CHAPTER 3

Investigating Cultural Producers

Aeron Davis

INTRODUCTION

This chapter is in four parts. Each of the first three parts offers a brief overview of the more common research approaches used to investigate cultural production. These are broadly categorised here as political economy, textual analysis and sociological/ethnographic work. The fourth part then concentrates on the third of these and the practical considerations involved. In both parts the discussion and examples draw on my own experiences of researching cultural production in the news industry and within the subcultures of financial and political elite networks. At the time of writing I have interviewed over 250 professionals employed in journalism, public relations, business and politics.

APPROACHES TO RESEARCHING CULTURAL PRODUCTION

Political Economy

In media and cultural studies there are several common approaches used for researching and documenting cultural production. These might be loosely placed into three categories. The first of these belongs, although not exclusively, in the domain of media political economy.[1] Under this remit cultural production is investigated on the macro level as an industry. Here it is assumed that the conditions of production shape cultural content. The researcher therefore attempts to link cultural outputs to the economic, industrial and political factors that shape the organisations and industries which then produce culture.

This often involves gathering quantitative data on those industries. What are the costs of production? What are the main revenue sources (advertising, sales, sponsorship)? How are the costs of production broken down and which processes, from research and development to distribution, cost what? How many competing organisations are there in the market and what is their audience share? Such figures are collected, aggregated and used to make inferences about the state of the cultural industry involved and the possible impacts on the cultural texts it then produces. So, for example, Curran (1978), Schiller (1989) and Garnham (1990) have looked at how advertising and other financial considerations are likely to have impacted on the cultural production and distribution processes. Doyle (2002) and Bagdikian (2004) have documented the pace of concentration and conglomeration across the cultural industries. For others cultural production is also linked to external, macro-level factors, such as politics, policy and regulation (Peacock 1986; Herman and McChesney 1997; Curran and Seaton 2003). Laws governing such things as media ownership, cultural content, licensing and levels of taxation are all likely to have a bearing on cultural outputs. In these accounts cultural outputs are in part shaped as a consequence of political and economic conditions. The negotiations and decisions of individual politicians, regulators and business owners and advertisers filter through to influence the choices and methods of those who make, edit, produce and distribute cultural products.

In other work, industry figures are simply used to trace new developments in production or the rise and fall of certain media or cultural genres. Post-Fordist accounts of the cultural industries (Christopherson and Storper 1986; Murray 1989) have observed such things as production outsourcing and flexible working practices which impact on outputs. Others have chosen simply to focus on how new technologies alter aspects of production and transmission (Downing 1984; Heap et al. 1995).

In each of these cases cultural production is investigated indirectly. The focus is not on those individuals who produce culture but on the structures, external factors and high-level decision-makers which come to influence and shape mass-produced culture. Research usually gathers data by obtaining and analysing documents from industry and/or government. These may be in the form of simple financial data sets, industry surveys and reports, policy and legislative documents or historical archives. The challenge of the researcher is to locate and access this data, which can then be collated, aggregated, cross-referenced, and so on. Such data is then used to develop a more macro account or to contribute to theoretical debates on aspects of cultural production.

Many of these data sources are produced by public bodies and are relatively easy to find. In the UK published legislative documents can be gained from HMSO (Her Majesty's Stationery Office). Historical records of past events and political discussions are obtainable from the National Archives. Debates in

Parliament are recorded in Hansard. In addition, government departments, from the DCMS (Department for Culture, Media and Sport) to the ONS (Office for National Statistics), are a source of statistics and industry overviews. Certain academic libraries keep hard copies of many of these documents. They are also obtainable direct from the public institutions. Increasingly, however, all recent documentation is published on the websites of these bodies and is downloadable without charge.

To access information on a sector in the media and cultural industries one can also seek out sources within that industry itself. The first question the researcher should ask is 'does the cultural industry in question have a professional or trade union body?' The second is 'do they have one or more "trade" or professional publications?' A third is 'do they have any regulators, official watchdogs or interest groups/associations which monitor them?' Each of these organisations or publications can be a potential source of data about the industry involved. As well as offering quantitative data about the sector, they are likely to offer very useful information for further investigation. Who are the main companies and the key figures in the sector? What are the latest developments and debates, and what are the important events that have taken place within the industry recently?

Lastly, one can go directly to the companies and institutions themselves. Extensive information on all aspects of the BBC is easily accessible from the Corporation and its website. Every commercial company doing business in the UK must publish its annual report and accounts and other information. Companies House keeps records on each company. Companies quoted on a stock market are also obliged to publish and circulate information about themselves on a regular basis. In most cases, once again, these days the company will also publish all such information on its website.

At the same time there is a large amount of commercial information on the cultural industries which is relatively inaccessible. Some reports and financial/industry data are produced by commercial research companies and expensive to obtain. Other reports tend to be produced and circulated only amongst industry specialists. Others still are regarded as very politically or commercially sensitive and are the hardest to access. In each of these cases the academic researcher must make personal contact with those involved and attempt to persuade them to pass on copies (see below on interviewing professionals and making contact).

When I began to research the rise of the public relations (PR) industry and its relationship to news journalism, I began with the industry journals and associations. I located and read through several years' copies of *PR Week* and visited the IPR (Institute of Public Relations – now CIPR) and PRCA (Public Relations Consultants Association). All three were a good source of industry and government reports and statistics about the profession. They directed me towards further academic and industry sources. When turning to journalists, I approached the NUJ (National Union of Journalists) and read through back copies of *The Journalist*, *Press Gazette*, and *British Journalism Review*, amongst others. As in the PR sector I was able to build up a macro picture of the profession from what I found. A comparison of aggregated data from the two professions offered some interesting findings. I also came to know much more about the main companies involved, high-profile individuals and the shape of the industries which, in turn, presented a list of potential interviewees and case studies for further research. I then began approaching some of the leading companies to gain further quantitative data and also to attempt more micro-level observations.

As an approach to research political economy assumes much about the influences on, and behaviours of, individuals involved in cultural production. Individual-level actions and cognitions cannot really be investigated closely. Many also object to the emphasis placed on political and economic influences and point out that statistical data may be interpreted and presented quite subjectively. On the other hand, it is very appropriate for developing a macro-level account of a cultural industry or individual firm. Findings may be more representative on a general level and the data collected more objective/representative than other research material (although this is vigorously denied by some).

Texts and Textual Analysis

A second research approach investigates cultural production through an analysis of cultural outputs. This involves applying forms of textual analysis to a series of printed, visual or audio texts. As with political economy approaches, cultural production is investigated indirectly. Wider deductions about the production (and also consumption) process are inferred from assessments of what is produced. In analysing texts researchers seek to highlight the common codes, terms, ideologies, discourses and individuals that come to dominate cultural outputs. What can be said about the individuals featured in the texts? Who are the contributors to the text? How are the texts framed and presented? What are the terms and phrases used and what is their symbolic meaning? What are the assumptions embedded in the texts? The answers to such questions, gathered from analysis, are then used to build arguments about those who construct cultural products and wider social, cultural and linguistic conditions.

The texts and research areas chosen vary considerably. Hall et al. (1978), Hall (1973) and the Glasgow University Media Group (1976, 1980) chose to look at the ideological 'codes' and 'primary definers' that dominate news coverage. Foucault (1975) and Said (1979) collected a number of historical, social and institutional texts and used them to deduce social discourses about 'disciplinary power' and 'the Other'. Fiske and Hartley (1978), Dyer (1982) and

Geraghty (1991) have decoded the language and symbolism of visual texts, in television and film, and made links to wider social and cultural values. Williamson (1978) and Goldman (1992) have deconstructed advertising texts and the means by which they attempt to appeal to consumers. Since culture and language are contained in all forms of social interaction, so texts for analysis can be found in a range of media forms and social settings (see Barthes 1972, for example). Musical lyrics, clothing, political speeches, posters, popular magazines and geographical layouts have all been recorded and analysed as texts.

The first concern of the researcher is to obtain and select the texts to be analysed. Are the texts recorded or recordable? Are there enough texts available for the kind of analysis proposed? Printed texts are usually the easiest to obtain. Thus news and magazine articles are commonly selected as the unit of analysis in research, although public documents, lyrics and political speeches are, in theory, not much harder to track down. Much material can be found in specialist libraries such as the newspaper section of the British Library in Colindale, London. The texts of key publications, going back several decades, can be found in paper or microfilm form. More recent texts are usually stored electronically and obtainable on database collections and websites. Companies such as LexisNexis offer larger news databases of multiple publications, thus enabling wider searches. Visual and audio text collection is a more hit-and-miss affair and more difficult generally, although digitalisation is making this easier. Films and popular television series are simpler to collect because they are easier to record, store and distribute. For other forms of textual analysis, the researcher has to be more creative in tracking down and recording the texts needed for analysis.

Having obtained the texts, the researcher then has to think about a number of other issues: How many texts should be analysed? How, if there are many to chose from, should a sample be selected? Is the analysis going to be quantitative or qualitative or a mixture of the two? The answers to these questions are reached by a combination of practical and theoretical considerations. Qualitative forms of textual or discourse analysis tend to look at far fewer texts but in more depth. Quantitative analyses usually generate large amounts of simple, numerical data from many more units. Whether the researcher wants to deduce conclusions about a single cultural product, such as a soap opera or a newspaper, or to make larger statements about soap operas or news has an impact upon the breadth and depth of selection. The key, practical considerations are that (1) the selection should be a representative sample of the texts under consideration – enough to support any wider conclusions; (2) the quantity is, in part, dictated by the amount of time and writing space needed per text; and, (3) in part, by the amount of texts available. Time spans, media formats, numbers of competing cultural products and key words can all be used to increase or decrease the sample number accordingly.

I conducted two studies involving textual analysis during research on public relations and journalism. Both were part of larger case studies and had quantitative and qualitative elements. They sought to document public relations battles that took place in large part through the print news media. The first was a conflict between trade unions, the government and the Post Office over proposed mail privatisation. The second was a large corporate battle as Granada attempted a hostile takeover of Forte. Both depended on contacting participants and, consequently, led to gaining access to their campaign documents (press releases, strategy documents, and so on) and all the press clippings covering the conflicts. The analyses sought answers to some of the following questions: What were the key elements and the main arguments put by each campaign, and who were the principal news sources? How were these reproduced in the news coverage during the period? I tried to locate the individuals, arguments, and associated factors which came to dominate press reporting. In each case samples of news coverage had to be selected, themes clarified and coded, and quantitative elements decided. Much of this became clearer after a more limited pilot study involving a smaller sample of news texts. This clarified to me what was possible and sensible in terms of the resources at my disposal.

As a research method, textual analysis often assumes rather more than it should about the conditions of cultural production and consumption. In the past rather grand claims about material and cultural relations have been deduced from limited and unrepresentative selections of texts. However, if properly applied, quite strong cases and historical accounts can be developed. The selection and collection of texts is relatively easy and this allows greater choice and flexibility for the researcher.

Sociological/Ethnographic Approaches – Interviewing and Observation

The third approach used to investigate cultural production might be broadly termed sociological/ethnographic[2]. It involves observing and documenting the actual processes and people involved in cultural production. In some cases work is on the quantitative and macro level and relies on surveys of professionals and companies involved in cultural production. Many surveys of journalists, for example, have been conducted over the years. However, the majority of sociological work in media and cultural studies has tended to be more qualitative and carried out at the localised, micro scale. It has usually involved a combination of interviewing and ethnography, most commonly in the form of limited participant-observation. In these cases the researcher is seeking to discover the practices, cognitive processes and social interactions of professionals involved in producing culture. How does an editor decide what stories, features or programmes are to be invested in and published or broadcast? Who are the new creative artists in film, music and television that are worth supporting and promoting? What makes a cultural product or individual a popular and/or critical success? How do creative artists interact with producers and marketing people?

These sorts of questions have been applied in interviews with, and observation of, journalists at work (Tunstall 1971; Gans 1979; Schlesinger 1987). Others, with an interest in news production, have closely recorded the relationships that develop between journalists and their sources (Ericson et al. 1989; Schlesinger and Tumber 1994; Davis 2002). There have been some detailed studies of the production process in television and how this influences the selection process and shaping of programmes (D'Acci 1994; Gitlin 1994). Similar studies have been conducted on the music business (Frith 1983; Negus 1992, 1999). For du Gay et al. (1997a, 1997b), in fact, the production of culture is inseparable from the culture of production. Once again, since culture evolves and is produced in spaces beyond the cultural industries, so researchers may choose to interview and observe participants in other settings. Hebdige (1979) and Thornton (1995) have used such methods to investigate subcultures. Others have attempted to document the culture and communications that take place in political or economic settings (Abolafia 1996; Herbst 1998; Knorr-Cetina and Bruegger 2002).

In conducting sociological/ethnographic forms of research there are several practical challenges and conceptual questions to engage with. One of these is selecting participants. Who and how many people should be interviewed and/or observed in order to get an account that can be said to adequately reflect the chosen topic? The answer tends to be determined by the parameters within which the research will take place. Is the study focused on an entire cultural industry, an aspect of that industry, a particular firm or subculture, or, on a specific case study example? The larger the parameters, the larger the number of participants needed. If a large industry or subculture, then a 'theoretical sample', one linked to the debates and theory being engaged with, needs to be identified. That sample should, if possible, be representative of the occupation in terms of, say, professional ranking, gender, age, and so on. If a case study approach is adopted, then the set of potential participants is limited and easily identified. A good case study will aim to deal with a range of candidates that can offer alternative perspectives. As with sampling texts, the time and resource limits of the researcher have to be factored in.

A second, fundamental challenge involves making and maintaining contacts with participants. If one cannot make contact and persuade participants to be interviewed or observed, the research is over before it has begun. As a result, the access question should be a key consideration when drawing up the research topic. Gaining access to, for example, groups of paramilitaries, sex industry workers, young children or high-powered elites might be problematic for all sorts of reasons (physical, social, temporal, ethical and legal). But interviewing any set of participants is never simple. In all cases one must think very hard about the initial contact. Researchers must ask themselves why participants might agree to cooperate as well as think about what might deter them from agreeing to allow access. Fears have to be allayed, cooperation must be made easy for the participant, and good relations must be maintained. It should also be remembered that the interviewees are, in many cases, not just the providers of an account. They are likely to be gatekeepers and/or sources of further information or interview contacts.

A third issue involves the ongoing collection and analysis of interview and observation material. Data collection and investigation tend to be different from political economy or textual analysis approaches. Data is generated during the research process rather than collected for analysis. Ideas, themes and theory evolve in interaction with participants rather than being confirmed/tested by an assessment of existing material. As a result, each single interview/observation has research implications. At each stage the interviewer has to ask which questions, lines of enquiry or forms of observation worked and which did not. 'Interview protocols' and research behaviours need to be adapted. Good sociological/ethnographic research regularly interrogates itself. Researchers have to keep asking themselves what their research hypotheses and aims are, and, how does what they are doing fit in with those (although all good research should do this)?

This is really how 'grounded theory' (Glaser and Strauss 1968) evolves during an extended period of interviewing and/or participant observation. Alternatively, in relation to a specific case study, it helps to construct a detailed, 'triangulated' account of the events, individuals and issues that are pertinent. Ideas and themes are noted and hypotheses developed. These can be further tested and then supported or discarded in later interviews and associated research. It is by such means that a number of interesting cultural findings have emerged. For example, Schlesinger (1987) realised that journalists adopt self-censoring practices to reduce the risk of their pieces being rejected by editors; something that can be as significant as externally-imposed censorship. Similarly, Herbst (1998) discovered that political staffers regarded news media and journalists as a public opinion indicator when making policy decisions, and usually found them more useful than opinion polls. It was also the way I made a key discovery early on in my research which still informs what I do now (Davis 2002, 2007). This is that elite groups can be as much concerned to communicate with each other through the mass media as they are keen to get messages across to larger mass audiences. Such findings appear relatively simple but each of them has also made a significant intervention in wider debates and evolving macro-scale theories of news production, politics, culture and power.

As a research method, the sociological approach to investigating cultural production is probably the most difficult and erratic but it can also be very rewarding. It relies on gaining access to, and the cooperation of, individuals who may be quite difficult to meet. It demands detailed and time-consuming work on the micro scale. Consequently, there is a high risk of being overly subjective and unrepresentative as well as saying little of consequence on the wider, macro level. However, it does look first-hand at cultural production in action. It makes fewer assumptions about individuals and social relations and is arguably more exploratory and/or innovative. Theory develops more organically as observations are amassed and collated as opposed to the situation where the researcher looks for financial or textual data to support a theory.

Multiple Methods and Case Studies

Lastly, the researcher may use any combination of the above methods. I have used all three approaches to varying degrees on different research projects. Each has its strengths and weaknesses in terms of what it assumes about cultural production, its macro or micro-level foci, the degree to which it can be said to represent a social phenomenon, and the simple practicalities involved in using it. Some are better employed to explore new ideas and social changes, and others are better employed to test existing hypotheses. All such issues should be borne in mind when planning and operationalising research.

If it is possible to use two or more approaches, and if this offers more evidence and strengthens descriptions and arguments, then that should be encouraged. This is often done in detailed case studies of particular organisations, cultural products, or subcultures. Schlesinger and Tumber (1994) and Miller et al. (1998) used several methods to observe the production of news about crime and health. Du Gay et al. (1997a, 1997b) applied a range of approaches to investigate cultural production at Sony. Deacon and Golding (1994) documented the media and communications surrounding the introduction of the 'poll tax' in the UK from a number of vantage points. Gitlin (1994) presents a well rounded, single case study of the development of the hit television show *Hill Street Blues*. In each of these cases multiple methods and observation points were used to record and cross-reference (or triangulate) an aspect or example of the production process.

SOCIOLOGICAL APPROACHES TO INVESTIGATING CULTURAL PRODUCTION: ACCESSING, INTERVIEWING AND OBSERVING CULTURAL PRODUCERS

This last section looks in more depth at some of the practical issues involved when adopting sociological/ethnographic approaches to researching cultural production. As argued above, such approaches are complex and difficult. The researcher is confronted with a number of conceptual and pragmatic questions. There are several good practical methods books which give useful guidelines here (for example, Hansen et al. 1998; Deacon et al. 2007). The following discussion complements these by drawing on the author's own experiences of interviewing some 250, mostly elite, individuals in a variety of settings. Two fifths of these were journalists or public relations staff involved in one cultural industry (news production). The rest were powerful individuals in the corporate and political sectors. In these cases cultural production was investigated within exclusive networks or subcultures.

Research Parameters and Participant Selection

Having selected a research topic, the first question is 'who and how many people should be interviewed and/or observed in order to get an account that can be said to adequately reflect the chosen topic?' The answer is determined by the parameters of the research. Does the researcher want to say something about a cultural industry, a particular firm, a group of professionals within that industry, or to produce a case study about the creation of a single cultural product? If one wants to make claims about the music industry in Britain, then interviewing five people (a music producer, two musicians, a music critic and a DJ) is inadequate. If the researcher wants to produce a case study of the processes involved in the production of a recent hit single in a new musical genre, then the material gained from interviewing five well selected people is likely to be more meaningful.

The parameters of the study also dictate practical issues like should one focus on a 'sample' of participants and, if so, how is that sample constructed? Should the same set of questions or observational procedures be applied to all participants? If one is wanting to talk about a sizeable group or industry, then one should aim to extract a 'theoretical sample' which is in part defined by criteria linked to the debates and theory being engaged with. To obtain a sample, the researcher should probably generate a potential list by starting with the industry involved. The professional association or trade union may well publish such lists. So might the trade journals or association newsletters. Sometimes they may exist in industry overviews and reports produced by the relevant government department. Having defined the sample, the researcher then draws up a single set of interview questions (an 'interview protocol') or observation procedures. Alternatively, if one is producing a case study, then a diverse range of involved individuals needs to be identified and specific sets of questions drawn up.

When I began investigating the influence of PR on news production, I attempted to generate a sample of interviewees on both sides determined by organisational types. I found several industry and association listings of the largest PR companies, cross-referenced them and initially approached the CEOs of the largest and most consistently listed. Later I took a specialist PR sector (finance) and approached directors of every recognised company within that sector. On the news side I decided to stick to national print journalists and approached one or two from each of the national papers. I then also chose to interview financial journalists, that is, those who had most dealings with financial PR companies. When producing case studies, I focused very specifically on the PR professionals and journalists who were centrally involved in those cases. More recently, when deciding to investigate the cultures and media relations of politicians, I was more critical in my sampling. I decided to aim for fifty MPs who reflected the contemporary balance of the party affiliation and gender. On a lesser level, I also tried to get a mix of ages and parliamentary experiences. Each of these 'samples' has obvious biases and omissions. However, they linked to the larger theoretical debates I was engaged with. The limits of the research, as well as the claims made, were, I hope, also fairly transparent.

Making Contact and Preparation

The hardest challenge is making contact and getting the agreement of subjects to participate. Good access is the key to this research. Increasingly, research institutions and funding bodies are imposing strict ethical and legal guidelines on research that involves human participants. Procedures have to be adhered to and permissions gained, either internally or from the organisations, parents and others who will be involved in the research. However, these formal obstacles often prove to be relatively easy to cross, compared with gaining participant cooperation.

For that the researcher must always consider why might subjects agree to participate or, conversely, what might put them off? Accordingly, a strategy must be worked out that can be used in the initial approach and that is likely to encourage cooperation: for example, a connection with the industry or people involved, a personal recommendation, experience within the sector, or personal links with the subculture. A bit of subtle flattery or evident interest/knowledge in the individual being approached and the industry might work well. One also needs to ask what will deter them from agreeing to meet you? They may want to remain anonymous. They may not have much time. They may be afraid of giving away information to rivals. They may be anxious of outsiders obtaining knowledge about them, their organisation or group. They may not want to be presented critically. The researcher has to allay all these fears and make any contact as easy as possible for them. All this information needs to be conveyed during the first contact and request for a meeting or interview.

Most professionals in the cultural and other industries I have contacted actually prefer a short printed letter with a single, supporting page with more details. Letters are then followed up with emails and/or calls a few days later. Contacting people involved in particular social groups or subcultures may be quite different. This may be more about personal contacts and gaining trust. It can work best through shared online spaces or talking to people directly at events. The research objectives may be similar but the practical approach is not. Above all, it is important to be patient and understanding with potential interviewees. Once contact has been made and an initial meeting or interview arranged, the researcher needs to be properly prepared. Do your background research. Find out, within limits, what you can about the interviewee and subject being investigated.

When approaching any potential participant I always write a one-page, three-paragraph letter. The first paragraph states what the research is about and why I am contacting them. The second has a couple of lines about why I am approaching them personally (a personal recommendation, what they do/have achieved, and so on). The third states all the conditions of the interview (time, anonymity if required, and so on) and offers contact details. I always have a second page with a short CV and other relevant information (for example, about the project and a list of past interviewees). When starting I always do some background research on my potential participants. Public figures, such as politicians, journalists and CEOs, normally have material published about them on websites and in news or trade journals. The longer one conducts research in an area, the more contacts and inside knowledge one collects, and these can then be utilised during later approaches.

Conducting the Interview/Observation

Take a small recording device with a separate, external microphone attachment (most recorders have poor internal microphones). Dress appropriately, which means dress in a way that participants will be comfortable with. At the start of the interview, ask whether they mind being recorded and, also, whether they want to be anonymous. Experienced interviewees will often start on the record and then ask for particular parts to be kept 'off'. Try to maintain a positive or neutral rapport with the interviewee throughout the meeting. Any negative reaction on your part is likely to hinder things. The same is true if any of your questions or terms are, in some way, antagonistic to the interviewee. Encourage responses that invite interviewees to talk about the positives rather than the negatives.

Be ready to adapt during the interview. Some participants will talk far too long on an issue or go off on a tangent. Others will give rather short, unresponsive answers. Both require you to be flexible, to adapt and prioritise questions. Often the most crucial issues and questions come towards the end. If the rapport is good and the interview is going well, then more sensitive questions and/or requests for further access can be put. As I have stated earlier in this chapter, it should be remembered that the interviewee is, in many cases, not just the provider of an account. He or she is also likely to be a gatekeeper and/or a source of further information. It may be that you want to access in-house documents, do another interview later, ask for recommendations and contact details of additional interviewees, or to gain permission for further observation.

Post-Interview Activity/Using Findings

What happens after the initial interviews and/or periods of observation? This kind of research tends to be more evolutionary. Data is collected through the research process rather than just being collected for analysis. Hypotheses and theories may evolve with the research. Consequently, interview questions and observation practices need to adapt too. Thus, early interviews/observations should be treated as a sort of 'pilot study'. Now is the time to be critical and make tough decisions if things are not working. The researcher must ask what themes are emerging? What questions are working and what are not? How are the findings supporting or contradicting the starting hypotheses? At regular points it is necessary to keep evaluating the research itself and, if necessary, to adapt and refocus.

I have gone through many such shifts during research periods. When I sought to investigate the social relations that developed between PR practitioners and journalists, I was initially guided by certain hypotheses and past studies – most of which did not employ this kind of interview-based work. I initially explored the popular idea that all-powerful 'spin doctors' were becoming more influential in news via a mixture of threats and manipulation. When I then interviewed both sides and asked such questions, I got regular denials. However, when questions focused on the changing resources and practices of the two professions, interview material was very revealing about how PR was infiltrating journalism in rather more subtle ways.

During interviews with financiers and politicians, I was not looking at wider cultural production but treating the two groups as subcultural networks. I simply wanted to see where and how the media (new and traditional) played a part in professional decision-making and behaviour. I began with very open questions such as: 'What are the main sources of information you use to inform yourself before making decisions in your job?' and 'What kinds of information are you looking for when you look at such a source?' After the initial interviews, certain themes and answers started to be repeated. I then adapted the 'interview protocols' to further explore these issues. Thus, one clear finding from this work has been that political and financial decision-makers use their specific relations with journalists, as well as some specific columns, to make assessments about what their rivals, within their political or financial sphere, are thinking and doing.

SUMMARY: KEY POINTS

Three general approaches are used in the investigation of cultural production:

- Political economy approaches investigate cultural production indirectly. They collect quantitative data and corporate/institutional documents to build a macro picture of the industry in question. Key practical operations involve locating, collating and aggregating data sources. Government institutions, corporations and corporate bodies, professional associations and trade publications are all potential sources.
- Textual analysis also investigates cultural production indirectly. Analysis is used to make deduction about specific, local or wider, social conditions in which cultural production takes place. A range of quantitative and qualitative forms of analysis can be applied. Key practical operations involve collecting and selecting texts, and clarifying which form of analysis and elements/coding to apply. Analysis can be applied to a variety of texts: mass media outputs and local (historical documents, reports, and so on) and textual forms (printed, audio, visual and physical).
- Sociological (and ethnographic) approaches investigate directly, and usually at the micro level. Most work in the field tends to be qualitative and involves interviewing and participant observation. Key practical operations involve selecting, accessing and working with individuals – either elite professionals in the cultural industries or those who are part of a subculture (or field or network). Data collection, hypotheses and analysis must adapt during the research period.
- Case studies of cultural production can involve any combination of the above methods.

When interviewing or approaching participants, the following must be kept in mind:

- The parameters of the research, its focus and hypotheses dictate the type and number of participants selected.
- How initial contact is made is critical. Participants have to be practically accessible. Most have to be persuaded with a careful and thought-out approach that encourages and allays fears.
- Patience and detailed preparation for interviews are essential. Interview questions, recording equipment and clothing must all be carefully chosen.

- Do what you can to make the interviewee comfortable and to build a rapport. The interviewee is also a source of further information and research leads.
- After each interview reassess what you are doing, your hypothesis and your next steps before proceeding.

FURTHER READING

Two classic political economy studies of the cultural industries are Garnham (1990) and Curran and Seaton (2003). Both collect data (archive/historical, official documents, and market figures) and use it to build an overview of the industry that ties into macro-level theory. For three different examples of textual analysis, which link texts to wider social and political relations, turn to Said (1979), Goldman (1992) or Herman and Chomsky (2002). Said offers a form of qualitative 'discourse' analysis, Goldman a qualitative deconstruction of visual, advertising images, and Herman and Chomsky a more quantitative analysis of news content. For sociological approaches that document cultural producers at work turn to Schlesinger (1987) or Gitlin (1994). For examples of work investigating subcultures turn to Hebdige (1979) or Abolafia (1996). Each of these builds up an account of cultural production through interviewing and/or participant observation. For some useful case studies that combine a number of research methods, see du Gay et al. (1997b) or Davis (2002).

NOTES

1. Many interpret 'political economy' as a critical or (post) Marxist approach. A large proportion of scholars in the field would position themselves accordingly. However, it should be noted that, political economy is broader than that, and there exist a range of ideological positions which adopt such methods.
2. Many would argue that the term 'ethnographic' is used too loosely when describing much social research. Ethnographies, conducted by anthropologists, have traditionally involved lengthy periods of immersion of the scholar into other cultures. However, media/communication academics tend to conduct rather more limited 'participant-observations' and/or interview series under the 'ethnography' label.

CHAPTER 4

Investigating Cultural Consumers

Anneke Meyer

INTRODUCTION: CULTURAL STUDIES AND CULTURAL CONSUMERS

Consumption in its many forms is not a new phenomenon (Storey 1999), but since the end of the Second World War, consumption in industrialised countries has proliferated to such an extent that the phrase 'consumer society' was coined. Arguably, *cultural* consumption has especially increased because technological advances have led to the development and spread of new forms of media and information and communication technologies (ICTs). These have in turn generated new forms of cultural texts and made cultural consumption more accessible. The term 'cultural consumer' refers to those who consume cultural texts or engage in cultural practices involving consumption. Key aspects of consumption are purchasing something and/or using it up (Lury 1996), but consumption cannot be reduced to these two activities because it includes a variety of other practices, such as listening, thinking or travelling. There is clearly a wide range of cultural products and practices of cultural consumption.

Cultural consumption is a complex phenomenon. Consumption is often juxtaposed to production as constituting the process of 'using up' what has previously been produced, but the two phenomena are deeply intertwined. Cultural consumption entails production in the sense that consumers have to make sense of products, hence they are producers of meanings. The complexity of cultural consumption is also rooted in its diffuse and often messy nature (Morley 1992); it occurs across various sites and is intended or focused to different extents. Some consumption, such as going to the theatre, is specific and planned, while consumption also happens 'automatically' and/or without consumers paying much attention, for example having the radio on while doing the cooking.

The analysis of culture encompasses the study of processes of production, consumption and circulation, as well as the products and practices (texts) involved (Ang 1996; Morley 1992). Cultural studies' conceptualisation of cultural products and practices as texts emphasises their polysemic nature, which means they contain various meanings and can be interpreted in different ways. Historically, cultural studies has tended to prioritise the analysis of cultural products (Johnson 1996), with the exception of audience research which concerns itself with the 'effects' of media consumption. More recently, cultural studies as a whole has become increasingly interested in cultural consumers, and it often uses qualitative methods to study processes such as attitude formation or meaning attribution. This chapter discusses two such methods, namely interviews and focus groups, which will be illustrated with examples from two research projects on cultural consumers. I conducted the first project myself (Meyer 2007), while the second project is outlined in Wendy Simonds's book *Women and Self-Help Culture* (1992).

PROJECT 1: PAEDOPHILIA

Since the 1990s paedophilia has been a high-profile topic in the UK, arousing great levels of interest and emotion. Media coverage is continuous, sensational and often demonising, and some newspapers, such as the *News of the World*, have taken on campaigning roles in which they have 'outed' child sex offenders (Critcher 2003). This begs the questions as to how the wider public responds to paedophilia, and how these responses are connected to media coverage. This research project aims to explore the attitudes and understandings of the wider public regarding paedophilia. It attempts to uncover popular opinions as well as the discourses and motivations underlying them. On a second level, research into popular understandings is connected to a textual analysis of media coverage of paedophilia in order to unravel discursive commonalities and variations.

PROJECT 2: SELF-HELP LITERATURE

Self-help books centre on a range of personal and social issues and provide readers with instructions on how to overcome any related problems. Since the 1960s self-help literature has proliferated, and as the majority of books are targeted at and consumed by women it has become perceived as 'women's culture'. Wendy Simonds's (1992) research into women and self-help literature aims to unravel the experiences and views of female readers of self-help books in order to address questions such as why women turn to self-help literature or how self-help literature is bound up with processes of gender and identity formation. On two further levels of research Simonds investigates the role of cultural producers (by interviewing editors of self-help literature) and relevant cultural texts (by analysing 122 bestselling self-help books).

Both projects are 'unspecific' in the sense of not focusing on the consumption of individual items. The paedophilia project is concerned with the impact of *overall* consumption of paedophilia-related media coverage and the self-help literature project explores generalised consumption as consumers have usually read numerous self-help books. Both projects aim to establish meanings and understandings regarding cultural texts, yet there are different levels of consumer involvement. Consumers of self-help literature directly and deeply involve themselves with the books, while most people consume media coverage of paedophilia in an indirect and piecemeal fashion. This further raises issues around intention and purpose: readers of self-help books purposefully choose books to 'match' personal problems while media stories on paedophilia are ubiquitous and near impossible to escape. Throughout this chapter the two projects will illustrate the respective strengths and weaknesses of interviews and focus groups.

A BRIEF HISTORY OF INTERVIEWS AND FOCUS GROUPS

In the social sciences, interviews are a key method associated with qualitative research (Platt 2002). Interviews involve an interviewer and an interviewee engaging in face-to-face conversation, with the interviewer guiding the conversation by posing questions related to particular topics in order to gain a better understanding. Interviews vary in terms of depth, focus, scope and degree of structure, but there is a common underlying idea(l) that interviews produce in-depth and complex knowledge of the human world by focusing on meanings and interacting with research participants and their life-worlds. Early academic proponents such as Merton and Kendall (1946) tended to see interviews as auxiliaries to quantitative research, but today interviews can be used as a stand-alone method as well as in conjunction with other methods. Historically, the rise of interviews and other qualitative methods in the social sciences is associated with the breaking of the dominance of positivist approaches, as well as the development of alternative conceptions of social knowledge as inter-relational and defined by meaning rather than quantifications (Kvale 1996). Within this framework research participants are seen as active meaning makers rather than passive information providers, and interviews offer a unique opportunity to study these processes of meaning production directly. The shared premise of the importance of meaning generates a particular affinity between qualitative methods and cultural studies.

Focus groups, which are originally a market research tool, have recently enjoyed popularity among social scientists. Focus groups involve an interviewer (moderator) and interviewees (participants) in a face-to-face situation in which the moderator asks questions relating to a particular issue in order to gain better understanding. But, as the new terminology of 'moderator' and 'participants' suggests, focus groups are more than simply group interviews. The presence of a group changes the research situation and the data produced; participants interact with each other as well as the moderator, and these group dynamics form part of the data (Kitzinger 1994). Moreover, data emerge from discussions rather than being 'answers' to interviewers' questions. Focus groups have become very popular with media researchers, in particular those interested in media 'effects' who combine textual analysis with focus groups of relevant consumers (Hansen 1998). Focus groups are relatively easy and cheap to set up and explore the views of a sizeable range of individuals, but their popularity is also rooted in more fundamental concerns. Group dynamics elicit debates, and as meaning-making is a social process it can be well explored through group situations (Alasuutari 1999). Despite the popular combination of textual analysis and focus groups, the latter can also be used as a self-contained method.

PROBLEMS WITH RESEARCHING CULTURAL CONSUMERS

This section largely revolves around media effects research which is concerned with the impact of cultural consumption. Media audiences and cultural consumers are of course not the same thing, but the terms are often used interchangeably because of their extensive overlap. Much of the culture we consume today is mediated, and cultural consumers, like media audiences, produce meanings and engage in a range of activities. They do more than just 'use (up)' products.

Research into cultural consumers requires both researchers and cultural consumers to be familiar with relevant cultural texts, experiences and practices. By the 1940s media effects research had arguably generated a particular kind of 'focused interview' (Merton and Kendal 1946) in which research participants need to have been involved in a *particular* situation or practice, such as having watched a particular television programme, about which they can subsequently be interviewed. Indeed, this format has been adopted by much effects research to this day, including various studies by the Glasgow Media Group (Philo 1990, 1999). However, this narrow type of interview is not suitable for many facets of cultural consumer research. For instance, it is not useful for researching popular attitudes to paedophilia, a topic which is widely covered by all media types, forms and genres. This context makes it impossible to locate the origin of any media impact in particular items. Hence the focused interview is only useful where consumption itself is focused and can be confined to a *particular* situation or practice.

A second problem concerns the terminology of 'audiences', 'consumers', 'messages' and 'effects', which implies a one-way model of communication in which texts are active producers of messages and consumers are passive recipients (Gray 1999). Texts and consumers, as well as their inter-relationships, are more complex. Texts both reflect and generate certain representations; they create and reproduce culture. For instance, women may consume self-help literature because they experience problems, but at the same time this kind of literature convinces them that they do have issues which need solving. Moreover, the books are part of a wider trend towards a 'therapy culture' (Simonds 1992) where therapeutic advise is increasingly offered and used in a commodity-like fashion. In this context self-help literature clearly reproduces and creates cultural values and consumption. Similarly, cultural consumers both consume *and* produce meanings (Gray 1999), which can be illustrated through paedophilia controversies. Paedophilia is a popular topic of everyday debate and in these instances people (re)produce certain meanings around paedophilia. They can draw on numerous ideas derived from media as well as non-media sources; consumers do not simply receive messages and they do not only obtain ideas from the media. Moreover, as both the media and consumers are not homogeneous groupings, there is never one unified message or response (Fiske 1996). In the media we find a range of interpretations depending on factors such as a political orientation or target audience. Cultural consumers are diverse groups of people whose diversity is brought to bear on cultural texts and the processes of meaning-making (ibid.). For example, the meanings which consumers derive from self-help books depend on their interpretations of the books as well as their own personal situations and backgrounds, suggesting that psychological advice found in books is woven into a complex web of interpretations and social relations and interactions.

The dynamics between cultural texts and consumers can be better conceptualised through discourses. The concept of discourse, which refers to a series of sanctioned statements that are circulated around an issue and used to make sense of it (Hall 2001), allows for the research of broader and therefore more adequate questions than the 'effects' of consuming media messages. We could, for example, ask through what kinds of discourses consumers understand topics such as paedophilia and in what ways these understandings are linked to media discourses. Discourses are constantly (re)produced across different sites in our culture. In this cycle of (re)production it is hard to identify points of origin or relations of cause and effect, which pose problems for media consumption research in terms of directionality. It becomes difficult to specify the media as the origin or inventors of discourses; we can only suggest that as institutions of mass communication, the media occupy a powerful position in the meaning-making process.

Indeed these problems are not novel or 'caused' by the discourse perspective, but rooted in the complexity of cultural consumption and the nature of qualitative research methods. Due to the diversity of the media and their consumers, any results regarding media impacts are limited to the groups researched, even though they may be treated as suggestive for other media or consumer groups if sufficient similarity criteria are fulfilled (Morley 1992). Hence analytical generalisation is possible, but qualitative research projects based on interviews and focus groups usually do not fulfil criteria of statistical generalisability (see Chapter 5). Their samples tend to be small and not informed by the systematic random-rule (Bloor et al. 2001), which means that they are not representative of the whole population. But statistical generalisability is not the main objective of qualitative research which aims to produce in-depth and complex understanding (Kvale 1996). The longstanding problems of generalisability and directionality have been obfuscated by a deceptively simple terminology of effects and messages; the acknowledgement of these issues can lead to research which is aware of (1) the limitations and benefits of different methods, (2) the complexity of the subject matter, and (3) the need to ask broader yet more qualified questions about the relationships between media and consumer discourses.

METHODS IN ACTION: FOCUS GROUPS OR INTERVIEWS?

The paedophilia and self-help literature projects are concerned with establishing meanings and understandings, and this makes qualitative research methods appropriate. Both interviews and focus groups can produce in-depth, detailed and complex data on attitudes, practices and experiences of cultural consumers, as well as the discourses and motivations behind their meaning-making processes. The choice of method depends on the nature and aims of the research, the advantages and disadvantages of different methods, and practical issues regarding time and finances. Taking this into account, interviews emerge as particularly suited to the self-help literature project while paedophilia research would be most fruitfully conducted through focus groups.

Focus groups fundamentally differ from interviews by involving a group situation in which data are produced through debates and interactive dynamics between participants (Morgan 2003). This is particularly useful for research into motivations and discourses behind attitudes and practices of cultural consumers because in discussions participants have to explain, justify and argue for their opinions. This happens through direct questions, open disagreements or challenges. For example, in the following extract one focus group participant, Miles, directly challenges Kerry to explain why she believes paedophilia to be a particularly serious crime deserving a lifelong prison sentence. Kerry's answer reveals that her opinion is based on a cumulative mix of factors including the crime being (1) sexual, (2) violent, and (3) committed against children:

> KERRY: I think they [paedophiles] should, should be locked up for life.
> MILES: OK, is a paedophile worse than rape then? Paedophilia?
> KERRY: Cause it's sex with children Miles . . . it's sex with *children*, it's . . . it is . . . that violence, it's not just sex, it's . . . it's violence against children.

This kind of information is usually difficult to elicit because a widespread consensus around paedophilia being *the* worst crime means that punitive attitudes do not require explanations (Meyer 2007). In an interview situation such rationalisations could be established through direct questions, but constant probing disrupts the interview flow while focus groups automatically produce clarifications as part of debates. Research into socio-cultural issues marked by significant consensus can particularly profit from focus groups because discussions are able to (1) stimulate the revelation of individual rationalisations, and (2) draw out the finer similarities and differences underlying the generalised consensus. By systematically comparing and contrasting attitudes and understandings within and between groups, the researcher can also gauge levels of diversity and consensus.

Focus groups can be specifically set up for inter-group comparisons. Practically, the groups would be kept homogenous apart from specific break variables to compare and contrast the impact of these variables on cultural consumers (Bloor et al. 2001). The usefulness of this strategy depends on the aims and nature of the research. For example, in the case of the paedophilia project, parenthood could be used as a break variable to establish whether and how parenthood impacts on attitudes and understandings. This promises to be insightful because paedophilia is perceived as a threat to children and media coverage directly addresses parents.

Focus groups are a particularly useful method for researching attitudes, experiences and understandings of cultural consumers because meaning production is a social and shared process. People develop their views and knowledge through social interactions and contexts, such as talking to neighbours or attending parents' evenings. Neither focus groups nor interviews tap into these 'naturally' occurring processes because they collect data by means of setting up artificial situations, but the interactive context of focus groups can illustrate how meanings are produced intersubjectively (Morley 1992). In the following example focus group participants discuss why the number of paedophiles in

their local area is rising. Various reasons are contributed by different participants to produce an *overall* story of a rise in paedophiles being caused by (1)
general inaction of the authorities, (2) authorities housing paedophiles in
poor areas, and (3) the lack of public access to the sex offenders' register,
which allows the authorities to house paedophiles without notifying the local
community:

SINEAD: It's increasing though, there's more and more . . . of them
    [paedophiles].
SARAH: And it's like nobody's doing anything about it . . . and all these
    children are getting abused.
BETH: That's why there's more of them [paedophiles] cause nothing's
    being done.
DONNA: Yeah, they [paedophiles] do it in their areas and then they get
    dumped here.
SARAH: Yeah, cause it's poor, well, classed as a poor area.
DONNA: Cause the people where they come from don't want them
    [paedophiles] . . . in their area.
BETH: *We* don't know about them [paedophiles].
CLAIRE: That's why there's more and more coming.

As reasons start to interlink, focus group debates show how participants *jointly*
produce coherent stories and make sense of their experiences.

A major difference between focus groups and interviews can be captured in
terms of breadth versus depth (Morgan 2003). Compared to interviews, there
is much less time for individuals to speak in focus groups, meaning that a topic
cannot be investigated in as much depth and detail. In contrast, focus groups
offer more breadth (in terms of participant numbers) and it is easier to explore
the experiences of a significant range of people. The importance of extra depth
or breadth depends on the research project. In the case of paedophilia research,
interest centres on establishing the *common* discourses which underlie attitudes
and practices of cultural consumers, and to this end breadth would be very
important. In contrast, interviews would be most suited to the self-help literature project which is concerned with the experiences and views of female consumers. Questions such as why women turn to self-help literature are likely to
be answered only through gathering an in-depth and comprehensive understanding of an individual's situation. This in turn requires a broad 'life' perspective and only interviews can provide the time and attention necessary to
produce this kind of understanding. For instance, in the following example an
interviewee's turn to self-help literature has been influenced by personal
experiences with religion. Having been raised a Catholic, Celia turned her back
on this religion as an adult, partly because of her life practices not fitting in with

the Church's teachings. This, however, left her searching for a 'replacement' spirituality which results in the consumption of New Age self-help literature:

> Celia: When I was younger I was a devout Catholic. And . . . unfortunately, through education, and just different experiences, I'm not as devout as I once was [. . .] I don't readily accept the standing of the Church's teachings at the present moment, and I cannot pretend I do and go along with it [. . .] Catholicism: you can only do it if you follow their doctrine. This [New Age philosophy] is not so rigid. It's not like you have to not eat meat on Friday. And I can be married twenty times, and it's not to say I'm a bad person. I'm looking for something more [than the Church] [. . .] I'm looking for something that's going to accept me *and* all my flaws. (quoted in Simonds 1992; 72; original emphases)

This kind of personal narrative, revealing details of an individual's practices, attitudes and experiences, can best be elicited through interviews. Morgan's dichotomy of breadth versus depth is slightly confusing because interviews can offer greater breadth than focus groups in terms of the range of topics covered; extra time allows for the exploration of wider issues. As a consequence, interviews are also particularly useful for establishing nuanced comparisons between individual cultural consumers; they ensure that all participants receive equal attention and time to tell their story. This is difficult to achieve in focus groups because of group dynamics. Even though moderators curb domination, certain individuals tend to lead debates, talk more and set the agenda while others remain quiet. If focus groups are good for establishing comparisons and contrasts between groups, interviews are useful for establishing them between individuals. And again these conditions suggest that interviews are a particularly suitable method for the self-help literature project. Women's reasons for and experiences of engaging with self-help literature are likely to vary, as a result of their vastly different personal situations and problems and because all interviewees have read a different selection of self-help books and interpreted them in different ways (Simonds 1992). Interviews offer to capture all these differences through the gathering of an encompassing understanding of individual situations.

Interviews are arguably also particularly useful for systematically studying the intricate connections between the social and the individual through particular cases. For instance, the self-help literature project is concerned with how a generalised culture of self-help becomes a personalised culture of consumption, focusing on processes through which self-help literature becomes something that women want to consume or choose at the expense of other forms of help. This in turn throws up further complex issues such as definitions of 'happiness' or conceptions of gender identity and selfhood. Simonds (1992), along with other feminists, has emphasised that 'true', individual selfhood remains somewhat elusive for women as their identities are to a large extent relational (for example, being a mother, a wife). Yet when women focus on their selves by reading self-help books they are often branded selfish and narcissistic. Interviews offer the opportunity to investigate how such social conditions work in conjunction with women's personal contexts to shape their consumption and experiences of self-help literature. We could hypothesise that these social contexts both encourage and condemn the consumption of self-help literature, generating a group of guilty female consumers. However, one strand of self-help literature is strongly feminist and readers who identify with the feminist movement may (re)fashion their focus on the self as a right. This interplay between social and individual factors is exactly what interviews promise to reveal.

The one-to-one research situation also means that interviews are well suited to exploring issues that are sensitive, emotive or controversial. Focus groups should not be ruled out per se because some individuals openly share personal experiences, but others may be inhibited by the presence of a group, fearing judgement, ridicule or questions. Group situations also make it more difficult for the researcher to deal with the effects of personal revelations, such as serious emotional upset or embarrassment. The self-help literature project is not the most controversial of topics (compared to, say, the consumption of child pornography) but it is sufficiently sensitive to be better researched through interviews. Self-help literature has long had a very negative press, both in the media and academia (Simonds 1992). Not only is consumption equated with narcissism, but many commentators treat self-help literature with disdain, judging it unscientific, shallow and simplistic. These attitudes are linked to a historical disregard of anything dubbed as 'women's culture'. Negative images of self-help literature may cause consumers to feel ashamed or guilty about their consumption. In the following extract one interviewee is obviously embarrassed by her continued belief in the power of self-help literature, a belief she calls 'stupid':

> Bonnie: I thought they [self-help books] had the answer. And I still do, in some stupid way. *Rationally*, I know these books don't have the answers; *emotionally*, I really think that if I find the right book, it will solve my problems. (quoted in Simonds 1992: 1; original emphases)

These kinds of emotions may make participants uncomfortable in group debates and unlikely to share their experiences and beliefs with others. Focus groups would consist of self-help literature consumers only, but the above comment illustrates that readers are still aware of cultural conceptions, and in group situations individuals can draw on these ideas to fight battles over status, image and morality. For instance, despite their own involvement, some consumers may portray *others* as undiscriminating and irrational consumers who cannot differentiate between good and bad self-help literature. Interviews avoid these complications associated with group presence, and this makes them a safer tool for exploring consumers of sensitive or controversial cultural texts.

PRINCIPLES OF RESEARCH AND CRITERIA OF ANALYSIS: HOW TO DO INTERVIEWS AND FOCUS GROUPS WITH CULTURAL CONSUMERS

The research processes involved in interviews and focus groups can be broken down into several key stages.

Design: Thematising, Sampling and Access

Any research project begins with thematisation, and this involves the acquisition of knowledge of the subject matter as well as the development of a clear research question and rationale (Kvale 1996). In the case of cultural consumer research, knowledge has to be acquired regarding relevant academic work as well as the objects of consumption. In this latter case, acquisition can take the form of a loose familiarisation with relevant cultural texts (such as conscious reading of self-help books) and/or rigorous textual research (such as an analysis of media discourses around paedophilia). This knowledge is useful at all stages because researchers need a thorough understanding of cultural texts to make sense of their consumers.

Thematisation informs the researcher's choice of method(s), and this impacts on sampling decisions. Sampling relates to finding research participants and the process throws up issues such as who to include, how many people to include and how to group them together. Probability sampling is the predominant strategy of quantitative research. Large-scale samples are generated on the basis of the systematic-random rule, which arguably makes them representative and produces statistically generalisable research results. However, qualitative research projects work differently. A key question concerns who qualifies as a participant. There are topics where respondents need to fulfil certain criteria in terms of possessing specialist knowledge or engaging in certain activities, such as reading self-help literature. In this case the researcher adopts a purposive sampling strategy which is driven by finding those who fulfil these criteria. When projects do not require participants with specialist knowledge, sampling is open and involves several decisions. The researcher may want to obtain a set of respondents which – if not wholly representative – covers a relevant range of people in relation to the overall population. This ensures that different social groups along major structural dividing lines are represented. However, certain social and cultural factors may be of particular importance on a given topic, in which case the research may be limited to especially relevant groups.

Research concerning cultural consumers always includes the option of sampling in terms of consumer groups, such as readers of a particular newspaper. Whether such sampling is useful depends on the research topic and aims. It is more helpful to use a specific consumer group for research into the impact of a *particular* newspaper's campaign than for research into the impact of *general* media coverage of a topic. However, consumer group sampling is often not as good or simple a method as it seems. Firstly, consumers tend to be exposed to various cultural texts in addition to the research project's key texts, meaning that patterns in attitudes or understandings cannot simply be explained through belonging to a particular consumer group. To use an example, you could interview readers of the *News of the World* to find out what they think about the newspaper's 'Name and shame' campaign. But this campaign has been widely covered by all major British newspapers and television channels, so that participants' views cannot be fully explained through readership of the *News of the World*. Secondly, consumer groups are a messy phenomenon which complicates the definition of 'belonging'. For instance, if people tend to read one particular newspaper, they often (1) do not read it daily, and (2) also read several other newspapers during the week, making it difficult to define consumer groups and operationalise them as a sampling strategy.

Sampling further involves a decision on how many participants to include in a research project. It is important to remember that projects have to be manageable because qualitative methods produce an enormous amount of complex data which need time to be transcribed and analysed. The researcher can fix the number of participants in advance or continually organise interviews and focus groups until a saturation point is reached where further research would yield little new data. However, this latter strategy requires considerable financial and temporal resources. In the case of focus groups, the researcher must also decide how many participants to include in one group: the 'ideal' figure is between six and twelve participants (Bloor et al. 2001), which is large enough to yield a discussion and small enough to allow for significant individual contributions. The number of groups in a research project directly depends on the number of break variables used. Any social or cultural factor can function as a break variable, which unites participants within one group and acts as a divider between groups. The more break variables are included, the more focus groups are needed.

Overall sample size is not the only concern regarding the grouping of participants. Break variables create homogeneity within and heterogeneity between groups, and can function to isolate certain factors and assess their influence through comparisons across groups. The usefulness of break variables depends on how interested the researcher is in (1) the role of a specific variable, and (2) comparisons between different groups of consumers. Moreover, it should be taken into account that intra-group heterogeneity can help stimulate debates. Focus group researchers also have to decide whether to use pre-existing groups, such as a football team. Market researchers have expressed fears that this strategy 'contaminates' data and diminishes control over break variables, resulting in diminished comparability. However, pre-existing groups have become increasingly popular in the social sciences, partly because participants tend to feel comfortable in familiar company, which is conducive to the production of data.

Any sample design raises the issue of access because researchers have to find participants who are both suitable and willing to take part. The difficulties associated with gaining access and consent depend on the nature of the research topic, where it is more difficult to find participants for sensitive research topics, as well as on the 'nature' of potential participants – for instance it is especially difficult to access elites (Hornsby-Smith 1993). Much research into cultural consumers tends to pose no *particular* access problems as the majority of consumers are not part of elites, but in the case of controversial cultural texts, such as child pornography, it may be very difficult to find people willing to identify themselves as consumers. If research projects require participants with specialist knowledge, sampling may be facilitated through contacting organised specialist groups. In the case of the self-help literature project, the researcher could contact suitable individuals via local support groups or websites. Generally speaking, there are many possibilities of generating access because sampling does not follow the systematic-random rule. Researchers can draw on their own wider social networks, find respondents by putting up adverts, or contact institutions and groups who are likely to include suitable participants, such as using nurseries to contact parents. This strategy has the potential to produce access to several participants at once, but dependence on gatekeepers such as nursery managers may be a disadvantage. All the different access strategies can be mixed as and when appropriate.

Doing it: Question Design, Interviewing and Moderating

Prior to interviews and focus groups, the researcher has to design an interview guide and decide on the degree of structure. Interview styles are usually categorised as structured (a list of set questions which must be covered), semi-structured (a list of topics to be covered, with some suggested questions) and unstructured (a list of very few rough areas). The relevance of respective advantages and disadvantages depends on the nature and aims of a research project. Generally speaking, a relatively unstructured approach has the advantage of giving respondents space to explore issues they consider important, while a more structured approach allows for easier comparison between interviews because the same topics have been covered through the same questions. In any case interviews and focus groups are guided conversations and not interrogations. It is important for interviewers and moderators to create an atmosphere where respondents feel safe and talk freely; this includes building a rapport and going along with the flow of the conversation, gently steering rather than domineering. Any issues which are not raised during conversations can be directly brought up at the end.

The more structured the interviewing approach, the more important the question design. In the unstructured and semi-structured varieties the researcher needs a list of topics to be covered to gather information on the specified research area. When corresponding questions are devised, they should be open-ended to invite elaboration and avoid yes/no answers. For example, Simonds's research into the consumption of self-help literature included topics such as the meaning of reading self-help books, which were covered through open-ended questions like 'What does reading self-help books mean to you?', instead of 'Are self-help books important to you?'. All questions should be brief and simple so that respondents can easily understand them. Especially at the beginning questions should be general; towards the later stages the interviewer can ask more specific questions, but they will have often been covered already. Throughout the conversation the researcher can ask probing questions which require the interviewee to explain or to elaborate further. Leading questions (such as 'Could your consumption of self-help books have started when your marriage broke down?') should be avoided because they are presumptive and suggestive.

The degree of structure of interviews and focus groups shapes the role of interviewers and moderators. The more structured the interview, the more direct and interventionist the interviewer's role becomes, both in terms of asking questions and steering respondents back onto research topics. As a general rule, interrupting or cutting off respondents should be avoided as this interrupts the communicative flow and has the potential to intimidate respondents and suggest that not all their experiences are valuable. Additionally, the moderator has to manage a group situation, which produces extra challenges such as domineering participants or heated atmospheres. Moderators are meant to 'moderate' a group, that is, mediate, guide and ensure its smooth running, rather than exercise direct control. Throughout the discussions the moderator aims to steer debates along the desired path, maintain a friendly atmosphere and keep participants involved. Market researchers insist that all participants contribute roughly similar amounts, but this is not the approach of academic researchers. In naturally occurring debates different people contribute different amounts, and this is reflected in focus groups. Of course, efforts can be made to include quiet participants but at the same time they should not be pressurised.

Transcription and Analysis

Interviews and focus groups should be tape recorded and transcribed, the transcription constituting the transformation of oral data into written data which can then be analysed. Oral texts do not translate neatly into written texts, for they contain many unfinished sentences, hesitations, pauses, fillers, silences and sentence fragments. These can be tidied up in transcripts or be copied down verbatim, the latter method being advantageous as characteristics of verbal speech convey meanings and help data interpretation.

The analysis of cultural consumers tends to take place on two levels. On the first level, analysis focuses on the transcripts. An ad hoc method of meaning generation (Kvale 1996), which combines a number of interpretive approaches, is commonly used. Researchers start by immersing themselves in the data, carefully reading and re-reading the transcript, making notes in the margins and highlighting certain elements which are recurring and/or important to the research question. In this way meanings are condensed into summarising statements in the margins of the transcript and categorised, as long statements or passages of speech are reduced to simple categories. 'Category' is a term which covers all kinds of general phenomena, such as concepts, constructs, themes or discourses (Lindlof and Taylor 2002). Group discussions about paedophilia have, for example, produced categories such as 'perversion' (a discourse through which people understand paedophiles as sexually deviant and incurable) or 'the cycle of abuse' (a theory people use to explain paedophilia in adults as caused by sexual abuse in their own childhoods). Categories can emerge from the data through recurrence or direct connections to research questions, or the researcher can discover meanings through knowledge of academic literature or 'pre-coded' topics which the wider public uses (Lindlof and Taylor 2002). Depending on the research project, certain categories or themes will emerge as more essential than others and become central to the analysis. Once categories have been identified, the researcher can assign all (relevant) chunks of text and use a form of coding to mark where text passages belong. Coding can be done through computer programmes or manually through colouring. Condensation and categorisation represent the beginnings of analysis and serve to reduce and structure data so that transcripts become more manageable. These steps are followed by a process of deep analysis or meaning interpretation, in which the researcher goes beyond what is obviously said in the transcripts. To this end the identified themes should be analysed in relation to each other, the overall research question and relevant academic knowledge.

These basic rules apply to all transcripts, but the researcher can adopt different analytical approaches, such as discourse analysis, content analysis, conversation analysis or narrative analysis (Marvasti 2004). Yet it is also acceptable for researchers to adopt no particular method and simply analyse transcripts through themes and their relations to wider knowledge contexts (Kvale 1996). Moreover, different analytical approaches can be employed and combined as and when useful, as long as the researcher is sufficiently familiar with them. For instance, an element of conversation analysis is always useful for focus groups where interactive dynamics are important for understanding what is being said, when, why, how and by whom. The analytical approach will be informed by the nature and aims of the research, for example the self-help literature project could be analysed using a narrative approach which is applicable to life stories of interviewees as well as self-help texts.

On the first level of analysis, focus groups have to include an analysis of the group dynamics in conjunction with thematic interpretations. Both group talk and interaction constitute research data, and the two are deeply connected. An analysis of group interaction can help understand why certain themes arise, the meanings of what is said (such as a hesitation indicating a lack of conviction) and how people construct knowledge and meanings intersubjectively.

Research into cultural consumers often also necessitates a second level of analysis in which the transcripts are explored in relation to an analysis of the cultural texts that respondents have consumed. This textual analysis should be carried out prior to interviewing to give the researcher a better understanding of both texts and consumers' responses. The intensity and scale of this second-level analysis varies, depending on the extent to which the research project requires comparative analyses of cultural texts and cultural consumers. For instance, the paedophilia research project centres on the relationship between cultural texts and consumers ('Does the public understand paedophilia through the same discourses as the media?'); this requires an extensive and *systematic* second-level analysis which compares and contrasts media and popular discourses. If a project requires a close analytic connection between two levels of research, it is helpful to choose a *common* method of analysis for examining cultural texts and consumers.

In the case of self-help literature, Simonds (1992) analysed an enormous range of bestselling self-help books, drawing out common themes and discourses, aims and promises as well as formal properties of books. She did not intend to assess in how far the books' features were 'taken on' by readers, but rather aimed to understand women's involvement with self-help literature by researching different aspects of this phenomenon. To this end, interviews with readers and textual analysis of books contributed knowledge of different aspects of the cultural phenomenon, and in fact Simonds went even further and included a third level of research into cultural producers by interviewing editors of self-help books. Given the conceptualisation of the research project Simonds did not need to engage in a systematic compare and contrast exercise between different levels of research. Nevertheless, all three levels are interconnected (for example, the promises of self-help books to bring about positive changes in readers' lives will shape consumers' expectations) and it remains the researcher's task to draw out these complex inter-relationships through an integrated analysis.

CONCLUSION: THE SUITABILITY OF INTERVIEWS AND FOCUS GROUPS FOR RESEARCHING CULTURAL CONSUMERS

Earlier in this chapter several problems associated with researching cultural consumers were discussed. These included (1) cultural texts simultaneously generating and reproducing culture, (2) cultural consumers being simultaneously producers of cultural meanings and texts, (3) cultural consumption being diffuse and messy, and (4) the diversity of cultural consumers and texts. These aspects are often identified as problems because they make it difficult to fit cultural consumer research into positivist conceptions of knowledge as quantifiable results. The production of neat and statistically generalisable findings is problematic because complex phenomena are difficult to code into variables in an equation and to isolate from other 'variables'.

However, this chapter has hopefully shown that qualitative methods are well suited to the complexities of cultural consumer research because they are open and flexible. In interview and focus group situations, participants can reveal themselves as producers of meanings and texts, as well as consumers who engage in certain practices and hold certain attitudes. And in this context cultural texts can emerge as both the products of people as well as constitutive of their culture. Similarly, the diffuse nature of consumption and the diversity of cultural consumers are open to be examined in qualitative research situations which give participants considerable freedom to explore issues in depth and detail and do not attempt to fit complexity into pre-fixed categories (Gray 1999). Of course in the analysis process making sense of complexity involves the development of themes and categories, and researchers are concerned to make some generalised observations and statements to avoid the disintegration of research into particularism and contextualism (Schroder 1999). But in interviews and focus groups such categories are not pre-imposed, rather they emerge from the data and the research framework. Hence, the complexity of researching cultural consumers is a challenge, but one for which interviews and focus groups are well-equipped.

SUMMARY: KEY POINTS

Research into cultural consumers tends to be concerned with the experiences, practices and attitudes of cultural consumers, and can be realised in research projects of various shapes and guises.

- There is no neat separation of processes of consumption and production, and cultural consumers are also cultural producers.
- Interviews and focus groups are excellent tools for researching cultural consumers because they are able to (1) elicit consumers' experiences, practices and attitudes through talk, (2) capture the dynamics between cultural production and consumption, and (3) take into account the diversity of cultural consumers.
- Focus groups and interviews are qualitative methods focused on meanings and concerned with the production of in-depth knowledge. Researchers can engage in analytical generalisations while statistical generalisations remain difficult and are not a key objective.
- Focus groups differ from interviews by including group interaction as data and producing shared meanings between participants.
- Focus groups and interviews possess their own sets of advantages and disadvantages which mean that they are more or less suitable to different forms of research into cultural consumers.
- Focus groups are particularly suitable for research into cultural consumers which:
  - aims to establish the social and shared production of meaning
  - explores a topic marked by much consensus or common-sense thinking
  - aims for breadth (in terms of numbers of participants), such as research concerned with how common an experience or attitude is
  - aims to compare and contrast different social groups.
- Interviews are particularly suitable for research into cultural consumers which:
  - aims for depth and detail
  - adopts a 'life perspective' covering various areas in an individual's life
  - aims to establish nuanced comparisons and contrasts between individuals
  - aims to explore the interplay between individual and social factors through the cases of particular consumers
  - explores sensitive or controversial topics where group dynamics may be unhelpful.
- The research processes involved in interviews and focus groups can be broken down into several stages which encompass a planning

phase, a phase of conducting interviews and focus groups, and subsequent transcription and analysis.

FURTHER READING

Qualitative research into cultural consumers is a specific topic which draws on several wider issues and fields. As a consequence students can choose which particular aspects they want to study further. Most relevant books are written from a social scientific perspective, though Alasuutari (1995) and Morley (1992) both explore qualitative research methods in the discipline of cultural studies. While Morley focuses on media consumption and provides very useful examples of audience research, Alasuutari's book is strong on methodological debates within cultural studies. For those particularly interested in interviewing as a research tool, there are plenty of social science books available which are relevant to the study of culture. Kvale (1996) is particularly recommended as it offers detailed, comprehensive and accessible accounts of practical issues on 'how to do interviews' and of the theoretical debates and backgrounds underpinning the method. For those further interested in focus group research, the 1998 *Sage Focus Group Kit* represents an excellent 'how to do' guide. This six-volume guide is lacking in theoretical discussion, but is clearly written and structured and covers practical issues extensively. The kit includes: Morgan, D. L. (1998) *The Focus Group Guidebook*, vol. 1; Morgan, D. L. (1998) *Planning Focus Groups*, vol. 2; Krueger, R. A. (1998) *Developing Questions for Focus Groups*, vol. 3; Krueger, R. A. (1998) *Moderating Focus Groups*, vol. 4; Krueger, R. A. (1998) *Involving Community Members in Focus Groups*, vol. 5; Krueger, R. A. (1998) *Analyzing and Reporting Focus Group Results*, vol. 6. In contrast, Bloor et al. (2001) is not as extensive but provides a concise and comprehensive overview of both practical issues and theoretical contexts and underpinnings.

Quantity and Quality

CHAPTER 5

Why Counting Counts

David Deacon

The contemporary field of cultural studies has little interest in, or engage-ment with, quantitative analysis. If you don't believe me, here are some numbers.

As preparation for this chapter – which explores the reasons for this disen-gagement and its detrimental implications – I conducted a content analysis of 130 refereed articles published in six recent editions of three major cultural studies journals.[1] In this analysis, I counted all and any references made to either primary quantitative data (that is, author-generated data) or secondary quantitative data (that is, statistics produced by other academic, official or cor-porate sources).[2]

The finding that 34 per cent of the articles contained some quantitative data may appear to weaken my initial assertion. However, this headline figure gives a misleading impression of the prominence of statistical evidence in the corpus of material analysed. Articles that presented quantitative data more frequently referred to other people's statistics rather than numbers the authors had col-lected themselves (29 per cent of the articles presented secondary data, compared with 8 per cent that presented primary data).[3] Furthermore, the pre-sentation and discussion of quantitative evidence tended to be fleeting: in the forty-four articles that contained any statistical data, the average amount of space dedicated to the presentation and discussion of the numbers accounted for less than 1 per cent of total article length (0.98 per cent), which represents, on average, less than a fifth of a published page.[4]

Quantitative content analysis was the most frequently conducted form of orig-inal statistical analysis (five of the ten original data collection exercises identified). In terms of secondary data, survey data was presented most (thirty-two of the fifty-seven presentations identified), followed by generic economic data (twenty-two appearances). The sources of these secondary data were, respectively, 'academic sources' (twenty-three appearances), 'corporate sector sources' (sixteen appearances), 'national/ international official sources' (thirteen appearances), 'opinion polls' (three appearances) and 'unclear' (two appearances).

The numbers quoted were never challenged nor interrogated. Not a single methodological, epistemological or ontological question was raised about any of the statistical results presented. Furthermore, contextual information that is normally used to appraise the reliability and validity of quantitative data (for example, sample size and procedures) was almost always absent. In the 2,276 pages I scrutinised, I identified only one reference to a significance test.

Such uncritical invocation of statistics could be indicative of a naïve acceptance, even reification, of the objectivity and authority of quantitative evidence. I am convinced this is not the case. Rather, I believe it further supports my initial point about a general disengagement and indifference in cultural studies towards quantitative modes of analysis. Although there may be occasions when the incidental use of a cherry-picked statistic can serve a general analytical (or rhetorical) function, in the main, the real intellectual work of cultural studies – the locations where meaningful reflexivity and debate is to be had – is seen to involve engaging with theoretical complexities or revelling in the richness of qualitative data.

Such assumptions are so widely accepted in the field that they are rarely openly articulated, but there are occasions when they surface. Take, for example, Simon During's observation about the rising influence of ethnography in cultural studies research: 'It can be "quantitative", which involves large-scale surveys and (usually) statistical analysis. However this kind of research ultimately belongs more to the social sciences than to cultural studies' (2005: 23). In challenging this kind of demarcation, this chapter explores three themes: the reasons why quantitative analysis is deemed *infra dig* for cultural studies; the relevance of this enduring disengagement; and its restrictive implications for the field as a whole. In addressing these issues, however, I am not advocating quantification as a preferable or more superior mode of analysis. Indeed, I am antagonistic to epistemic prioritisation of this kind, just as I am to its mirror opposite, which vaunts qualitative analysis as the only legitimate mode of analysis (Deacon et al. 1998). As shall be explained, both perspectives are informed by a flawed and outmoded methodological determinism.

Reasons

To understand the reasons for cultural studies' disengagement with quantitative methods, there is a need to appreciate the broad and specific historical contexts in which the field emerged and established its presence. In wider terms, the rise of cultural studies in the 1960s constituted just one condensation funnel in a multi-vortex tornado that transformed the human sciences. Across the disciplines, this period was marked by a resurgence in anti-positivism, in which earlier hermeneutic traditions were rediscovered, reasserted and extended (Morrison 1998: ch. 4). In this new *zeitgeist*, positivist epistemology and methodology were not only identified as philosophically untenable but also as politically reactionary, complicit in the legitimisation of capitalist exploitation, racism and sexism (for a recent statement of this position, see Steinmetz 2005). Particularly influential in this respect were feminist critiques that identified androcentric traits in the development and application of statistical methods and, as a consequence, prescribed a methodological agenda orientated exclusively around qualitative methods (Cook and Fonow 1986; Miles 1983; Stanley and Wise 1983; Harding 1987; Lather 1988; Reinharz 1992). Such critiques resonated powerfully with the political inclinations of cultural studies pioneers, and their affiliation to humanist Marxism, interest in identity politics and support for subaltern groups (Inglis 1993: 131). Thus, the field readily and willingly aligned itself with what van de Berg has disparagingly labelled 'the epistemological left' (2006).

There are additional, specific reasons why an elective antipathy to quantitative methods became part of the rote and routine of cultural studies. All of the key founding figures had backgrounds in literary studies, rather than the social sciences, and their intellectual orientations and methodological predilections soon became formalised in the teaching and research activity of the field. In theoretical terms, this disciplinary infusion helped vitalise previously moribund debates about communication and media, providing new and exciting ways of conceptualising the 'production, circulation, distribution/consumption [and] reproduction' of meaning (Hall 1973/1993: 91). Carey characterised this change as a shift from a 'transmission' to 'ritual' view of communication, which saw 'the original or highest manifestation of communication not in the transmission of intelligent information but in the construction and maintenance of an ordered, meaningful cultural world that can serve as a control and container for human action' (1985: 19).

Methodologically, however, this change provided an additional reason for rejecting quantitative methods, as their development and deployment had been a central feature of the dominant 'transmission' paradigm (Gitlin 1978). For example, in a chapter outlining the conduct of media studies at the Birmingham Centre for Contemporary Cultural Studies in the late 1970s, Stuart Hall confidently asserted: 'Audience-based survey research, based on the large statistical sample using fixed-choice questionnaires, has at last reached the terminal point it has long deserved – at least as a serious sociological enterprise' (Hall 1980: 120, quoted by Morrison 1998).

In this new fixation with questions of representation and meaning, traditional quantitative methods were rejected as intractably inflexible and ill-conceived.

Quantitative content analysis, with its emphasis on cross-textual denotative aggregation, was criticised for ignoring the immanent complexities of textual meaning and how it 'derives from relationships, oppositions and context rather than the quantity of references' (McQuail 1987: 189). Experiments and sample-surveys were shunned for their failure to engage people's with complex interior lives or their situated cultural and social experiences. As Inglis remarks:

> [O]ne is seeking out the presence and power of intersubjective meaning and value. These are not quantities in people's heads, retrievable by social surveyors. They are the evaluative atmosphere or ethos which the members of a society must breathe in and out by virtue of being human and sociable . . . Common or intersubjective meanings and values, therefore, are not . . . available to hard data and social-survey analysis. (1993: 148)

An important element of such critiques is the proposition that frequency of occurrence should not be seen as the definitive measure of significance or, indeed, signification (for example, Burgelin 1968). Although cultural studies defined itself, at least initially, as a political project asking major questions about capitalist hegemony (Hartley 2003; Rojek 2002), it sought to do so by interrogating the particularities of culture rather than its generalities. This orientation remains prevalent to this day. For example, in her recent book on cultural studies research methods, Ann Gray emphasises the 'uniqueness' of textual and ethnographic investigations and their incompatibility with traditional social scientific concerns about 'generalizability' and 'representativeness' (Gray 2002: 74, quoted in Barker 2003). In a similar vein, John Hartley described his methodology for his study of journalism, modernity and popular culture:

> I tend to concentrate on what I take to be emblematic texts or moments, using these to tease out the implications and significations involved, rather than attempting objective methodologies like sampling, surveying or statistics. This is because I am interested in meanings, which are rarely expressed in the form of generalities. You can reduce a kiss to information for the benefit of scientific enquiry, of course, but it is not a method which yields complete understanding of what a given kiss means in specific circumstances to its participants and onlookers. So the methods employed in this book are documentary, historical, argumentative, metaphorical and textual. (1996: 6)

More recently, Hartley has also acknowledged the general indifference of cultural studies to questions of 'scale': 'Thus, where sociology and anthropology were generalising, classifying and theorising disciplines, cultural studies retained some of its literary-critical mind-set, with a devotion to detailed and passionate engagement with the particular' (2003: 124).

This emphasis upon particularities and emblems helps identify a further reason why the field has been so resistant to quantitative methods. Cultural studies is orientated to the deconstruction of meaning, whereas statistics are fundamentally about the construction of meaning. Numbers do not arrive unbidden, out of thin air; they rely on defining and operationalising concepts and categories, and choosing and applying procedures. This constructive process is often obscured in the presentation of the resulting data, which results in the simulation of 'an objectivity that in reality depends on the legitimacy of the questions asked' (Gadamer 1996: 301). Both of these factors are guaranteed to invite the scepticism rather than the interest of cultural studies' analysts, although it is significant to note that this rarely extends to a detailed deconstruction of actual statistical evidence. Most typically, it amounts to a high-handed dismissal of quantification *per se*, as inevitably lacking ecological validity.

A final point of relevance here is that the field's resistance to quantitative analysis varies. Almost all of the statistics I identified in my content analysis of recent cultural studies journals were descriptive statistics, that is, the numbers were used to 'describe' wider social, economic and cultural trends. Their uncritical use suggests a degree of tolerance for this kind of empirical evidence, even if its contribution is marginalised and uninterrogated. Such acceptance does not extend, however, to statistical inference: the realm where statistics are used for hypothesis testing and extrapolating wider population estimates on the basis of what has been observed (Deacon et al. 2007, ch. 5). Certainly, this is the facet of statistics that has attracted most criticism from feminist theorists (for example, Hughes 1995). Two findings from the content analysis confirm this antipathy is shared in cultural studies: the almost complete lack of any reference to statistical significance tests, and the total absence of experimental research-based evidence. Tests for statistical significance make assumptions about the stability and predictability of social, cultural and psychological patterns ('because we find it here, we can predict confidently its existence and extent elsewhere'). Experiments are methods designed specifically to establish and measure causality. Both propositions are an anathema to a field that is shaped, at root, by 'the literary affirmation of human singularity' (Inglis 1993: 131) and that valorises the capriciousness, creativity and particularity of human expression. Textual poachers are not amenable fodder for regression analysis.

RELEVANCE

Having identified the main reasons for cultural studies' resistance to quantitative modes of analysis, I now want to consider the relevance of this situation.

For, although a dismissal of quantification remains largely unchallenged in the cultural studies mainstream, elsewhere in the human sciences such assumptions have been subjected to considerable revision, particularly regarding the extent to which one can 'read off' epistemologies and politics, on the basis of methodological choice.

Reading off Epistemology

At the core of the hermeneutic turn in the 1960s and 1970s was an 'incompatibility thesis' (Howe 1988: 10). This held that methodology and epistemology existed in an iron embrace, and as a consequence qualitative and quantitative methods could never be combined satisfactorily (for example, Guba and Lincoln 1982; Smith 1983). More recently, however, interest has grown across many disciplines in the combination of qualitative and quantitative research methods, which suggests opinions have altered on the 'epistemology/methodology' link. The sociologist Alan Bryman has been at the foreground of debates about the reconcilability of qualitative-quantitative methods for many years (for example, Bryman 1988) and in a recent study examined (1) the prevalence of multi-method studies in refereed journals across the human sciences and (2) the views of senior academics on the pitfalls and benefits of combining qualitative and quantitative methods (Bryman 2006). On the basis of this investigation, he concluded that, although pockets of resistance remain:

> [T]he paradigm wars [of previous decades] have been replaced by a period of paradigm peace. In this new era, there is a tendency to stress the compatibility between quantitative and qualitative research and a pragmatic viewpoint which prioritises using any approach that allows research questions to be answered regardless of its philosophical presuppositions. (2006: 124)

This shift in emphasis from 'means' to 'ends' is the product of several related developments. First, it can be seen as a measure of the success of the hermeneutic critique of positivism in the 1960s and 1970s. Without question, it was a vital intervention and few, if anyone, would now subscribe to beliefs about the objectivity and value freedom of statistical evidence, nor fail to appreciate the limitations of quantitative methods.[5] However, once purged of their epistemological pretensions, quantitative methods become amenable for inclusion in more reflexive and interpretative research activity. Second, this interest in incorporating quantitative methods in multi-method investigations also reflects a growing appreciation of the limitations of interpretivism – in particular, concerns about the research issues it closes off, the methodological inhibitions it can create, and the spectres of solipsism and relativism that haunt the paradigm. Third, it has been argued that the incompatibility thesis overstates the antinomy of positivist-orientated and interpretivist-orientated research concerns. For example, Murdock notes that many qualitative and ethnographic studies within cultural studies, despite their resistance to more formal forms of statistical measurement, 'often fall back on loose statements of how many people did or said something or how often' (1997: 181) (see also Lewis 1997). The legitimacy of this observation was confirmed by my own experiences in conducting the content analysis of recent cultural studies journals. Time and again, I encountered quasi-quantitative statements in the articles, not only in the presentation of qualitative empirical evidence, but also in authors' general rhetorical and theoretical discourse. A small selection from the plethora of comments I encountered are set out in Table 5.1, for illustrative purposes. My point in presenting them is not to suggest that they all needed more specific and rigorous quantification, but rather to demonstrate a prevalent, if tacit, acceptance that in political, analytical and rhetorical terms, 'frequency of occurrence' does count – even when it is not counted.

Table 5.1 Quasi-quantification and cultural studies: some recent examples (emphasis added in all cases)

'In *almost every instance*, [the programme's] wrongdoers fit this description'

'*The majority* of quiz shows to emerge in recent years depend on "general/academic" knowledge'

'The Italian audience has been offered *an increasing number* of home-grown serials'

'*Most of the interviewed club culture practitioners* . . . seemed acutely aware of these more general and, in particular, local contexts and instances of racialised power differentials in the City's club culture economy'

'In recent times we have witnessed *a growing attention* to global flows of information and telematics and their post colonial implications'

'I was struck by the fact that *almost all* the interviewees spontaneously referred to [the programme]'

'Technologically mediated communication *is frequently* only a supplementary mode of exchange supporting geographically dispersed family members'

'There is certainly *a well-established association* between middle-class gay men and the gentrification of inner city housing stock'

'The study of media pleasure *was once widespread* in media studies'

'Not surprisingly, *many of the interviewees* saw economic globalization as an exploitative process'

'*Some of our interviewees* seemed to prefer not to get too immersed'

'[the central character] *was described almost unanimously* as the embodiment of the new social group (or class) of career woman'

Despite the general growth of interest in multi-method research in the human sciences – and indeed its popularity within related branches of communication and media studies – cultural studies remains strangely impervious to its appeal. This is a surprisingly outmoded stance for a field that has long vaunted its cutting edge interdisciplinarity and reflexivity. As Justin Lewis comments:

> Research within cultural studies has consistently been qualitative rather than quantitative . . . While such a preference was initially both well-conceived and fruitful, the lingering suspicion of numerical data has degenerated into habit. It is as if the argument with these methodologies was so comprehensively settled that one can be spared the time and effort of any further thought on the subject. (1997: 84)

In criticising this 'doctrinal' rejection of quantification, Lewis also questions whether quantitative audience research should be as readily dismissed for its theoretical inadequacies. For example, he argues that agenda-setting research provides a 'germ of an analytical model' (1997: 93) with its interest in reality construction and analytical distinction between 'deep ideological structures – the social encyclopaedia of common knowledge – and the more overtly ideological discourse of attitudes and opinions' (ibid.). Similarly, he applauds the cultivation analysis research of George Gerbner and colleagues, which 'for all its shortcomings . . . remains the only comprehensive body of research to have systematically demonstrated that television plays a clearly defined hegemonic role in contemporary culture' (1997: 89). Furthermore, Lewis sees no reason why other public opinion data cannot be appropriated and integrated within 'a thorough going analysis of the evolving ideological character of cultural industries and institutions,' and be used 'to provide the rough contours of a complex ideological map' (ibid.).

Reading off Politics

Just as views about the intrinsic epistemological flaws of quantification are being challenged, so questions are being raised about the accusations that statistics are always the refuge of reactionaries.

As noted, feminist critics have been very influential in this political assault on quantification (for example, Belenky et al. 1986; Reinharz 1984; Harding 1987; Gilligan 1982). For example, Hughes argues that, 'The politics of domination are integrated into the scientific method and used as a political agent for those in power' (1995: 395). She supports this appraisal by providing fascinating historical details about the early inventors of statistics and their broader intellectual and political concerns:

Statistical methods were invented as a way of knowing by men motivated by eugenic politics . . . While enabling investigation in every field of study, statistical analysis has also aided in the social construction of dominance by giving scientific authority to the construction of reified categories which lead to the objectification of oppressed, subjugated groups. (1995: 401)

These are grave accusations. However, I have two reservations about her critique. First, although there have been many occasions when the analysis of 'statistical difference' has been used to objectify and stigmatise marginalised groups, it does not follow that this is invariably the case. Indeed, it has been argued by other critical scholars that the identification of difference is a vital component for democratic progress (see, in particular, Nancy Fraser's work on the politics of recognition (1995)). On a more applied level, it is widely recognised within the public policy literature that the identification, naming and categorisation of marginalised social groups is an essential precondition for them to receive appropriate support, resources and respect. Second, Hughes provides many examples where statistics were developed for patriarchal and racist purposes, but fails to demonstrate precisely what it is within the statistical procedures themselves that are inherently inscribed by prejudicial values. Furthermore, couched within her critique is a major concession: 'This does not make the mathematics incorrect, or nullify knowledge that has been gained by the use of statistical analysis' (1995: 396).

Her attack, in other words, is focused on the political (mis)uses of these procedures and delusions of their creators, rather than on their intrinsic deficiencies. Quantification is thus declared guilty by association, which is rather like condemning the development of the internal combustion engine because of its use in machineries of war, so neglecting its equally vital role in improving the efficacy of ambulance services.

This may seem a trite analogy, but the essential point would be supported by those who question the historical veracity of the claim that statistics have always privileged patriarchy. Ann Oakley (1998) warns against the 'dangers of simple histories', and argues that it is not 'clearly the case that "quantitative" methods have served no relevant feminist goal' (1998: 721–2). Against Hughes' invocation of eugenicists such as Francis Galton, Karl Pearson and Ronald Fisher, Oakley cites a long list of feminist reformers like Jane Addams, Harriet Martineau, Florence Nightingale and Beatrice Webb who all conducted sample survey research to generate 'policy-relevant knowledge as ammunition for social reform' (1998: 722). A particularly valuable aspect of Oakley's critique is how it highlights the fact that what is sometimes referred to in an undifferentiated way as a 'feminist' methodological critique is actually based on a specific form of feminism: the 'difference' feminism of theorists such as Carol

Gilligan, which subscribes to the existence of fundamental psycho-biological differences between women and men. This second-wave feminism has been subjected to considerable subsequent criticism by other feminist theorists (for example, Lister 2003), and many would concur with Oakley's identification of the damaging political implications of such methodological monism:

> The case against quantitative ways of knowing is based on a rejection of reason and science as masculine and an embracing of experience as feminine; but this is essentialist thinking that buys into the very paradox that it protests about . . . The result is likely to be the construction of 'difference' feminism where women are described as owning distinctive ways of thinking, knowing and feeling, and the danger is that these new moral characterisations will play into the hands of those who use gender as a means of discriminating against women. (1998: 725)

A related point here is the unquestioned assumption that qualitative methods are always used for progressive purposes. For example, in his definitive study of the politics of marketing of the British Labour party, Dominic Wring (2005) demonstrates how a self-styled modernising tendency used qualitative focus group studies strategically to justify the jettisoning of social-democratic policies and shift the party towards the political right. Apart from questioning the rigour of these studies, Wring demonstrates that a major reason for their appeal and influence for the Labour leadership in the 1980s was their *qualitative* nature. During this period, the party leadership was desperate to connect with the concerns and aspirations of key marginal voters, and focus groups were seen as offering a magical solution to this conundrum. Not only did these studies amplify the influence of these 'quality minorities' on the shaping of party policy to the detriment of others, the findings were also used to legitimise a centralisation of control, erode the party's democratic structures and give prominence to disturbingly reactionary discourses. For example, in 1987 the then communications director of the party used focus group findings to claim that Labour was out of touch and associated with 'gays', 'Marxists' and 'strange things' (Wring 2006: 79).

RESTRICTIVE IMPLICATIONS

Implicit in all of the criticisms I have raised is a belief that cultural studies' aversion to quantification is closing off academic avenues and political options. In this section, I want to identify more precisely what I believe these restrictive implications to be.

The first relates to methodological difficulties that can be created by imprecise 'quasi-quantification'. As noted, it is possible to detect a latent quantitative impulse in many pieces of cultural studies research, but there are occasions where this reluctance to engage in systematic counting creates analytical vagueness, and even internal contradictions and logical inconsistencies. Graham Murdock furnishes an illustration of this point with reference to a study of audience responses to a television drama documentary about IRA bombings in Birmingham (Roscoe et al. 1995). Although the study was based on the qualitative analysis of twelve focus group interviews, Murdock identifies two pivotal quantitative statements in the analysis:

- 'There are *many occasions* in the group discussions where participants drew on their classified group membership to inform their reading' (Roscoe et al. 1995: 96; emphasis added)
- 'There were *many instances* of participants moving outside of the particular "interest" and "non-interest" classifications used in this study as they made sense of the issues.' (Roscoe et al. 1995: 98; emphasis added)

As Murdock notes, without additional quantitative elaboration, these statements appear mutually contradictory:

We are not told how often each practice occurred, whether one was more common than the other, who was most likely to engage in them and in which contexts, or even whether they were different people or the same individuals at different points of the discussion. All of these features of the situation could be very simply expressed in numerical form. Far from reducing the complexity of the analysis, calculating these figures would deepen it by establishing the patterning of practice and by suggesting new dimensions of interpretation. (Murdock 1997: 182)

A second restrictive implication of cultural studies' disengagement with quantification is that it limits the capacity of the field to deconstruct statistical evidence *on its own terms*. This displays an odd incuriosity for an enterprise so wedded to deconstruction. More seriously, it can become a form of political abdication. To dismiss all statistics as artificial constructs is to assume that all are as bad as each other, which is patently a fatuous generalisation. It is certainly true that statistics do not speak for themselves and should never be taken on face value. They need to be read critically. But, to acknowledge the constructed nature of statistics is not the same as saying they are inevitably corrupt. The validity of numerical evidence is determined by the competence of its conceptualisation, the meticulousness of its collation and the rigour in its interpretation. These can only be ascertained by close and careful scrutiny. Moreover, we cannot ignore the pervasive belief that numbers have greater scientific rigour and objectivity than other kinds of evidence, however much we might want to challenge it. Indeed, it is because statistics have this rhetorical power that critical analysts must have the capability to engage in an internal critique of statistics when identifying and confronting their rhetorical and political abuses. As Inglis remarks:

> [A] student of culture must be statistically numerate. This is even more intractably true when the student is preoccupied by questions of power . . . Power, crude coercive power, will always try to wrest numbers for its own purposes, like the bastard it is. Freedom will always oppose it, and discover the uses and abuses of statistics with which to affront power. (1993: 123)

A third restrictive implication of avoiding quantification is that it disengages cultural studies from wider public policy debates. For example, Tony Bennett has long argued that if cultural studies is to have any political influence in the formation of cultural policy, it must have the capability to understand and engage with 'governmental calculations' (1992: 35). One example he provides is of the need to be able to challenge official 'performance indicators' in cultural policy that are rooted in economic rationalist criteria: 'In this regard, people with the capacity to do sophisticated statistical and economic work, have a major contribution to make to work at the cultural studies/policy interface – perhaps more than those who engage solely in cultural critique' (1992: 35).

A similar point has been advanced by Angela McRobbie in her criticism of the tendency within cultural studies to dismiss empiricism (along with ethnography and 'experience') as '[an] artificially coherent narrative fiction'. In her view, such purism makes it difficult for researchers:

> to participate in facts and figures oriented policy debates, or indeed in relation to the social problem whose roots seemed to lie in innovative cultural practices, for example, the rise of rave and dance cultures and the consumption among young people of E's (i.e. Ecstacy). It has instead been left to sociologists like Jason Ditton in Glasgow to do the dirtier work of developing policies on youth cultures like rave, which necessitate having access to reliable facts, figures and even 'ethnographic accounts' to be able to argue with angry councillors, police and assorted moral guardians. (1996: 337–8)

A fourth major limitation of non-engagement with quantitative methods is the ability of the field to adequately address questions of power. As discussed, cultural studies privileges fine-grained analysis. This is valuable in many respects, not least in offering a corrective to over-generalised and deterministic structural analyses of power. However, a theoretical and methodological orientation that is exclusively orientated to micro agency and complexity can easily lead to a negation of the structural forces and inequalities that circumscribe these activities (Ferguson and Golding 1997: xxvi). This can then transform into overly optimistic celebrations of the semiotic autonomy of cultural consumers and the 'cool' of capitalist culture (McGuigan 2006). As Oakley notes, with regard to feminist research:

> Women and other minority groups, above all, need 'quantitative' research, because without this it is difficult to distinguish between personal experience and collective oppression. Only large-scale comparative data can determine to what extent the situations of men and women are structurally differentiated. (1999: 251)

The incorporation of extensive methods also provides a more legitimate basis for extrapolating implications beyond the particular, which remains a latent impulse in much cultural studies' work, whatever might be said about the evils of generalisation. Crucially, it would provide a corrective to what John Hartley acknowledges as the 'not entirely positive habit' cultural studies has inherited from literary studies of universalising from particularities (2003: 124).

It is important to appreciate that the combination of qualitative-quantitative methods is not just about providing checks and balances to the excesses of each. We should also be alive to the creative possibilities of their combination, in which insights and findings from one strand inform directly the design and development of others. An excellent example of the fruitful combination of qualitative and quantitative methods is offered by Livingstone et al.'s research into audience reception of audience participation talk shows. In the first phase of their research, a series of focus group interviews were conducted in conjunction with a textual analysis to explore the complex relations between 'reader, text and context' in this genre (Livingstone et al. 1994: 376; Livingstone and Lunt 1994). These were followed up by a survey of a random, representative sample of 3,000 adults, who were asked to fill in a self-completion questionnaire that enquired about their viewing of, and views about, these TV talk shows.

The results of the focus discussions directly informed the design of the questionnaire: insights derived from unstructured questioning provided guidance for subsequent structured questioning. Furthermore, the aim of the second extensive phase of the research was intended to test the general applicability and representativeness of the initial conclusions. This was because, in the authors' view, questions about the generalisability of findings from small-scale qualitative reception studies were a matter that had 'largely been avoided' in previous focus-group based studies (Livingstone et al. 1994: 376). Finally, although these different methods produced many *complementary* insights into audience perspectives about TV talk shows, in some areas they generated unique perspectives. On the one hand, 'the focus group interviews identified more complex connections between text and reception, [and] identified contradictions within audience readings' (ibid.). On the other hand, the self-completion questionnaire survey 'highlighted what had been missed in the focus group analysis, namely, the importance of the viewers' age compared to, say, gender or social class' (ibid.).

CONCLUDING REMARKS

This discussion has examined the reasons, relevance and restrictive implications of cultural studies' disengagement with quantitative analysis. Some may reject my criticisms as being yet another example of an attack from a hostile sociological 'outsider', but this would misrepresent my view of the field and ignore the fact that many of the concerns I raise have also been articulated by theorists more closely associated with cultural studies (for example, McRobbie 1996; Lewis 1997; Inglis 1993; Bennett 1992; Livingstone et al. 1994).

It is true that my discussion has focused exclusively upon what quantitative methods can bring to cultural studies. In view of this, I would like to end on a more positive note, and invite consideration of what cultural studies could bring to quantitative analysis. It is undoubtedly the case that statistics can often be dry, prosaic and of such banality as to be prime candidates for what a sarcastic journalist once defined as the WIND award ('Well I Never Did!'). I am convinced that 'the cultural studies imagination' has much to contribute to enriching the rationale, design, presentation and interpretation of quantitative evidence. But this can only be achieved by waking up to broader developments in the human sciences and embracing the potential of these methods rather than fixating on their limitations.

SUMMARY KEY POINTS

- The chapter identifies cultural studies' long-term and enduring rejection of quantitative research methods.
- This repudiation is now so widely accepted that it is rarely commented upon or justified. However, it is clear that the greatest antagonism is towards inferential statistics.
- Despite this, many cultural studies investigations engage in quasi-quantification, both empirically and rhetorically. On occasions, this can lead to a lack of precision that produces confusing or contradictory conclusions.

- The reasons for the field's dismissal of quantification are rooted in its literary-studies foundations and its historical links to anti-positivist movements that gained prominence during the 1960s and 1970s.
- However, the methodological determinism that infuses such perspectives (that is, that epistemology and methodology exist in an iron embrace) is increasingly falling from favour in many other areas of the human sciences.
- Cultural studies' doctrinal disengagement with quantitative analysis means that analysts are unable to deconstruct statistical evidence on its own terms, or to evaluate the comparative merits of statistical data. This inhibits their ability both to critique the ideological misuse of statistics and to participate in broader cultural and public policy debates.

FURTHER READING

For a broad introduction to statistical uses, principles and procedures which makes no assumptions about prior knowledge, see ch. 5 ('Handling Numbers') of my co-authored methods textbook, *Researching Communications* (Deacon et al. 2007). Chapter 14 ('Using Computers') of the book also provides an introduction to SPSS (the Statistical Package for the Social Sciences), which is the most widely used computer software for statistical analysis in the social sciences. For more extensive introductions to statistical methods, see Coolidge (2006) and Fielding and Gilbert (2006). Bryman and Cramer (2005) valuably combines a clear discussion of statistical procedures with descriptions of how to conduct analyses using SPSS. Krippendorff (2004) remains the definitive textbook for those interested in quantitative content analysis procedures. For further reading on the epistemological and methodological value of integrating qualitative and quantitative methods see Hammersley (1996) and Bryman (1988).

NOTES

1. *Cultural Studies* volume (editions): 19 (4 to 6), 20 (1 to 2, 4); *European Journal of Cultural Studies*, 8 (2 to 4), 9 (1 to 3); *International Journal of Cultural Studies*, 8 (2 to 4), 9 (1 to 3).
2. I did not code all numerical references (for example, '9/11', 'The Top Ten' etc.). To be included the numbers had to represent some formal observation, collation and analysis.
3. These are not mutually exclusive categories, which is why their addition exceeds 34 per cent.

4. It should also be appreciated that these averages were inflated by the presence of three articles that dedicated more than five pages each to the presentation and analysis of statistical evidence. If these 'outlying values' are excluded from the calculation, the average proportional presence of statistical data per article drops to 0.75 per cent.

5. It is also unfair to assume that all of the pioneering positivists were oblivious to these concerns. See, for example, David Morrison's fascinating reappraisal of Paul Lazarsfeld's intellectual career (1998).

CHAPTER 6

Why Observing Matters

Virginia Nightingale

> Materiality conveys meaning. It provides the means by which social relations are visualised, for it is through materiality that we articulate meaning and thus it is the frame through which people communicate identities. Without material expression social relations have little substantive reality . . . (Sofaer 2007: 1)

Observation-based research relies on interactions and exchanges between researcher and research participants, and it is this expanded vision of observation – observation that explicitly designs and accounts for the impact of the research process on the fieldwork experience and the data it produces – that the chapter explores. It is based on the premise that communication is a material process in the sense that it is something that can be observed, recorded, documented, analysed and written about. Fieldwork involves finding ways to transform the fleeting character of communication and social relations into durable analysable forms. Other research practices – for example, textual analysis, image analysis, historical research, archival research, market research – may be used to complement the materials produced by the primary engagement with research participants. These research practices use forms of mediation other than observation by a researcher, and usually play a supporting role to the observation-based fieldwork. These secondary research materials are increasingly important today because in effect they replace some of the contextual information previously revealed through the extended time commitment required by a traditional participant observation.

In observation-based research, 'exchange' between the researcher and the research subjects is the medium that assists the transformation of ideas and thoughts into the words and activities recorded. Exchange also acts as a corrective to the assumptions inherent in the researcher (his or her predisposition to counter-transference) that might otherwise be projected onto the research subjects. Dracklé has noted that, 'We talk with others about our ideas – and weave our ideas and images into stories so as to translate them for others. To do this, exchange is required, exchange amongst several people' (Dracklé 2004: ix). In other words, observational research involves interacting with research participants, finding ways to transform *their* ideas and images into forms the researcher can observe, record, document and analyse, and then finding the place where the researcher's experience meets that of the research subjects. In this sense observation needs to be an active process, aimed at facilitating the enactment of ideas and their translation into material form (recorded or recordable research data).

Observation-based research is highly dependent on the exercise of self-reflexivity – critical reflection by the researcher about the impact the observer has, or is likely to have, on the sorts of things that are said or done while the fieldwork is in progress. Self-reflexivity is also important during the analysis and writing of the fieldwork experience, since it is in these activities that the researcher's power to shape the representation of the research exchanges is greatest. It is where sensitivity to the meaning for the research subjects of the observer's presence can potentially be best integrated into the research report.

THE LIMITS OF OBSERVATION

Imagine this: a group of people sit silently in a room. The room, the group and the silence are observable, recordable and can be documented. Clearly, the fact that these people are sitting silently in the room means something. How might an observer work out what is going on: who are these people, why are they silent and what does their silence mean? The sitting and the silence may be because the group is depressed, alienated, or afraid. They may be meditating, or recovering from tonsillitis. They may have taken a vow to sit silently together for several hours each day. They may be waiting for something to happen – the end of the world or a terrorist attack. Or they might just be stubbornly refusing to speak.

One approach might be to research the group and its silence by covertly observing the group – through a keyhole, open doorway or one-way mirror. This would allow the researcher to document and speculate about what each person is wearing, what their facial expressions indicate about their inner states, how frequently they make eye contact with each other, how often particular group members make trips to the bathroom and what happens when it is time to eat. This research activity produces analysable data, but it is not very rich data in terms of explaining what is, or is not, going on. And it does not allow for the fact that the silence may be generated by the group knowing or suspecting that they are being watched.

Alternatively, the researcher may observe the group by sitting silently with the group – effectively *embedding* herself (sic) in the group. *Being with* the group, in this way, produces richer research data. The researcher shares the physical experience of the 'environment': the air quality and temperature, the smells, the hardness of the chairs, the aches and pains of sitting too long in one spot, perhaps even the sounds of laboured breathing by some members of the group. By sharing the silence and the sitting long enough, the researcher might develop a sense of solidarity with the group and, given enough time, reach some conclusions about the effects of silence on a human group or formulate assumptions about why this group has chosen to sit silently.

However, unless or until there is some exchange (either verbal or behavioural) between group members or between group members and the researcher, any explanation of our hypothetical group remains speculation. Even though embedded in the group, the researcher cannot produce an adequate account of the phenomenon without assistance from the group members or from informants either inside or outside the group. The researcher may produce an absolutely accurate and evocative account of what it is like to sit with the group in that room yet still fail to explain why they are there and why they stay. To produce good qualitative research, accurate observation has to be combined with communication and exchange of information and ideas, both between the researcher and participants and among research participants. This is why sociologists have argued that:

> The most complete form of the sociological datum, after all, is the form in which the participant observer gathers it: an observation of some social event, the events that precede and follow it, and the explanations of its meanings by participants and spectators before, during and after its occurrence. (Becker and Geer 1972: 102)

Being there as observer is the first step. Assessing how best to combine observation with participation and exchange in ways that make it possible for the participants to enter into productive exchange with the researcher, and vice versa, is the second.

PARTICIPANT OBSERVATION AND ETHNOGRAPHY

It is interesting to compare early social science descriptions of participant observation with its use today and with anthropology's use of ethnography, since *being there* is central to both, and ethnography has been the source of observational strategies and tactics now widely practised in social science generally. For Becker and Greer, the particular value of the participant observation lay in the wealth of contextual and experiential information resulting from combining observation and interrogation over time.

> By participant observation we mean that method in which the observer participates in the daily life of the people under study . . . observing things that happen, listening to what is said and questioning people, over some length of time. (Becker and Geer 1972: 102)

Somewhat paradoxically today, the capacity to devote time to observing has been dramatically reduced because of its cost and complexity. A notable recent exception is Georgina Born's (2004) excellent ethnographic observation of the BBC which provides fascinating evidence to support the value of contextual information in the evaluation and analysis of primary research data.

Cowlishaw (2007: 1) has suggested that for anthropology, ethnography involves, 'writing that is based on extended, empirical field work, the "being there", "going elsewhere", immersing oneself in some *other* social space with *other* social subjects in order to *change your mind*'. Participant observation, as the term is used today in cultural studies, more usually focuses on problem *behaviours* or *attitudes*. It frequently addresses problems in the researcher's own culture – where separation from the known and the embedded aspects of ethnography cannot be achieved. On the other hand, participant observation may involve prolonged engagement with people of different class or status (Hobson 1980) or, as in Born's case, being intermittently embedded in an institutional setting over a period of several years. The current widespread use of the term 'ethnographic' to describe most examples of participant observation today reflects this influence. However, ethnography – and, *inter alia*, participant observation – is associated with characteristic weaknesses that the researcher using observational methods needs to recognise and manage appropriately.

A recent BBC television series, *Tribe*, provides a useful opportunity to explain the complex issues raised for observation-based research by ethnography and its history as a social research method. Bearing in mind that the aim of *Tribe* is to entertain the British television viewer, it is not surprising that the programme transforms ethnography into spectacle, a performance, rather than research. While the programme is broadcast primarily on subscription TV (at least in Australia where I live), information about *Tribe* can be accessed at its website. The show's host, adventurer and film-maker Bruce Parry, provides an interesting echo of Cowlishaw's definition of ethnography when he describes the programme as follows:

> *Tribe* is about looking at the way other people live and asking questions about the way we live. It's about family values, joie de vivre, free time,

gender, sex, drugs, health and sustainable living. It's about everything
that we talk about down the pub. Not just me and you but everyone. All
our lives. But it's also about the global environmental and cultural threats
that we know exist but that we don't know what best to do about. It's
about commercialism and corporations and perceptions of our
individual, materialistic world. It's about politics and social organisations.
(Bruce Parry, http://www.bbc.co.uk/tribe/bruce/index.shtml, accessed
1 April 2007)

Tribe combines reality TV with documentary and travel genres. Parry visits
tribal communities throughout the world. His involvement with the tribes
often includes being adopted by an appropriate family. For up to a month he is
expected to meet the requirements of group membership in terms of work,
social life and leisure, living as the tribe does – at least when in front of the
camera. Parry and his team are, in these senses and to the extent that the camera
reveals, *embedded* in the life of each tribe for a month.

Brad, London
Saw the Dassanech episode last night purely by accident. A brilliant
programme, it's great to see someone involved, instead of the usual
patronising and insular voice-overs. What wonderfully warm people;
thought your 'mum' was great Bruce! I was riveted to the croc hunting.
Best TV I've seen in months. (*Tribe* website, accessed 1 April 2007)

Each episode involves Parry and his production team in complex negotiation with tribal elders and community members. These negotiations are sometimes but not always revealed to the viewer. When they are revealed, they are
used to heighten the drama and create cliff-hanger uncertainty. Parry is filmed
eating and sleeping, working and playing with representatives of the tribe, and
each episode features Parry in one or several tribal rituals: a hunt; a feast; a marriage; a sacrifice; an initiation.

Neil, Brighton
Bruce's face when he was told that he would be the one to sacrifice the
bull – a classic Parry moment! (*Tribe* website, accessed 1 April 2007)

Each tribe becomes a site of discovery and self-discovery for Parry – and
through identification with Parry, for the viewer.

Lorna B, Bristol
I absolutely love this programme. I always find it so thrilling to see such
a realistic and rustic view of different ways of life. I find the traits of

certain tribes albeit slightly uneasy still very interesting and begin to understand due to the way this programme is made. (*Tribe* website, accessed 1 April 2007)

Each episode ends with sadness, and often tears, that the visit is ending and the newly adopted family member is leaving. The viewers, it seems from the comments logged at the website, also regret the fact that Bruce is leaving, even if only for another week or until another series. The programme co-opts fieldwork practice from ethnography but bends it to the service of compelling television entertainment and the delivery of an armchair tourism experience that tries to make the lives of others, their beliefs and values less 'strange' to the Western viewer.

But something strange does happen in this complex communication process. In the viewer comments (quoted above) the focus of the programme shifts from the tribe it was to 'document' onto Parry himself. Bruce Parry becomes the subject of the programme rather than the tribe. It is Bruce's reactions that viewers remember and comment on. Only one of the comments listed at the site wonders what *they* (the tribes) must make of *us*! And Bruce is credited with diplomatic powers that far exceed any skills demonstrated in the programme – viewers log comments that encourage Parry to act as a 'peace broker' and thank him for 'helping' the tribes when in reality the tribe has made it possible for Parry and his team to deliver another successful episode in the BBC series.

Emma Cave, Dorset
I thought Bruce was extraordinary and hit all the right spots. (*Tribe* website, accessed 1 April 2007)

Amsale Tibebu, Essex
This is quite simply the best TV programme of the 21st century. Bruce is just brilliant and he lived among the tribes as one of them. Bruce, I sincerely honour you for what you do. I'm originally from Ethiopia. Thank you for all that you do for these lost tribes. (*Tribe* website, accessed 1 April 2007)

Rob A., Manchester
The most fascinating thing is that no matter how different any tribe appears on the surface, Bruce is still able to relate and connect as on the basic level the people are not very different at all. (*Tribe* website, accessed 1 April 2007)

In *Tribe*, Parry plays the ethnographer, the student of human nature and cultures, but cannot help but replicate the ethnographer's plight. As in ethnographic fieldwork, the embedded commentator remains at all times a representative of the developed world. There is no chance of mistaken identity: the ethnographer may be adopted for a short time into a tribe, but everyone (Parry, his production team, the tribe, and the viewers) knows they will leave again. The tribe's generosity, forbearance and loss of privacy is repaid with gifts and money, but the stature of the visitor is incommensurably enhanced in the world where the product of the ethnographic practice is consumed. Representatives of the tribe may assist and guide his fieldwork experience but it is Parry and the production team who control the manner in which the story of the encounter with the tribe is interpreted to the developed world. The presenter/ethnographer, rather than the tribe, becomes the 'expert' on this tribe and tribal culture in general. And most importantly, the programme is silent about the pressing social, political and ecological issues facing tribal cultures throughout the world today.

This (mis)use of ethnography by *Tribe* reveals the differences in cultural power that shape the ethnographic encounter. As Rosaldo (1986) has noted, from the moment of first contact – in this case, the arrival in four-wheel drives with state-of-the-art recording equipment and resources – the scene has been set for the enactment of an unequal engagement that cannot be changed by good intentions, empathy, generosity or goodwill. However Cowlishaw (2007) has also pointed out that in regard to ethnographic research,

> the element of exploitation in such relationships, particularly with the colonial subaltern but also with any informant, is not produced by the ethnographic enterprise itself, but is a prior condition of the world. As a privileged segment of the nation, we participate in exploitation. Any writing about the world entails an author's power to represent others. That is, the power relations entailed in ethnography are not created by and nor are they resolvable through any academic practice.
> (Cowlishaw 2007: 2)

Here Cowlishaw correctly indicates that it is not the fieldwork in and of itself that is likely to trouble the research subjects, but the manner in which they are presented and represented. In the case of *Tribe*, for example, the programme is singularly successful in erasing the difference of the other, the differences between tribes, and most importantly any critical perspective on the tribal condition. The communities of *Tribe* are represented as having freely chosen their lifestyles and as being content with their choice. No sense of exclusion from the benefits of development, no sense of loss or injustice related to former tribal power and authority penetrates the veneer of the programme's format. In addition, the production team is represented as visiting and leaving without any effect on the ongoing patterns of life or the aspirations of the tribe. The 'apologetic' face of ethnography is revealed here, and it is this type of representation of ethnography that Cowlishaw argues has caused anthropology to lose its political and policy edge and become subservient to a fashionable and superficial post-colonialism.

POWER AND POLITICS IN OBSERVATION–BASED RESEARCH

Today global development and communication systems are changing the cultural research landscape. As a result, the problem of differences in cultural power between researcher and researched is not unique to *Tribe* or to ethnographic fieldwork. Researchers are as likely to face interrogation by those researched as by their academic colleagues. Diaspora communities challenge the right of career academics to speak for and of them. In qualitative research, would-be recruits feel freer to refuse the consent that ethically researchers are bound to seek. And in some forms of own-culture research the power balance can shift almost completely to the research participants, as in Born's research where securing permission for the fieldwork could not guarantee that her presence would be welcome (Born 2004: 12) or her stature as a researcher respected. In all observation-based research the power of the researcher is constrained by ethical and legal requirements, and by strict permission and access rules, that demand that the safeguards and the benefits of the research for the research participants are adequately addressed before the fieldwork can begin.

So the encounter with ethnography has enriched observation-based research to the extent that it now draws on an expanded palette of research methods and tactics to translate communicative exchanges into researchable data. The more limited interventions of traditional social science – the interview and focus group, the questionnaire and survey – have been enhanced by drawing on ethnographic research strategies and tactics, and by a more adventurous use of recording media such as video, digital still cameras and mobile technologies – by both the researcher and the research participants. This has aided the development of research designs that:

1. Encourage the sharing of power between researcher and research participants, even to the point where the research participants author the design.
2. Integrate digital technologies in the research process in addition to their use to record significant research moments and interventions.
3. Involve the research participants in activities that complement the usual focus group and interview with the production of research materials (photo collections; art work; podcasts; videos).

4. Involve the research participants as co-producers of the research outcomes using image work, play and other constructive activities.

The aim of such practices is to produce richer research data by ensuring that opportunities exist for more equal participation. And in return, social science and cultural studies have provided signposts for re-imagining anthropology as a science of the urban cultural environment – studying micro communities rather than tribes, castes and classes.

SHARING POWER

While alert to the difficulty of managing power in observational research, nothing softens the blow of realisation when the imbalances of power are revealed. In the first media research I carried out (Nightingale 1982) I used a semi-structured individual interview format to discover what media and information sources British high-school students drew on to shape their ideas about other countries. In the private schools where I interviewed, students easily expressed themselves. In the working-class rural comprehensive schools the story was very different. Students found the individual interview challenging, and I lost count of the number of times the answers 'don't know' or 'can't say' were given. When I followed up the few questions they did answer by asking where they had come across their information, the answer was often simply 'eavesdropping' or 'overhearing'. In this case, both the choice of the individual interview and my outsider/class status created a distance too great for some (though not all) low socio–economic status participants to bridge. While this research allowed me to trace the broad schemas the students used to categorise other countries and provided some important outcomes, I became convinced that I had failed to provide appropriate opportunities for some students to share their ideas about other countries and how they discovered that information.

COLLABORATION

Working with a collaborator as a way of sharing the authoring power inherent in research is routine in ethnography, but less common in own-culture research. Several of my projects have used collaborators/informants to increase the participatory aspects of the research, so here I draw on three examples to demonstrate the gains and losses involved in collaboration. In 1990, as a pedagogical exercise, I co-opted my undergraduate students as research collaborators. As part of their coursework, they were required to observe a friend or fellow student watching a television programme on three separate occasions, then to interview the friend about the programme, and finally to document what watching it had meant for that friend. I subsequently read the transcripts of observation and interview, and in turn interviewed the student collaborators. This multi-layered approach revealed the extent to which choosing a television programme is motivated by personal history and everyday context. From an educational context, discussing the research outcomes established how well the student had handled the research process.

In subsequently writing about this process (Nightingale 1992) I selected three examples where students had observed people watching rugby league on TV. Their efforts produced three very different stories about the meaning of watching rugby on TV and about the ways that gender is implicated in sports viewing. The collaborations increased the complexity and richness of the available data but at the same time removed me (as researcher) from the scene. The accounts of the sights and sounds of the observation available to me were of necessity second-hand. My power as researcher to speak with authority about the research process was reduced. I was as much a hostage to my student collaborators as the participants they had interviewed and whose stories I could not verify. It was therefore essential to share my account of their work with the student collaborators to negotiate a mutually agreeable account of what had happened. In this case, the use of collaborators and their social networks allowed the inclusion and publication of the stories of people and experiences that would otherwise never have been told.

THE COLLABORATOR/INTERPRETER

For another project (Nightingale 1997) I adapted an ethnographic strategy called cross-cultural juxtaposition (Marcus and Fischer 1986: 157–63). The research design involved a series of individual discussions with Japanese and Australian participants. My collaborator, Chika Otsuka, managed the recruitment of participants, the language translation, and acted as a guide to the cultural texts the participants talked about. She was of similar age and background to the Japanese participants and had experienced the trans-cultural shift on which the research focused. The Australians were asked to talk about their experiences of watching Japanese TV when in Japan, and the Japanese were asked to discuss watching Australian TV in Australia. This time the research revealed the ways the ephemera of television viewing are associated with discourses of national identity that in turn were used by both groups to justify pre-existing beliefs about 'own-culture' superiority (Nightingale 1997). The cross-cultural juxtaposition intensified the emphasis on the similarities and differences between Japanese and Australian culture. As a researcher, I again found the collaborative method disconcerting, not only in regard to establishing what had really happened between the collaborator and participants, but also in regard to the communication between researcher, collaborator and participants. My lack of familiarity with the language and culture of the Japanese participants intensified my feelings of powerlessness to assess the validity and generalisability of the research outcomes. This insecurity was offset by increased reliance on secondary sources such as off-air tape recordings of Japanese television programmes and advertisements, and on English-language scholarly research and writing in Japanese studies.

More positively, the project led to recognition that the research situation can be expanded when secondary sources recommended as significant by the research participants are included. The participants in effect use pre-existing textual materials as guide-posts or signs that point to meanings they find difficult to articulate. This process reverses the more usual procedure of identifying a text/programme as significant, before finding and researching its audience (Nightingale 1996). By sharing power with the collaborator and also by allowing the research participants to shape the subsequent investigation of texts, a richer sense of the complexity of intercultural media communication was revealed in the links participants suggest between nominated texts and their experiential world.

THE COLLABORATOR AS AUTHOR

My third example is drawn from a very different type of research. In 1999, working with documentary film-maker Maryella Hatfield, I conducted research for the NSW Breast Cancer Institute that interviewed and videotaped the stories of Sydney women of diverse ethnic backgrounds. As it happened each story dealt with different aspects of the importance and need for breast screening programmes, and the ease and difficulty of accessing such services in the Sydney region. The women selected the settings for filming and some allowed us to include family photographs as part of the documentary. Families and friends of the production team became involved when their parents and friends offered their stories. Women of Greek, Italian, Turkish, Lebanese, Egyptian, Chinese and Korean backgrounds were interviewed. The women previewed several iterations of the film and their feedback was integrated into the final version. In addition to the video and the research report, the women's stories were rewritten in magazine story format and printed as a booklet in both English and the native language of the woman involved (*To Tell My Sisters*, 1999). The research in this case involved translating the women's stories into popular video and print genres.

In all these examples, and in collaborative research in general, the researcher both loses and gains. By relinquishing some authoring power, the researcher is compromised in terms of the capacity to control what is said and done. On the other hand, the researcher is rewarded by a freshness and emotional depth to the research data, and by access to new ways of understanding the problem being investigated. Participant authoring opens up avenues for new research and ways of thinking about the research problem that are more relevant for the people involved.

PARTICIPANT COLLABORATIONS

The types of activities research participants undertake may involve drawing, photography, videotaping, blogging. Participant-generated research data provide new challenges for social researchers, since they are now *observers* of both interactions and the created products.

Types of creative activities used as research tools have included:

1. Video diary (Pini and Walkerdine 2005): teenage girls were given access to a video camera and asked to prepare a video diary of their daily experiences. The girls chose what to reveal to the diary and how to tell their stories – including what camera shots to use. (Bloustein (2003) has also used video diary in ethnography.)
2. Audio recording (Bird 2003: 65–86): in the late 1990s Bird mailed videotapes of television news to participating households who audio recorded their subsequent discussion of the news and mailed the audio cassette back to the researcher.
3. Imagework (Edgar 2004): dreams, daydreams and other imaginings are drawn, painted, written or audio recorded.

The acceptance of creative work as research data introduces new challenges for understanding observation in research, not the least because it adds to the researcher's list of required skills. Here the researcher needs skills to interpret and analyse these new forms of documentation (drawings, photos, podcasts, text messages, and so on). There is a sense then, in which new communications technologies (particularly digital technologies) are revolutionising observational research and facilitating the shift of responsibility for the production of research data from the researcher to the research subject.

For example, in the two images in Figure 6.1, Courtney and Taisha, both eight years old, were asked to draw a picture of a favourite advertisement. The drawings, scanned and digitised, are based on a McDonalds advertisement. Courtenay situated herself at the centre of the action, as the goalkeeper at a kids Saturday soccer match. Taisha copied Courtenay's drawing of the soccer net, but situated herself alone and behind it – an outsider. Here Taisha represented graphically her experience of the group process, and possibly of Australian

Figure 6.1 Courtney and Taisha's favourite advertisements.

culture. While happy to be included, her drawing is suggestive of the differences of ethnicity, class and cultural capital that she felt in the group. The images reveal an emotional aspect of the focus group process that was not obvious in the verbal transcripts (author's unpublished research data from 2002).

EMBEDDED OBSERVATION

Observational research is also often disconcerting and painful for the researcher. In reflecting on her observation of a family viewing *Rocky II*, Walkerdine (1990) described the alienation felt by the embedded researcher.

> I was struck by the fantasies, anxieties and pain triggered in me by being perceived as a middle-class academic confronting a working-class family. Although I invested considerable desire in wanting to 'be one of them' at the same time as 'being different', no amount of humanistic seeking for the 'beyond ideology' would get them to see in me a working-class girl 'like them'. (Walkerdine 1990: 195–6)

Walkerdine had grown up in a working-class family, yet Joanne, the six-year old subject of this investigation, and her family treated her as an outsider. For the family, Walkerdine's similar cultural origins were overshadowed by her role as observer/researcher – a role she describes as voyeuristic in 'its will to truth' and in its dedication to 'imposing a reading on the interaction' (Walkerdine 1990: 172). The strategy Walkerdine adopted to overcome this methodological problem was to offset the observation of this interview with reflection on contemporary academic debates about voyeurism and reflections on her own childhood experiences. The researcher has no option but to 'impose a reading'. This is an integral aspect of the way social science research is organised – part of the structure of research. However, in this case the researcher's self-reflexivity and family background are drawn on to enrich the analysis by providing diverse positions from which the reader is able to evaluate the research observation.

A similar dilemma is documented in Edgar's more recent *Guide to Imagework* (Edgar 2004: 63–70). Edgar sought to 'observe' the imagework that is an integral but often invisible aspect of everyday life and identity formation, and to translate it into a form that could be analysed. He began by immersing himself in a situation devoted to imagework.

> We are immersed in imagery. We have images of ourselves and images that we portray to the world. We rehearse future action and decision by imagining how things would be if we did this or that. We reflect on and evaluate the past through weighing up and sifting through our memories, just as with a set of old photographs . . . experiential research methods, such as imagework, can elicit and evoke implicit knowledge and self-identities of respondents in a way that other research methods cannot. (Edgar 2004: 1–2)

Edgar co-facilitated and participated in a dreamwork group that had met for over five years. On the basis of his long-term immersion in the group, he adopted a dual role – as embedded researcher working on his own academic project, and as participant in the group experiences of dreamwork. Edgar made no secret of his dual leadership/researcher versus participant roles, but for at least one group member, 'There was, for whatever reason, considerable animosity towards me as a researcher' (2004: 66). For this group member, the recording device seems to have represented an embodiment of Edgar-the-researcher as opposed to Edgar-the-group member.

This example draws our attention to an as-yet-unmentioned aspect of embedded and immersed research. Where most embedded ethnography still focuses on identifiable groups – like an indigenous community, a class formation or subculture, or a club or organisation – Edgar's dreamwork research was not about the group, but about the process of dream interpretation that developed within the group. The immersion of a researcher therefore has the capacity to shift the research focus from the group and onto an activity, behaviour, or experience that is shared by group members – and possibly, though not necessarily, by people outside the group.

EMBEDDED VERSUS IMMERSED RESEARCH

The point of collaborative strategies such as those described above is to assist the transformation of interactions, experiences and thoughts into observable forms. They are also intended to increase the quality of participation by the research subjects, to motivate cooperation with the research task, and to minimise differences of culture and status that characterise research in general and research that employs observation in particular. They can be summarised as *embedded* research practices in that the researcher is in some way aligned with the research subjects, while not actually belonging to the group. However, the very existence of *embedded* research also suggests the possibility of even closer alignment between the researcher and the researched group: the possibility of the group as author of its own research and of group members as preferred researchers. I will refer to this type of research as *immersed* research. The *immersed* researcher is (1) often a member of the group, (2) authorised (either tacitly or explicitly) by the group to undertake the research, and (3) pursues a research task that serves interests the group has identified as important.

The knowledge immersed research produces serves a dual purpose: it represents the group to itself and it allows the group to position itself, to pursue action outside the group to achieve group goals. In *fan research* a group member claims the specialist task of researcher for the group, while in *activist research* the group controls the *research* which is defined by the group's needs and history rather than by the interests of the academic community.

IMMERSED RESEARCH — THE CASE OF FANDOMS

The distinction between researching the group and researching some aspects of group process can be seen in fan research, where a fan claims the role of academic researcher for either fandom in general (Jenkins 1993; Hills 2002) or for a particular fan community (Baym 2003). Fan-academics are often academics who decide to base their research on a phenomenon or community of which they have first-hand knowledge. They claim the privilege of researching and writing about their fannish passions and interests. Henry Jenkins, a self-confessed fan-academic, has identified this occupation as a fan specialisation, alongside other occupational specialisations in fandom such as fan editor, writer, composer, artist, convention organiser, activist – the list goes on. The size, diversity and global reach of a contemporary fandom promotes such specialisation. Furthermore, drawing on the work of Lévy (1997), Jenkins insists that fandom is exemplary of how social networking can promote and enhance the collective intelligence that will become the *modus operandi* of the digital age (Jenkins 2003). However, fan-academics are accepted by fandom primarily as apologists for fans. Their writing normalises fan interests and activities and informs a larger audience about the nature of fan involvements with fan texts. They are part of the process by which fans, who often consider themselves to be misrepresented by mainstream media and by demeaning stereotyping, consider their reputations to be justified, if not redeemed.

Fans, by definition, have a primary attachment to a particular text and its characters (for example, *Star Trek*; *Buffy*; *Zena*) or to a celebrity (Nicole Ritchie; Beyonce; Elvis) that can compromise the fan-researcher's capacity for critical analysis, and even for defining the research problem. This limitation is most evident in the love-hate relationships that characterise the interaction between fans, media industry employees, and the industry itself. This relationship is expressed as competition over ownership – ownership based on love and service versus ownership based on copyright, control and surveillance – or as Jenkins describes it, over 'the informational economy' of a show (2006: 57). Jenkins describes how, in the case of the show *Survivor*, fans invented a spoiling game designed to reveal the show's location. The show's producers 'wanted to direct traffic from the television show to the Web and other points of entry into the franchise', while the fans 'were looking for ways to prolong their pleasurable engagement with a favourite programme' (2006: 57). The game was played out in deadly earnest when the show's producers joined in the game and began to manipulate the group. The result, however, was that the fans lost interest in the show and the programme was discontinued. This example demonstrates the co-dependence of fans and industry – a co-dependency that draws attention to the exploitative nature of television's systems of production–consumption and the role fans play in sustaining it. This co-dependency compromises the fan-academic in that too severe criticism of the industry that produces the fan texts is neither welcomed nor acceptable to the fan communities. Solidarity with fandom is essential to success for the fan-academic. So even immersed research presents the researcher with drawbacks that need to be documented and integrated into the fieldwork analysis.

IMMERSED RESEARCH – THE CASE OF MEDIA ACTIVISM

The term media activism refers to the use of communications media to bring about social and cultural changes desired by a community or group. Here the researcher is totally identified with the group and it is at this point that the limits of 'observation-based' research are reached. Media activism is directed at establishing and/or operating community radio or television stations, creating websites, community information services, news or podcasting services, or making documentaries and films that express the world-view and values of a particular community. Documentation and analysis takes second place to the establishment and operation of services and the production of creative works. The 'research' itself is immersed in the relations of production and its processes, and is revealed in products – the films, documentaries, web-based archives and stories – that in turn provide evidence of the success or failure of the community activity. Yet here the process of exchange and communication between the researcher and the research subjects, and by extrapolation between the research subjects and those to whom and for whom the researcher writes, has been displaced by a social action or community building agenda. The need for observation and observational strategies ceases to exist.

CONCLUSION

Observation in research is dependent on strategies and tactics that transform interactions, words and gestures, thoughts, ideas and daydreams into material forms that can be recorded and are therefore available for analysis. Observation is not a passive process, but should include active exchange between researcher and research subjects. Today the researcher's reliance on note-taking is being replaced by audio and video recording, and by digital photography. Digital recording technologies have expanded the types of activities research subjects may use to represent themselves for the research. By offering the research participant opportunities for self-documentation, the researcher is released from some of the personal distress that is inherent in observational research: distress associated with acceptance and rejection, belonging and being an outsider; certainty and self-doubt. Yet the communicative power of the observation is eventually compromised if the research ceases to take the form of communicative exchange between two different groups of participants: the researcher and her culture and the research subjects and their culture.

Participant observation matters because it occurs in a terrain characterised by insecurity, uncertainty, self-doubt and mistrust by both parties. What is observed, what it means and how it might best be translated is an ongoing challenge for the researcher. How they are being observed, what it means for them and how the position of the researcher can best be influenced also represents an ongoing challenge for the research subjects. These characteristics force the researcher to continually experiment with innovative ways of establishing and maintaining communicative exchange with the research subjects. It is through such exchange that the experiential worlds of research subjects can be expressed and recorded for analysis. Observation matters because it is vital for the production of new knowledge of the many worlds of experience.

SUMMARY: KEY POINTS

- This chapter argues that observation matters in cultural research because (1) it situates the researcher in direct interaction with research subjects, and (2) it provides opportunities for discussion and negotiation between them.
- Observation-based research borrows strategies and tactics from ethnography that reflect a desire by researchers to minimise the imbalance in authorial power created by the research situation. They have included various forms of collaboration, embedding and immersion.
- Such strategies are helpful to the extent that they enable research participants to more easily express their ideas and opinions in forms that can be recorded and analysed. However, they also pose the problem of the point where the negotiation between the social formations represented by the researcher (and whose ideas the researcher seeks to inform through the research) and the social formations represented by the research participants is erased by the transfer of authorial power.
- Observation-based research produces new knowledge through the exchange of ideas and debate between researchers and research participants. It requires recognition and management of differences in power and authority to generate new knowledge.

FURTHER READING

In recent years researchers have preferred to use the term 'ethnographic' to describe participant observation. To gain a sense of the importance of participant observation in social and cultural research it is useful to read older work, such as Manis and Meltzer (1972). The Canadian scholar Erving Goffman was one of the leading exponents of observational methods in cultural research. Three of his books are particularly recommended: *The Presentation of Self in Everyday Life* (1959); *Relations in Public: Micro-Studies of the Public Order* (1971); and *Interaction Ritual: Essays on Face-to-Face Behavior* (1976). In the 1980s a critical reappraisal of ethnography was spearheaded by James Clifford and George Marcus in *Writing Culture* (1986). In addition, George Marcus and Michael Fischer (1986) are extremely helpful in challenging the preconceptions that inform the researcher embarking on observation-based research. More recent description of the methods used in such research can be found in Angrosino (2002) and in Bernard (2002).

Texts and Pictures

CHAPTER 7

Analysing Visual Experience

Sarah Pink

PROLOGUE: A STORY FROM THE FIELD

I arrived at David and Anne's house one morning in autumn 2005, to interview them about the community garden project David was involved in. I was ready with the tool kit of a contemporary visual researcher: digital video and stills cameras, audio recorder, and pen and notebook. My research involved photography, audio-recording our interview and collaboratively exploring the garden site with David on video. It also led me to attend closely to the visual elements of the project itself. When I interview people about their experiences, projects and passions, they usually pull out visual images with which to tell me stories about their lives. So I was not surprised when David began to narrate the story of the community garden project in spoken words, interjected at times with Anne's comments, written word-processed documents, drawings and plans through which the local residents had visualised their ideas about the garden, and printed photographs. I was gripped by the story and this was partly because it gained my attention through multiple media. The combination of spoken words and visual images provided me with multiple ways to start imagining how the garden already was, how they planned to create it and what it would feel like when it was finished. This was not simply visual imagining since our discussions of the garden included plans for a 'sensory' area with sweet smelling plants and for a brickweave path – a textured route through the garden that, although it could be represented visually in photographs, would also be a haptic experience, felt underfoot by those who walked in or through the garden.

Before I photographed David and Anne, we discussed the composition of the image. Since the choice of a brickweave path for the garden was a key issue at that moment in time, we agreed they should be holding the photographs that illustrated the type of path they hoped for (Figure 7.1). David's communication

Figure 7.1 David and Anne Gibson at home. Photo © Sarah Pink 2005.

with me about the community garden project in this interview provides an excellent example of how people often communicate to others about their experiences as part of everyday life. The images that David showed me had not been made for my benefit, but were part of the process of developing and planning the project. By photographing David and Anne with the photograph, I hoped to make this point; what they told me was not simply expressed in words but was a multimedia narrative that included visual images.

After our interview David took me out into the garden site. As it was pouring with rain, Anne lent me a jacket and an umbrella which I held over my video camera as I filmed David showing me around the garden. By the time I write I have repeated this process three times, at different points in the project's progress. The first time I walked around the garden with David, the development had not begun, but the residents' ideas had already been mapped out in their minds and on paper. I could gain ideas about how David intended the garden to be experienced once it was completed. As we stood in the long wet grass, he explained that it was difficult for people to walk through and that with a new path mothers with pushchairs would find it much more accessible. The garden site would not only look different, but it would feel different under foot. Although the addition of a path might seem quite mundane to some, it is actually very significant. For the anthropological theorist Arjun Appadurai, 'the organisation of paths and passages, the remaking of fields and gardens' forms a vital element of the production of a sense of 'locality' (1996: 11), and the architecture and design theorists Malnar and Vodvarka have argued that greater attention needs to be paid to 'the generative role of the path, and its sensory character' (2004: 119). Walking through and video-recording David's spoken and embodied commentaries on the garden site allowed me to understand the nature of the garden site without a path and to imagine how it might be once it was installed. The video tape did not of course record the feel of the garden underfoot or the dampness of the rainy atmosphere. However, it did enable me to represent these audio-visually in a document that I would later use to invoke these experiences for myself as a research text, and for others combined with written or spoken words in presentations or in a future multimedia text. Video (and film) has the potential to evoke empathetic responses in its audiences. By showing on video, rather than just describing verbally, the experience of walking through the garden, soaked by the pouring rain and the wet grass underfoot, I intend the audiences of my work to gain a sense of how it felt to be there (see Pink, forthcoming).[1]

I give David and Anne copies of the videos and photographs I take of their garden, and copies of the texts in which I write about and visualise them (including this one). I also use visual images to communicate with the people who participate in my research. By showing people my written notes, I would be asking them to battle with my handwriting and incomprehensible sentences scribbled quickly in note form, whereas by sharing these images I communicate with them about how I am representing them. As is usual in most contemporary ethnographic research contexts, I, the visual ethnographer, am neither the only image producer nor the only person using images to communicate. When David showed me the garden, he also photographed me videoing him; it was, as he put it, 'tit for tat' (see Pink 2007).[2] He had already photographed me sitting at the table in their home and I, like the other project participants, was featured in his PowerPoint file about the project.

This short account of my research experiences invites an important question: why, if the visual is so central to everyday narratives and provides us with such great opportunities to evoke something of the sensory embodied experiences of research, does so much ethnographic research rely on aural narratives, or written accounts of people's multisensory experiences? Given that visual images, texts and metaphors play such a central role in our everyday practices and ways of communicating with each other, should researchers not attend to them more closely? In this chapter I explore possible applications of visual ethnographic methods for cultural analysis. I do not cover all the visual methods that could possibly be used (the nearest I get to doing that is in my book *Doing Visual Ethnography* (Pink 2007)). Rather, drawing from key examples, I offer a taste of the potential of collaborative visual methods in cultural

Figure 7.2 Up the garden path. That winter David photographed the whole process of laying the path, and when it was completed, Monica, who was supporting the project, emailed me his photograph of it. Later in the year David posted me a hard-printed copy of a set of photos of the path being built. David has regularly photographed the garden as it has progressed and kept a PowerPoint digital diary of the project. Photo © David Gibson 2006.

analysis. Where appropriate, I direct readers to my two main works in this area: *The Future of Visual Anthropology* (Pink 2006) and *Doing Visual Ethnography* (2007).

INTRODUCTION: VISUAL METHODS IN CULTURAL STUDIES

Although some disciplines and fields have been more successful in ignoring it, cultural studies has always implied the analysis of the visual. Indeed, since cultural studies is concerned with 'how culture is produced, enacted and consumed' (Lister and Wells 2000: 61), it is inevitable that scholars working in this area would engage with the visual. As Martin Lister and Liz Wells argue, 'it is seldom, if ever, possible to separate the cultures of everyday life from practices of representation, visual or otherwise' (2000: 61). Most scholars working in the field of visual studies agree that any analysis of culture would benefit from attention to the visual experience, knowledge and practice that in part constitutes what culture is (Pink 2007).

Figure 7.3 David at work in the garden. The following summer I continued my video walks with David (and sometimes Anne too) through the garden. I walked along the new pathway, photographed David at work in the garden and met other local residents as they also passed through the garden or came over to chat. Photo © Sarah Pink 2006.

However, situating a visual methodology within cultural studies is a complex task. Cultural studies itself is an academic field that is defined by its theoretical and substantive area of interest – the power relations and institutions of modernity (and if one wants to use the rather contested term, also postmodernity), colonialism and postcolonialism rather than by its methodology. Whereas, for example, social anthropology was historically associated with the long-term fieldwork method developed since the mid-twentieth century (although it is less so now) and sociology with interviewing and survey methods, cultural studies methodologies have tended to be eclectic (McGuigan 1997), drawing from different disciplines as and when appropriate. Thus, one way to approach the question of visual methodologies in cultural studies is by investigating how visual approaches have developed in the disciplines that have generated the methodologies cultural studies draws on. Indeed, with the recent expansion of texts on visual research and analysis across the social sciences and humanities, and the interest in ethnography in cultural studies, a wide range of methods and approaches to the visual that are relevant to scholars working in cultural studies is now documented. Some such texts focus on the analysis of visual images (for example, Rose 2001), some advocate a broader 'visual' approach to understanding culture (for example, MacDougall 1998; Grimshaw 2001), and others advocate the visual as a method of research (for example, Banks 2001; Pink 2007; Grimshaw and Ravetz 2004; Pole 2004; Knowles and Sweetman 2004; Halford and Knowles 2005) or representation (for example, Pink 2006, 2007; Grimshaw and Ravetz 2004; MacDougall 2005).

Aside from these developments, Lister and Wells have proposed a 'visual cultural studies'. Visual cultural studies is closely identified with its parent field of cultural studies in its approach to images through 'the circuit of culture' model (see du Gay et al. 1997) and attends to 'the many moments within the cycle of production, circulation and consumption of the image through which meanings accumulate, slip and shift' (Lister and Wells 2000: 90). Indeed, the 'methodological eclecticism' that characterises cultural studies means a visual cultural studies is similarly non-prescriptive about method. It encourages scholars to draw from a variety of methods and to 'bring into play their own experience' (2000: 90). Lister and Wells's own characterisation of visual cultural studies, as drawing on diverse methodological traditions, offers a starting point for the approach I take here. Among the key disciplines that cultural studies draws from are social anthropology and sociology. In this chapter I shall take the visual subdisciplines of visual anthropology and visual sociology as key sources for the theoretical and methodological approaches and practices of a visual cultural studies. There are two reasons for this choice. First, within the visual methodology literature by far the most enduring and prevalent influence is that of visual anthropology. Second, correspondingly in the interdisciplinary area of 'visual culture', one of the strongest influences has come from social anthropology. The academic field that has been called 'visual cultures' grew up in the later twentieth century as part of the British cultural studies tradition, drawing largely from art history and media studies approaches (for example, Evans and Hall 1999). However, Jessica Evans notes that in 1996 the editors of the cultural theory journal *October* carried out a questionnaire regarding the concept of 'visual culture' and came to the conclusion that 'the interdisciplinary project of visual culture is no longer organised on the model of history (as were the disciplines and fields of art history, architectural history, film theory etc.) but on the model of anthropology' (October 1996: 25, quoted in Evans and Hall 1999: 6). This suggests that a visual approach to cultural studies might draw further from anthropological understandings. The original formulation of visual anthropology set out by Jay Ruby and Richard Chalfen (1974) outlines three key concerns: (1) the study of visual elements of culture, (2) the use of visual media and images to produce ethnographic knowledge, and (3) the production of visual representations of research. This three-stranded approach has the advantage that it not only represents the visual cultural studies interest in analysing images (outlined by Lister and Wells 2000) but also links with the enthusiasm for ethnography that has developed in cultural studies and implies a methodology for visual ethnographic research and representation. To understand any one of these three strands of visual anthropology practice, one needs to situate the visual in three ways. First both researcher and research subjects' uses of visual methods and visual media are always embedded in social relationships and cultural practices and meanings. In any research situation these need to be reflexively unpacked. Second, no experience is ever purely visual, and to comprehend 'visual culture' we need to understand both what vision itself is, and what its relationship is to other sensory modalities. Third, in academic analysis and representation we are never really dealing with 'visual' subdisciplines. The idea of a visual anthropology, visual sociology or visual cultural studies is itself misleading. Although the labels are likely to persist, we are usually actually dealing with audio-visual (for example, film) representations or texts that combine visual and written texts. Thus, the relationship between images and words is always central to our practice as academics.

In this chapter, following Michael Pickering's point in the introduction that textual analysis has been overplayed in cultural studies texts at the expense of a broader use of ethnographic approaches, I attempt to redress this balance. Following my own existing work on visual anthropology and visual ethnography (for example, Pink 2006, 2007), I outline a visual approach to cultural studies research. This is embedded in a sensory understanding of culture and society, and in an intersubjective and participatory approach to the production of knowledge.

HISTORICAL CONTEXT: UNDERSTANDING WHERE VISUAL METHODS COME FROM

Detailed versions of the histories of visual anthropology (for example, Ruby 2000; Grimshaw 2001; Pink 2006) and visual sociology (for example, Chaplin 1994, and see also Pink 2007) have been developed elsewhere. Here I provide a brief summary of the aspects of this history that are most relevant to a visual ethnographic approach for cultural studies.

Early uses of photography and film in anthropological research were developed in the late nineteenth and early twentieth centuries by Alfred Cort Haddon in the Torres Straits, Franz Boas in the United States and Baldwin Spencer and Frank Gillen in Australia. Embedded in the scientific approaches of their historical period, they treated vision as an observational tool and the camera as an objective recording device. In the twentieth century uses of the camera in anthropological research included the photographic work of Bronislaw Malinowski and the later work of Boas. However, their uses of photography in the 1930s were incompatible with the scientific approaches to the study of culture and society that were dominant at the time (Grimshaw 2001: 67) since photographic or filmic recordings were considered too subjective and limited.

Later in the twentieth century Margaret Mead used photography and film within the strictures of this scientific paradigm, insisting that visual methods could support the objectives of observational social scientists in their search for objective data that could be subjected to systematic analysis (for example, Mead 1975). However during the latter part of the twentieth century ethnographic documentary film-making became the dominant method in visual anthropology. Two main approaches can be identified: the scientific approach that sought to represent 'whole cultures' and whole scenes, used little or no editing and aimed to produce an objective record of human activity (for example, Heider 1976); and the more cinematic approach that made greater use of narrative devices, and recognised the inevitable subjectivity of the film-making process and of filmic representations. The latter has most influenced the visual research methods I discuss below.

Since the 1980s approaches to social research have increasingly stressed reflexivity and subjectivity, thus becoming more compatible with the collaborative and reflexive approaches already developed in the work of participatory ethnographic filmmakers. In visual anthropology, participatory and collaborative methods are central to the process of knowledge production during both the research and film-making processes. The work of the anthropological filmmakers Jean Rouch and David and Judith MacDougall have been important influences. Rouch's work is particularly interesting in relation to the focus on postcolonial identities and power relations in cultural studies. In his films Rouch was often concerned with shifting the locus of power by giving voice to those who had been disempowered by colonialism, and with the implications of colonial rule. *Les Maitres Fous* (1954) represents a ceremony 'in which the oppressed become, for a day, the possessed and the powerful'. The film makes a powerful statement that uses 'unsettling juxtapositions to jolt the audience' (Stoller 1997: 126) and perhaps change how they perceive the realities represented in the film. Rouch's work was not simply intended to communicate to Western audiences about the experiences of people living in developing countries. His idea of a 'shared anthropology' considered the 'first audience' for his films to be the film subjects themselves (2003 [1973]: 43). Their comments on the viewing permitted Rouch to receive a form of 'feedback' which 'enhances participation and allows the ethnographer-filmmaker to mediate openly and self-critically on his or her role' (Feld 2003: 18–19). Rouch saw this 'feedback' as fundamental to a 'shared anthropology' (2003 [1973]: 44), creating, as Paul Stoller has suggested, films in which 'no one voice dominates' (1992: 195). Often made in contexts that were wrought with the inequalities between anthropological film-makers from colonial powers and the subjects of their films who were usually from the colonised, Rouch's approach limited the extent to which these power relationships could permeate his research and film-making process.

Around the same time the ethnographic film-maker David MacDougall proposed a 'participatory cinema' involving 'collaboration and joint authorship between filmmakers and their subjects' (1998 [1973]: 136), later redefining this as '*intertextual* cinema' (original italics) which would have 'a principle of multiple authorship' (1998 [1992]: 138). He suggested film-makers might put 'themselves at the disposal of the subjects and, with them, inventing the film' (1998 [1973]: 136) and that multiple authorship might allow ethnographic film to 'address conflicting views of reality in a world in which observers and observed are less clearly separated and in which reciprocal observation and exchange increasingly matter' (1998 [1992]: 138). Such approaches may not only even out aspects of the power relations implied by economic inequalities between researchers and research subjects, but also shift the emphasis from the idea of doing research about/on a group of people or person, to that of doing research with/for them. These notions of 'shared' and 'intertextual' visual anthropology, developed originally within ethnographic documentary film-making practice, continue to inform contemporary visual ethnography methods. For instance, in the research experience I described in the prologue we can start to see how collaborations are developed in practice.

The last decade has seen an impressive expansion in the literature on visual images and methodologies across the academic disciplines, often borrowing from visual anthropology (this is detailed in Pink 2006: ch. 2), but with limited discussion of visual methods in cultural studies. Above I noted Lister and Wells's (2000) discussion of a visual cultural studies approach to analysing images. Their focus is on the situated analysis of visual images, in terms of 'the many moments within the cycle of production, circulation and consumption of the image through which meanings accumulate, slip and shift' (2000: 90). Drawing from a cultural studies methodology, they analyse the material and social histories of images in culture and society. Their focus recognises the institutional and contextual meanings embedded in images, the conventions that inform their production, and the role of situated human agents as viewers and interpreters of images.

In this chapter I build on and depart from this existing work to offer a visually orientated methodological framework that applies to the whole research process. If cultural studies scholars are to understand culture through attention to the visual and to visual aspects of human experience, knowledge and meaning, this requires rethinking existing understandings of academic research, analysis and communication in the field. A decade ago the anthropological film-maker and theorist David MacDougall was arguing for 'a shift from word-and-sentence-based anthropological thought to image-and-sequence-based anthropological thought' (1997: 292). I suggest that likewise, for cultural studies scholars, to engage with the visual beyond the existing treatments of image-as-text, requires more than simply the use of a camera during research.

Rather it implies rejecting the idea that the visual can be objectified through words, and re-thinking how the sorts of visual and sensory embodied experience and knowledge that is the essence of ethnographic research can be represented and communicated by combining images and words. A collaborative (audio-)visual approach to researching, analysing and representing culture offers cultural studies scholars a privileged way of understanding and communicating about other people's knowledge and experience.

WHAT IS EXPERIENCE? HOW MIGHT WE ACCESS OTHER PEOPLE'S SENSORY EMBODIED EXPERIENCE?

What is experience? The term is very popular in academia, partly in connection with the current enthusiasm for phenomenological approaches across the social sciences (for example, see Katz and Csordas 2003). There have been several attempts to define it over the years, from the perspective of social anthropology (for example, Turner and Bruner 1986) and cultural studies (Pickering 1997; and see Chapter one of this book). However, academics often refer to experience with no explanation of what they actually mean by it, and even those who have in the past debated the question have found it hard to agree on a definition. In fact two of the contributors to Victor Turner's co-edited book *Anthropology of Experience* (1986) note how the contributors to the volume could not agree on what either the theory or subject matter of experience should be (Bruner 1986: 13; Geertz 1986: 375). As Jason Throop (2003) summarises, the main disagreement was between Victor Turner and Clifford Geertz. Turner, who distinguished between 'mere "experience" and "an experience"', argued that 'mere experience is simply the passive endurance and acceptance of events' whereas 'an experience' is circumscribed with a beginning and end (Turner 1986: 35) and thus a defined event. Geertz, in contrast, and in line with the argument that culture might be read as text, proposed that 'mere experience' does not exist, since experience is always interpreted as 'an experience' (Geertz 1986: 380). Throop suggests that since both these understandings have some merit, experience should not be seen as being *either* found in the relationship between the incoherent flow of 'mere experience' and its reflective definition *or* always being interpreted. Rather, a flexible model that incorporates both, as well as several in-between, understandings is more appropriate. Such a model thus recognises that experience takes many different forms which may include 'the indeterminate, the fluid, the incoherent, the internal, the disjunctive, the fragmentary, the coherent, the intersubjective, the determinate, the rigid, the external, the cohesive, the conjunctive *and* the unitary' (Throop 2003: 227). By arguing for a phenomenological model of experience that integrates the 'immediacy of temporal flux and the mediacy of reflective assessment' (2003: 233), Throop sensibly suggests that experience need not be defined as either/or undetermined narrative or interpreted event, and that there may be variation in how and when experience is reflected on (see Pink 2006: ch. 3 for a discussion of this).[3]

An approach to ethnographic research that places human experience at the centre of the analysis also implies the importance of attending to the sensory and embodied nature of experience. Scholars across the social sciences and humanities are currently acknowledging the benefits of accounting for the senses (see Howes 2005) in a research agenda that emphasises the inevitable interconnectedness of the senses and the multi-sensoriality of human experience. As I noted in the prologue to this chapter, the experiences of the community garden project I was seeking to understand could not be understood only visually and verbally; rather, the physical sense of 'being there', feeling the wet grass underfoot, the sound of the rain on the umbrella, and the firm texture of the new path underfoot were essential to this experience. This body of research has demonstrated the impossibility of separating the visual from the other senses in human perception, knowledge, understanding and practice (see Howes 2005). It has brought into doubt the viability of a *visual* anthropology (see Pink 2006: ch. 7), visual sociology or cultural studies and of purely visual research methods (Pink 2007). Some sensory approaches include the analysis of literary texts as their subject matter. For example, working in design and architecture studies respectively, Malnar and Vodvarka (2004) and Pallasmaa (2004) draw from analyses of literary texts to highlight how we experience our environments not only visually, but also through touch, sound, smell and taste, and they argue for a sensory focus in the design of buildings and cities. However, recent ethnographic studies have provided the most convincing demonstrations of how we might understand cultural experience, knowledge and practice through a focus on the senses (for example, Guerts 2002; Desjarlais 2003; Pink 2004).

An emphasis on sensory experience presents a methodological question: given the complexity of experience itself, how can we ever hope to understand other people's experiences? We cannot get inside their heads or under their skins to think or sense as they do. If we are interested in how they see, we cannot be their eyes. We cannot follow the processes from undefined physical or emotional sensation to reflective assessment that they may be (sometimes unconsciously) involved in. The closest that we can get to feeling as they feel is through our own limited capacity to empathise with their embodied experiences. Given these inevitable limitations, one of my tasks in the remainder of this chapter is to outline some of the methods that can take us closer to other people's sensory embodied experiences. Throop has already proposed that the different types of experience he identifies might be researched using different methods, suggesting that some methods, like interviewing and questionnaires, are more likely to reveal 'those explicit reflective processes that *tend* to give coherence and definite form to experience'. Others, like 'video-taping and/or systematic observation of everyday interaction', can 'capture' the '*often* pre-reflective, realtime unfolding of social action' (Throop 2003: 235). While I broadly agree with this distinction, here drawing from the 'shared' and participatory visual anthropology research tradition outlined above, I take a slightly different approach, dividing the methods I shall discuss into two categories. First, those that encourage people to reflect on and thus define their experiences to us as researchers. Second, methods that provide researchers with opportunities to experience similarly and use their own sensory embodied knowledge as a basis from which to make assumptions about that of others. I suggest that (audio-)visual methods of research and representation can play a key role in the production of these types of ethnographic knowledge.

CASE STUDY 1: (AUDIO-)VISUAL MEDIA IN A COLLABORATIVE ETHNOGRAPHIC STUDY OF SLOW LIVING

Researching (in) Visual cultures

Since summer 2005 I have been doing ethnographic fieldwork as part of a research project about the Slow City (Cittàslow) movement in the United Kingdom. The research involves both analysis of the various texts (online, multimedia, printed and so on) produced by the movement, and an in-depth ethnographic study of the everyday and ritual practices through which Slow Cities themselves are constituted 'on the ground'. The community garden project discussed in the prologue is a Cittàslow project being developed in Aylsham in Norfolk (United Kingdom). My research explores the sensory, social and material aspects of the garden's development. This entails both analysing the images produced and used by research participants themselves and my own production of video and photographic images of them. This propensity of images in the research context itself allows me to follow Lister and Wells's (2000) interest in the production, circulation and consumption of local images. For example, some of the images are professionally drawn-up plans. They have been sent to the council with a planning permission application for the garden development and are archived in David's records of the project. They serve as both official and memory documents. Other images, such as David's brickweave photographs (Figure 7.1), have been used in various contexts – including showing other project participants and funders the proposed style of path, and communicating this to me. Again, they become memory documents as they are archived. These images are embedded in and communicate as part of a complex network of personal, social, economic and bureaucratic contexts according to which their meanings can shift. When they are part of an interview, they perform simultaneous functions. First, with spoken commentary, they form part of the narratives through which people reflect on and define their experiences. For example, when in 2005 David showed me the plans he had been drawing for the garden, he explained that they were part of a process of visualisation:

DAVID . . . the committee was formed obviously from the people that was doing the regular attendances and we were all asked to put forward our ideas at various meetings and that was my plan of the field and what I would like to see and there was one or two others and at the end of the day I think there's been a compromise from several ideas to what we've actually got at the moment.

SARAH Right.

DAVID Like a pathway to start with from the Close to the Wood end at the end of the Way and obviously at a later date once that project has been completed putting in other things. Now this plan that I've got here hasn't necessarily been approved because there's other ideas now.

SARAH Right.

DAVID I think we've got that in this letter.

SARAH So other people have been drawing plans as well.

DAVID Oh yes.

Second, images become evocative of the different contexts for which they hold intersecting meanings. Indeed, as the sites of intersecting (perhaps conflicting) meanings, visual images can provide researchers with important starting points for understanding the complexities of the social and cultural contexts they are working in.

Video as a Research Method

The second method I introduced above was that of using video collaboratively to explore and understand other people's understandings of the environments in and objects with which they live. Existing writings have discussed using the camera to learn how to understand the visual sense by focusing on how other people see (for example, Pink 2007; Grasseni 2004). These works also stress the role of the camera as a catalyst. For example, Cristina Grasseni describes how by using video in her research about cattle breeding in Italy, she learned about the 'skilled vision' of cattle breeders. When she first started to tour farms with a breed inspector, she 'did not know what to point the camera at, because I could not *see* what was going on' (2004: 20), but under the guidance of the inspector and by showing her research participants the videos she recorded, she gradually learned how they saw cattle. It was not simply a matter of seeing, but also a method in which video was important. Rather than simply looking at the cow as she was instructed to, Grasseni video-recorded this vision; as she puts it 'the camera functioned as the catalyst of my attention, tuning my eyes to the visual angles and the ways of framing the cow through the inspector's gaze' (2004: 21). If we are to understand how other people see their worlds and how they evaluate and interpret what they see, video and photography can play an important role in the collaborative processes through which we learn about their viewpoints. It provides us with a visual reference point when doing research, allows us to produce a visual record to share with the participants in our research, and provides a visual text in which to focus the collaborative discussions with research participants through which knowledge is produced.

Above I described the 'walking with' video recordings I made with David and Anne. Although the visual was important in this work, I was not only interested in exploring how they saw the garden site, but in the garden site as a multisensory context. Using video, I was interesting in both recording the experience of being in and walking through the garden, and exploring how, as well as vision, other sensory modalities were part of this. For example, when David prodded the soil with his foot and discussed its texture, my visual focus on this ensured that I remembered his tactile form of expression. These enabled me to produce a particular type of research knowledge (see Pink forthcoming for an in–depth analysis of this method). This involved what Throop (2003) has referred to as capturing the pre-reflective flow of action as it occurs, in that the video recordings represent an actual reality of which I (with my camera) was a part. However my emphasis here is on the role of such video-recording as a process through which I could experience something similar to what my research participants were both describing and experiencing themselves. On video I recorded aspects of my own experience of this and simultaneously how they used their whole bodies to represent the experience of the garden site, not just words and visual pointers. These types of performance when recorded on video perform two roles as research materials. First, they are records of pre-reflective experience as it flowed in our research encounter. Second, when engaging in these sorts of research task participants tend to reflect on their experiences, thus leading them to think about, define and articulate their experiences anew (see also Pink 2006).[4]

CASE STUDY 2: ANALYSING THE WWW.TELEMADRE.COM WEBSITE AS PREPARATION FOR EXPERIENTIAL RESEARCH

Much ethnographic research nowadays commences with web searches and email contacts. The Slow City research discussed above was initiated when I searched the web to find out more about the Slow Food movement and discovered that Aylsham in Norfolk had become a member of the Slow City movement. The project I now discuss implies a two-stage research process. The first stage, which involves the analysis of a key text – a website – is complete and reported on, and could in itself be considered a finished piece of work. However, this research begs the undertaking of a second stage. Although the textual analysis implies a good many things of interest and significance, it also demonstrates what is *not* known and implies that until ethnographic research follows up the questions it raises, the analysis will be incomplete.

In 2005 I began a project with Ana Martinez Perez, a Spanish anthropologist based in Madrid. We were both interested in how Spanish gender roles, lifestyles and food knowledge were changing, and the project was inspired when we visited the website telemadre.com. We realised that this new media form could be analysed in relation to the existing research knowledge we had from our respective ethnographic research projects, and that it begged fascinating questions about the changes occurring in Spanish culture. Often contemporary Spanish cultural studies focuses on film, art and fashion, seemingly neglecting the question of how everyday sensory practices and new uses of culinary knowledge are involved in processes of social and cultural change. We wanted to respond to this by using an analytical approach that both drew from existing ethnographic knowledge and recognised that visual texts are inevitably embedded in, and cannot be understood in isolation from, complex and changing social and cultural contexts. Our analysis of the www.telemadre.com website (published in full in Pink and Martinez Perez 2006) echoed Lister and Wells's (2000) framework in that we explored the following areas.

Why was it developed and by whom: www.telemadre.com was developed by a group of young advertising professionals who run an agency called mmmm . . . (see www.mmmm.tv, accessed 12 October 2006). Ana Martinez made contact with the agency and, on the basis of an interview she carried out, documents they supplied and media reports, we discovered that the site was established when they identified a need amongst busy young professionals for good traditional home-cooked food. The story is that fed up with eating out in restaurants every day, they asked the mother of one of the group's members to regularly cook lunch for them, sending the meals out by taxi. The idea caught on and they set up telemadre.com to enable retired housewives to cook meals and send them, for a fee, to busy young professionals who want to eat well but have no

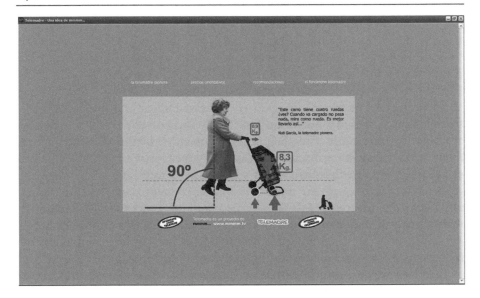

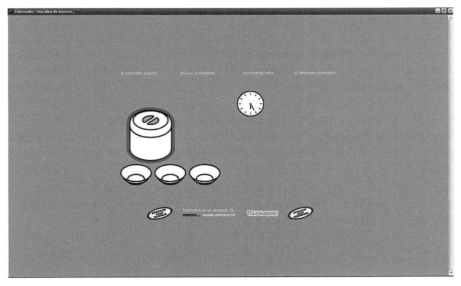

Figure 7.4 Three web captures from the 'recomendaciones' section of the www.telemadre.com website, showing the shopping trolley, Thermos flask and Tupperware.

time to cook and shop. The site is professionally designed and, as I discuss below, as well as providing factual information about this system, it uses a number of visual images that refer to aspects of traditional Spanish culinary culture.

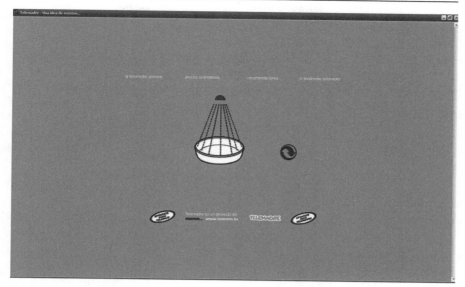

Figure 7.4 *(continued)*

Having established the aims and origins of the site, our next task was: *to iden-tify the wider social and cultural context in which it exists*. We now used our own (for example, Pink 2004; Martinez 2000) and other authors' existing ethno-graphic and statistical research to identity connections between the aims of and practices surrounding the activities represented on the website and the demo-graphic, economic, social and cultural context for these practices. In contem-porary Spain retired housewives can have low incomes, a growing amount of young women are entering the labour market, many young women reject learn-ing the traditional domestic skills and knowledge kept by their mothers, and an increasing number of young people live away from their mothers, meaning they cannot access the domestic services their mothers would provide. The tele-madre.com model seemed to suit this climate well.

Next we *analysed the meanings of the visual content of the text*. To understand how these images become symbolic of and meaningful about particular aspects of Spanish culinary culture required a good understanding of the role of the 'traditional' Spanish housewife and mother. We had both covered these ques-tions in our existing research and we identified three key images: the shopping trolley; Tupperware containers (also discussed in Pink 2007: figure 2.2); and Thermos flasks. All represented as 'recommendations' on the website, each of these images is connected to the everyday practices of traditional Spanish housewives who shop for, cook and store food for their children, and often continue to do this for long after they have left home. These visual representa-tions, in our interpretation, serve to emphasise the link between the role of the retired housewives – the telemadres – and the role of the traditional Spanish mother.

These stages of analysis allowed us to understand both the written narratives and discourses that were promoted by the website, and how the visual images added meaning to and strengthened these narratives. The images also helped to evoke the notions of home, mothering and familiar tastes that the words of the text implied. Thus, we were able to understand both how the content of the text fitted with contemporary shifts and changes in contemporary Spanish culture and society, and suggest how the text actually worked to generate such meanings by using a combination of images and words. Nevertheless, an analysis centred on the text and other existing materials and knowledge is limited. Although it suggests a set of connections between textual discourse, content and representation and 'traditional' cultural practices and social relationships, it does not reveal how this website connects with people's actual every day realities. Therefore, the analysis invites a taking the research a step further through a visual ethnography that would explore the experiential elements of the site: how do people actually use it? And what are the sensory and emotional effects of this – both for the telemadres and the young professionals who pay them to cook for them? The example reveals two points: first, it shows how the analysis of cultural texts invites questions about the cultures in which they are embedded; second, it suggests how preparation for visual ethnographic research might be carried out through textual analysis.

Together both case studies, the Community Garden project and telemadre.com, demonstrate how ethnographic and textual analyses of visual images tend to imply each other. In my study of the community garden project, my interest in finding out about the social relationships and process of the project led me to the production of photographs and video and the analysis of visual images produced by others – maps and photographs. In the telemadre.com study, Ana Martinez and I started with the study of a visual text – a website – which led us to re-examine our existing ethnographic studies of Spanish cultural values and social relationships.

COMMUNICATING VISUAL RESEARCH

Visual research methods offer cultural studies scholars an excellent means of communicating with research subjects and academic audiences about their work. In existing work, visual images have often been used simply to illustrate points already made in written descriptions or arguments; as 'evidence' (numerous examples exist in twentieth-century social anthropology texts). Critical perspectives on this objectifying practice which involved the modern Western researcher visually framing their research subject abound (as discussed in

Pink 2006, 2007: ch. 2). The approach to visually representing other people and their environments taken here again recommends a collaborative approach. Rather than simply using images as illustrations, researchers should seek innovative ways to (audio-)visually provoke responses in their viewers that might lead them to reflexively question their pre-existing assumptions.

Photographic representations

Photographs produced as part of visual ethnographic research might be used to represent knowledge in multiple ways, including in printed texts, interwoven with a written narrative in a photo-essay, in a Powerpoint presentation, or as part of a multimedia hypermedia representation of a research project (see Pink 2007: ch. 4 for a full review). Whatever the context, it is unlikely they will be used in isolation from written words. In this section, by way of example, I discuss two images from my own research.

People to whom I mention my Slow City research often initially assume that the term 'slow' refers to places cut off from the mainstream – a misunderstanding also identified by people involved in promoting Slow Cities. To counter this notion of slowness, I created the image shown in Figure 7.5 which I use in seminar presentations and intend to include in both printed articles and

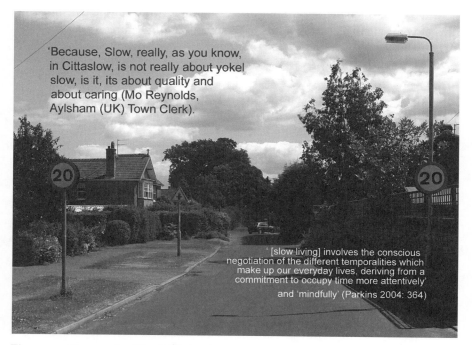

Figure 7.5 Representing Slow Living

digital multimedia publications. In developing this image, I aimed to invite viewers to draw on their existing assumptions about slowness, by showing a quiet residential lane with a 20 mph speed limit. Because 20 mph signs are rarely used in Britain, this implies the town has a slow pace. However, the written text inscribed on the photograph aims to challenge such preconceptions. At the top of the photo I quote from an interview with Mo, a leader in the local Cittàslow process. By stressing that Cittàslow is not about 'yokel slow', her words suggest we should look beyond existing stereotypes of rural Britain to define what is meant by 'Slow City'. At the bottom of the photo I quote a cultural studies perspective: Wendy Parkins discusses how the concept of time is implicated in the Slow Living movement, concluding that this involves not doing things slowly, but making 'a commitment to occupy time more attentively' (Parkins 2004: 364).

Whereas Figure 7.5 was deliberately produced to represent my research and the concept of 'slow', other photographs are produced spontaneously as part of the visual ethnographic research process. For instance, Figure 7.1 was taken on the basis of my discussions with David and Anne during our interview. Above, and in presentations, I have used Figure 7.1 for two purposes: first, to represent the project and the importance of the path; and second, to represent the collaborative ethnographic moment of its production, showing how David and Anne's and my own perspectives were joined in the image, since although I framed it, they shaped its content. Its captioning is not simple labelling, but aims to combine images and words in the creation of meaning.

Video Representations

Digital video is used increasingly as an ethnographic research method. Its ability to represent both the experiences of research participants and the actual research process itself in ways that cannot be expressed in written words is fundamental to this. The best-known use of (audio-)visual media to represent culture is ethnographic graphic documentary film. A number of texts cover the history, production methods and analysis of ethnographic film (for example, Loizos 1993; Barbash and Taylor 1997; MacDougall 1998). Yet one criticism that frequently remains unresolved is that, as stand-alone audio-visual documents, they often fail to sufficiently contextualise their representations culturally or theoretically (discussed in detail in Pink 2006). Ethnographic films can represent aspects of other people's lives, experiences, everyday practices and routines, emotions, spoken narratives, embodied actions, and more. However, while their importance in the above role should not be downplayed, they are inevitably limited and need to be contextualised verbally, both theoretically and often culturally.

Other ways of presenting video to academic audiences, such as showing video clips as part of a spoken presentation, can fill these gaps to some extent.

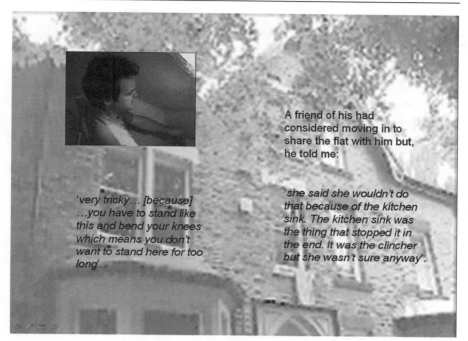

Figure 7.6 PowerPoint Slide. In this slide (produced for the Interior Insights conference in 2005), I combined a background of the house where my research participant lived at the time of our interview with a video clip of him washing up, and quotations from our interview where he discussed the physical and social implications of this material context. The video clips from this project have also been screened as part of spoken presentations (see Pink 2007 for more detailed discussion of this presentation).

However, such video presentations are also limited since, interjected with theoretical arguments and cultural contextualisation, they do not tell a story in the same evocative way that a documentary film narrative might. Nevertheless, these limitations should not be deterrents from using video to communicate about ethnographic experiences. Showing video clips in talks can foreground new aspects of the research process and of research participants' experiences. Above I noted uses of photographs to challenge audiences' existing assumptions and stereotypes; similar uses of video clips could create powerful challenges to audiences' understandings of the people or practices presented.

Video can also be used in multimedia digital presentations. Both PowerPoint and web page software provide useful ways of showing and linking video to other texts. However, video need not be produced only for face-to-face audiences. It might also be combined with other media in hypermedia projects to be used on a computer by one user.

Hypermedia

In their published work scholars are increasingly communicating not only through academic writing, but also by using (audio-)visual texts in relation to their written words. Some academic publications now include CD Rom or DVD supplements which show (audio-)visual texts that could not be printed in the book or journal. Examples include a special issue of the journal *Media International Australia* (2005) including a DVD Rom featuring web pages, a hypermedia project sample, photography and video relating to its articles. Amongst these were a series of web pages from the telemadre.com website to support an article where Graham Murdock and I discussed this work (Murdock and Pink 2005). The edited volume *Reflecting Visual Ethnography* (Crawford and Postma 2006) also includes a DVD, here containing pertinent clips from the documentary films discussed by the book's contributors. These forms of publishing that link books and (audio-)visual texts provide a new route for those who wish to integrate visual knowledge into their discussions.

More 'complete' digital multimedia hypermedia texts have also recently been developed by scholars from the social sciences and humanities spanning documentary art, social policy research, and social anthropology. The CD Rom *Cultures in Webs* by the documentary artist Rod Coover (2003) combines written narrative, video, sound and photography to represent Coover's video and photographic projects in Ghana and in France as well as a theoretical essay embedded with film clips (see Figure 7.7). The CD Rom *Sexual Expression in Institutional Care Settings* (Hubbard et al. 2003) represents the research process, findings and policy implications of research about sexuality amongst older people in residential homes. Visual anthropologists have also started to produce anthropological hypermedia texts on CD Rom. The earliest of these was Biella Changon and Seaman's (1997) *Yanomamö Interactive: The Ax Fight* CD Rom and book, an excellent, complexly structured and encyclopedic project housing a digitalised film, photographs, written text and other data sources, produced as a didactic text. More recently the visual anthropologist Jay Ruby (2004, 2005, 2006) has developed a series of CD Roms that combine video, photographs and written texts to represent his study of Oak Park, a residential area in the USA (see Pink 2006: ch. 6 for detailed analysis of these hypermedia projects).

Hypermedia enables academics to combine written theoretical and descriptive discussions with video and photographic representations in the same text, and in relation to each other. Because hypermedia allows the creation of representations that are multimedia, multilinear, multivocal and interactive, it offers an incredibly flexible environment for researcher creativity. In doing so, it permits academics to make links between, on the one hand, video clips with

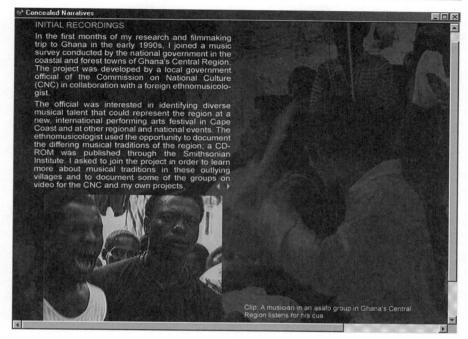

Figure 7.7 A screen capture from Rod Coover's *Cultures in Webs*. Here we can see how Coover has combined video, written text and still images on the same page. In fact, on this particular page he also uses slow motion video and sound in extremely evocative ways that serve to isolate and thus emphasise the different elements of the sensorial experience of the performance.

their evocative potential and ability to generate empathetic understandings in their viewers, and on the other the theoretical arguments and explanations that make these experiential texts meaningful in academic terms (see Pink 2007 for a discussion of contemporary ethnographic hypermedia practice).

SUMMARY: KEY POINTS

- Since so much human communication involves the use of images, it is appropriate that cultural researchers should also use the visual to learn about and represent other people's experiences.
- With the exception of Martin Lister and Liz Wells's (2000) formulation of a visual cultural studies, little attention has been paid to developing a visual research agenda within cultural studies. Visual anthropological practices provide a starting point for thinking about collaborative and non-hierarchical methods appropriate for cultural studies research.

- A collaborative (audio-)visual approach to researching, analysing and representing culture offers cultural studies scholars privileged ways of understanding and communicating about other people's knowledge and experience.
- Visual ethnographic research methods can (1) encourage people to reflect on and thus define their experiences to us as researchers, and (2) provide researchers with opportunities to experience similarly and use their own sensory embodied knowledge as a basis from which to learn about that of others.
- Ethnographic and textual analysis of visual images often imply each other.
- Rather than using images to illustrate written points, researchers should seek innovative ways to (audio-)visually provoke responses in their viewers which might lead them to question pre-existing assumptions.

FURTHER READING

Banks (2001) provides a good overview of visual ethnographic methods in research and representation, while the volume edited by Knowles and Sweetman (2004) demonstrates the various uses of visual methods in sociology. Another edited collection, Pink, Kurti and Afonso (2004), offers a selection of visual anthropology methods in research and representation. Among my own publications, Pink (2006) develops an argument for a visual anthropology that engages with the senses, digital media and its potential for social intervention, and Pink (2007) delivers an overview of the visual ethnographic process. Lister and Wells (2000) gives a good outline of a visual cultural studies.

NOTES

1. The example of the video tours of the community garden project are analysed in a journal article (Pink forthcoming) through a detailed discussion of different parts of the research process, and a theory of place. Readers interested in this analysis are recommended to read this article.
2. Elsewhere, this form of participant practice and reflexive engagement is discussed in detail; the reader is recommended to *Doing Visual Ethnography* (Pink 2007) for further reading.
3. This paragraph is paraphrased from a similar discussion in my book *The Future of Visual Anthropology* (2007). It has been necessary to incorporate it

here since the principles it outlines similarly support my discussion of visual methods in cultural studies

4. Readers are recommended to follow this up by reading my detailed analysis of how the video tour method was used similarly to research the sensory home (Pink 2006: chs 3 and 4).

CHAPTER 8

Analysing Discourse

Martin Barker

The seemingly inexorable rise of the concept of 'discourse' has made it almost unavoidable for cultural studies researchers, particularly since its invitation to theorise culture as 'like a language' coincides with so many impulses within our field. But not without substantial costs. Looking at the cultural studies field from my angle as an audience researcher, some troubling features within discourse work come into view. For all the multiplicity of approaches, and the attendant variations in attached modes of 'discourse analysis', there are some powerful unifying features in 'discourse talk'; and these features presume the *very things* that as an audience researcher I have to question. Very crudely, if the predominant theories of discourse are correct, my research field becomes 'impossible'. There are embedded assumptions about the 'powers' of discourses, about how discourses 'work', which are powerfully disabling. There is a further problem, seemingly unrelated to the first, of the 'convenient sample': that is, the choice of cases which suit a researcher's pre-given position and purpose, and which cannot allow a test of these. How do researchers know what 'texts' or bodies of materials to choose, for analysis? To whom are they relevant *other than* to the analyst? This too has dangerous entailments for the possibility of audience research. It is time, in my view, to expose these assumptions and to unshackle discourse research from their influence.

These issues have become particularly alive for me in the last four years, as I began with colleagues to plan for, conduct and assemble, and then analyse a vast body of materials within the international project on audience responses to the film of *The Lord of the Rings*. This project, which is being published in a range of forms and places, has required us to find or develop very detailed methods of discourse analysis in order to bring into view the differing orientations of a great range of kinds of audiences in varying cultural and country contexts. In this chapter I draw upon the insights I have gained, from being involved in these processes, without either directly addressing our detailed solutions or reporting any of the resultant findings. For any who are interested, I have footnoted some of the main places where these can be found.

THE GROWTH OF DISCOURSE WORK

Over the last thirty years discourse theory and analysis have grown from a minor specialist area to one of the most pervasive and multifarious academic fields. WorldCat is the nearest we have to a complete database of all publications in the English language. As Table 8.1 shows, a simple search at five-year intervals for book titles containing the word 'discourse' suggests a steady rise to its current prominence. This accelerating growth across the period 1980–2000 is striking, albeit it may be stalling now. But if we consider related journals, which emerge as a field consolidates and becomes organised, the picture becomes more complicated:

Table 8.1 English language book titles including the word 'discourse'. Source: WorldCat

1965	1970	1975	1980	1985	1990	1995	2000	2004
70	144	157	327	360	449	651	762	616

Discourse (founded 1980)
Discourse Processes (1981)
Text: an Interdisciplinary Journal for the Study of Discourse (1981)
Discourse and Society (1990)
Discourse Studies (1999)
Discourse Analysis On-Line (2003)
Critical Discourse Studies (2004)
Journal of Multicultural Discourse (2006)

The first 'clump' of development marks the emergence of sociolinguistics, and of the cognitive sciences, but my suspicion is that these are only weakly related to the kinds of book publication then appearing. In that period of accelerated book publication in 1975–85, a large number of the books derive from the crisis in academicist Marxism, and its replacement of 'ideology' by 'discourse'. The delay before the second round of journals emerges arises precisely from the fact that this was less a research tradition than an expression of altered political concerns. The 'field' that emerges thus acquired some distinctive, peculiar qualities:

- A considerable amount of *renaming* went on – in various parts of the field, from 'ideology', or from 'text', or from 'structure of feeling', to 'discourse'.

- This field is very self-aware, philosophically and epistemologically – it is not easy to work in it without entering fundamental debates about the relations between 'discourses' and the non-discursive.
- It is a field of *contentions*, with sharp and continuing clashes between, for instance, sociolinguists and conversation analysts on the one hand, and discourse theorists and critical discourse analysts on the other.
- It is a field very concerned to be culturally and politically *relevant*, yet deeply worried about its warranty for taking political positions.

In fact, we might characterise it as a motley domain, made up of scholars who probably cannot agree on any fundamental definitions, yet all of whom are drawn to certain questions, which are seen as having particular relevance today. These questions concern the nature and role of language and other meaning-systems in the operation of social relations, and in particular the *power* of such systems to shape identities, social practices, relations between individuals, communities, and all kinds of authority. And the reason for the centrality of this topic of power surely arises from the ways in which discourse work emerged from the collapse of academic Marxism, the rise of alternative social movements theorised by near-simultaneous academic constituencies, alongside the 'cultural turn' in various fields of the social sciences.

Just about every writer about discourse theory acknowledges the diversity within the field, although they may cut the cake differently.[1] Whilst acknowledging the helpful distinctions various authors have made, I have found it most useful to ask a series of questions of different kinds of discourse work. This has led me to distinguish seven main tendencies[2] and to tabulate their different answers to my questions as shown in Table 8.2.

This way of thinking the field has at least two advantages. First, it addresses the relations between definitions of discourse, their ontological and epistemological assumptions, and the associated questions and methods. Second, it brings in the one approach that other accounts tend to leave out – that deriving distinctively from the work of Valentin Volosinov. Work deriving from Volosinov still considers issues of power to be crucial, but because of its general theorisation of language, the nature of that power has to be considered an *empirical* question.

By contrast, and with the one exception of conversation analysis, the other strands tend to treat 'power' as the central 'given' of discourse.[3] It is this I wish to address. But rather than address this purely at the level of theory and definitions, I prefer to look in detail at actual examples of discourse analysis. For this purpose, I have chosen two books as test cases.

Table 8.2 Main Approaches to Discourse

THEORIES OF DISCOURSE	Saussurean Structuralism	Lacanian Post-structuralism	Foucauldian Theory	Rhetorical Psychology	Conversation Analysis	Critical Discourse Theory	Volosinovian Dialogism
What are its key founding claims?	Language is an arbitrary system of differences	The formation of language is the formation of gendered self	Institutions construct their subjects as objects of knowledge	Language is always a function of contexts of talk	Spoken interaction is a complex *achievement*	Linguistic *forms* are constitutive of ideological positions	People use language to form groups & conduct social struggles
What forms of language are seen as primary?	Forms of classification, descriptive systems	Constructions that relay 'Self' and its many relations to 'Others'	Language embodying institutional processes and knowledge	Ordinary talk embodying social arguments and beliefs	Ordinary talk expressing patterns of exchange	Embedded grammars expressing power/ideological relations	Shifts between linguistic struggle and conceptual sedimentation
What is the main purpose/function of speech in society?	As samples of current synchronic structure	To embody Self in its relation of Desire to Others	To constitute subjects through institutions, shaping their responses	To respond appropriately to social contexts	To be and to embody complex social relations	To fix or to challenge the fixity of linguistic codes	To form and carry through social projects, and form communities
How is linguistic and conceptual change explained?	Secondarily, as a function of shifts in synchronic order	With difficulty, mainly by 'consciousness-raising' techniques	As a function of shifting institutional imperatives	As social contexts change	Change is the norm, fixity only relates to general speech patterns	As a result of struggles between 'langues' and 'paroles'	As an outcome of social struggles, emergent communities

Table 8.2 (*continued*)

THEORIES OF DISCOURSE	Saussurean Structuralism	Lacanian Post-structuralism	Foucauldian Theory	Rhetorical Psychology	Conversation Analysis	Critical Discourse Theory	Volosinovian Dialogism
How is language related to thought?	Language *is* thought, virtually	Language *is* identity/ies, virtually	Language is related to regimes of truth which *measure* thought	Language is determined by public contexts and knowable, thought is unresearchable	Language is the 'front-end' of back-region unseeable processes	Language shapes and 'determines' thought	People orient to languages, actions provoke us to check them by critical thought
How is 'power' in language conceptualised?	As a direct function of structures, 'langue' precedes parole	Language is a function of desire which powerfully constructs the world and identities	As a function of regimes of truth, constituting forms of resistance also	'Contexts', both lived and ideological, are powerful	Power is over the situation of talk, directing the flow of exchanges	As embedded grammars which remain unexposed, hence unchallenged	As persuasion in real situations, tactical control of concepts and exchanges
What can discourse analysis reveal, and what can it prove?	Reveal synchronic systems (their power is already 'known')	Reveal the operation of gendered constructions (their power is already 'known')	Reveal institutions at (their work existence is already 'known')	Reveal contextual/ ideological determinants, and strategies of response	Reveal how people manage their social interactions, proving little beyond that	Reveal social/ ideological grammars (their power is already 'known')	Reveal new aspects of processes and terms of struggles, and how people orient to them
Exemplars of each approach's ways of analysing	John Hartley, *Approaches to News*, Judith Williamson, *Decoding Advertisements*	Frank Burton & Pat Carlen, *Official Discourse*	John Tagg, *The Burden of Representation*, Stephen Heath, *The Sexual Fix*	Jonathan Potter & Margaret Wetherell, *Discourse and Social Psychology*	Charles Antaki, *Analysing Everyday Explanation*	Gunther Kress & Tony Trew, 'Ideological dimensions of discourse'	Marc Steinberg, *Fighting Words*; Chik Collins, 'To concede or contest?'

CHRIS BARKER AND DARIUSZ GALASIŃSKI, *CULTURAL STUDIES AND DISCOURSE* ANALYSIS (2001)

Barker and Galasiński offer a useful test-case. Their book is, if you will, a manifesto, urging upon cultural studies scholars the benefits of complementing a presumed-to-be-agreed set of theoretical positions, with methods for close empirical analysis of cultural materials.[4] The recommended method is critical discourse analysis. But these methods will not test any of the core theoretical claims – these are 'known' on other grounds. They include a range of philosophical positions (about self and identity, about the nature and role of language in society, and about the wish for cultural studies to 'give voice' to disadvantaged and silenced groups), and which derive from a pantheon of recognised theorists (Saussure, Pierce, Wittgenstein, Barthes, Hall, Foucault, Lacan, Butler, and so on). The role of methods is limited, it seems, to detailed illustration. The rest is 'interpretations', which are essentially a matter of position.

At the heart of the authors' approach is a stance that I would want to challenge, as either endlessly ambiguous or just plain wrong, a stance which is captured in their summative acceptance of the 'argument that language is constitutive of subjectivity, identity and our cultural maps of meaning' (2001: 47). There are many issues buried in here, but the one which concerns me here is the deterministic language. Throughout the book it is possible to find repeated instances of words assuming specific kinds of causal relations at work within culture: people are apparently 'constructed', 'impelled', 'constituted', 'interpellated', and so on. The book's first three chapters lay out what the authors regard as this 'agreed territory', followed by an account of critical discourse analysis, and then some extended applications to a CIA document; some interviews with men about fatherhood; and some interviews with elderly Poles about their attitudes to Ukrainians. For the sake of focus, I look at their first example.

Over fourteen pages, they scrutinise a Credo posted on the CIA's own website, using various CDA tests for social grammars (in particular focusing on the recurrent use of 'we', and the self-attributions this implies). This scrutiny unquestionably leads to a richer description of the document. But then comes a claim which goes beyond description. Here is what they say:

> Let us take a look at the thematic and information structure of the CIA Credo, beginning with the first sentence: 'We are the Central Intelligence Agency'. As we pointed out earlier, the theme of the clause is the recurrent 'we'. However, unless we can actually see a group of people, we cannot simply accept the 'we' as given. Who, we might ask, are the people saying this? There is no way to tell. So why

not start by saying 'this is the Credo of the Central Intelligence Agency'. The answer lies precisely in the given status of the theme. The text proposes that we, the readers of the text, know who is talking. This is a strategy quite consistent with opening a web site and working on an image of legitimacy, law-abidance, and transparency. What follows from this is an interesting exercise in locating the CIA as the given of the text and the rest as the new. In other words, the CIA assumes that its audience knows merely of its existence and nothing about what it does. This is a fascinating finding when one considers that the Credo, like other corporate texts, is displayed for public consumption on the Internet. Yet, we would speculate that this apparent glitch in the form of the Credo is probably well worth it. Thanks to it, the CIA not only establishes itself as a known, taken-for-granted part of American life, but presents itself as a unity defending American values. The average American can sleep peacefully knowing that the CIA is out there making sure that American interests are well-served. (2001: 83)

There are several problems with this account, and its implicit moves. The most obvious is the slipped-in rhetoric of this 'average American' who appears to be someone who can be 'spoken' to by the CIA. An abstract figure, what qualities might s/he have? And what is it that makes her/him so open to being consti-tuted into comfort by this document? It is not just that we do not know, but there is no interest in finding out. This aside, other implicit assumptions underpin this move. The most troublesome are these. It seems that the capac-ity to be affected by these discursive elements is a function of a *motiveless encounter*. Readers are not looking at this web document for any reason, or with any purpose – they are just looking. It also seems that they have never before seen a document of this kind. If they had, generic knowledge that 'this looks like one of those Mission Statements' might kick in, making otiose the dis-tinction which is vital to their move: that 'we' might only know of the CIA's existence but know nothing of its nature. If we recognise this as a Mission Statement, we probably know something about the rhetorical functions of such statements, and a number of things about the *kinds of organisation that produce them*.

This example not only illustrates just how deeply embedded are these moves and implications. It also suggests that they gain their persuasiveness because they are backed by those wider philosophical position-takes. Discourse analy-sis naturally generates 'images of the audience' which require no testing. Let's see how this works in a more determinedly 'empirical' book.

CARLA WILLIG (ED.), *APPLIED DISCOURSE ANALYSIS* (1999)

Willig's collection is an example of the best that critical discourse analysis offers to cultural studies. I do not mean that cynically. The book contains much that is very valuable and instructive. Even so, each of its essays reveals blind-spots. In her introduction, Willig is acutely aware of the many epistemological and political problems of 'applying' discourse analysis to live problems. But two things are strikingly missing from her worries: any examination of the issue of the 'power' claims in discourse theory; and any consideration of how the truth-claims of discourse analyses might be tested. These absences re-emerge in the essays, which I want to examine.[5] I spend longer on the first, only because close attention to that saves time on the remainder.

In his essay, Steven D. Brown explores the discursive organisation of self-help books – the kind that tell you how to cope better with stress, and to make the most of yourself, especially at work. He asks, 'how do these texts exert their effects?' (1999: 24). He notes their near-didactic organisation, their constant 'prompts, suggestions, encouragement' (23) to examining yourself, seeing stress as something to be addressed within yourself (as against, for instance, challenging stressful working environments). This leads to him locating an idea of a 'serviceable self', a managed production of oneself that will cope, be flexible and productive, and have a sense of self-worth from achieving this. But all the way through the essay, the analysis of the books is accompanied by an unanalysed figure. 'The reader' enters at the moment when s/he opens one of these books, after purchase: 'Let us leave aside for a moment what motivates people to buy or read a self-help book about stress. Consider instead what happens as they work through the text' (23). Thereafter this figure gradually accretes attributions. Some are soft and casual: regimes are 'presented to the reader' (35, no implications of response); the books 'encourage readers to develop a particular relationship with themselves' (37, slight implications). Others slide further: 'The reader must accept the serious nature of the choices that he or she is making . . .' (31); 'the use of devices such as heat serve to make stress visible in a way that is immediately explicable to the reader' (32); 'computational metaphors . . . impress on the reader the importance of under-standing mental operations during stress . . .' (34) – with the curious implication in the last two that these rhetorical resources are *evidently effective*, a claim I find curious to say the least. This is perhaps Brown's strongest version:

> A grand gesture of extending wisdom and guidance is played out. The reader must further accept the serious nature of the choice he or she is making, and that this involves assuming an active role: 'This is not a book for hypochondriacs. It is for people who enjoy being healthy and

are prepared to help themselves to remain healthy' (Eagle 1982: 6). The work of staying healthy is purely a matter of personal responsibility. The texts offer help, but on the proviso that readers fully accept that the problem lies within themselves. (1999: 31)

Thenceforth, this 'reader' becomes increasingly a textual construct, an 'addressed' and 'positioned' empty figure – only becoming nearly three-dimensional in the closing paragraphs, where Brown asks: 'Clearly we need to understand just how this transformation then plays out when it becomes an accepted feature of labour relations' (38). But notice how readers' motivations, and uses of the books, have now been subsumed within a *disciplinary* model: they meet these books *within the context of labour relations*. Indeed he makes the curious assumption that those most likely to read these books are the victims of such work environments, rather than (as I suspect) their managers, trainers, supervisors. The books' 'power' is thereby virtually guaranteed. Thus Brown's safety clause ('Readers do what they will with them' (40)) becomes a rhetorical closure, instead of an invitation to possible testing research. And that to me is the real issue.

Let me summarise the problems I am pointing to. Brown's interpretation of these books only works if we share certain premises with him.

1. *Premises concerning unity and coherence:* he is *forming them into a genre*, assuming that the average 'reader' will receive them as working and meaning in the same way. That makes two further assumptions: (a) it assumes that readers will not see important distinctions among them – perhaps in *style*, or in *applicability of metaphors, examples, and regimes* – and thus generate their own genres, responding to some and perhaps rejecting others; (b) it assumes that there will thus be *cumulative influence*: '[t]he more readers begin to revise their grasp of their personal circumstances in terms of stress' (24), the more they will be 'positioned'. Treating them as unified allows Brown to claim a 'discourse', and thence to presume without evidence their 'power'.

2. *Premises concerning persuasiveness:* Brown has presumed on the effectiveness of their rhetorical organisation. For example, he writes that 'it is the very vacuousness of the terms stress and energy which makes the mixing up of these discourses possible' (37). That permits him to move to arguing that this emptiness allows the books to be 'all things to all people'. The assumption here is that what *he* as discourse analyst can see as vacuous, not only is not visible to 'readers', its invisibility is the *very ground* of their incorporation. Thus, discourse analysis perversely builds in a presumption of the effectivity of the patterns it 'discloses'.

3. *Premises concerning investigative completeness and testability:* all these
are posed in ways which hide the possibility of testing. The
implications are there, but are never sign-posted. They remain half-
buried, with the protective stricture that this is 'only an
interpretation'. This for me points to two further sub-questions:
(a) the issue of researchers' responsibility for consequences and
implications of their strong claims. It cannot be right that at the first
point of critical enquiry an analyst is entitled to say 'This is only an
interpretation, you are pushing my account too far'. That would lead
to the most sterile form of relativism imaginable. (b) A further
assumption, less evident in this case but vital later, is that his own
method of analysing the books is *trustworthy*. Of course, the essay
format makes it hard to demonstrate methods in depth. But that
cannot remove the questions involved here: what larger investigation
of their meaning-making processes underlies his presentation? What
guided his list-making, and how complete was this? Has Brown
examined the books *rigorously*, in the sense of attending to their
overall organisation and direction, rather than lifting for quotation
favoured but marginal elements? Has he examined *differences* as well
as *similarities* within his 'genre'? All these have to be taken on trust in
a way that they would not be in more 'conventional' modes of
research.

These issues are replicated, albeit with differences, in other essays. Timothy
Auburn, Susan Lea and Susan Drake offer an account of the discursive practices at work in police interviews. They look in particular at moments of
explanatory disjuncture, when an interrogator points to discrepancies in a
suspect's account, and demands s/he account for these. Using recorded interviews, they draw attention to a series of rhetorical devices used by the police –
such as urging suspects to be honest with themselves, or to see how another
person would look at their account, or to think how an expert would evaluate
their explanation. From this they develop an account of the police interview as
the discursive work of producing an administrative knowledge of the events,
and they suggest that discourse analysts should 'take sides' by teaching this
kind of understanding to groups (gays, mental health advocates, trade union-
ists) who suffer regular harassment by the police. All this is interesting, but the
revealing 'slip' comes when they sum up a police line of questioning as follows:

This concern about the lack of intersubjective agreement on 'what
really happened' is warranted by a particular selection of features of the
event which give rise to inferences that there are discrepancies between
the two available accounts. The production of a discrepancy in turn

relies upon carefully crafted fact constructions so that the discrepancy becomes a plausible inference from the selection and meaning of the 'facts' as part of a wider narrative of the events. (54)

Pause on this. Just what would a 'carelessly crafted' or 'implausible' version look like? Is there any way in which, for discourse analyses of this kind, rhetorical moves can *fail*? I do not think they can, because these accounts *assume* the productive coherence (as against the tactical, and contestable nature) of official discourses. (It is interesting that the extract which precedes and leads to the above quote ends with the suspect simply repeating, 'No I didn't do it'.)

Val Gillies explores women smokers' argumentative strategies for not giving up in the face of their acceptance of health arguments about smoking. Using quotes from four women, she draws attention to the way they talk about 'addiction'. This is a discourse, she argues, whose 'most powerful effect . . . is to provide a deterministic explanation that emphasises the smoker's lack of control over her actions' (71). This couples with her talk of discourses such as 'addiction' 'containing' and 'positioning' individuals. Their use of these languages shows they are victims because of their discursive domination. However, with one woman at least, 'Mary', she notes that 'addiction' is only one among a number of other strategies. Mary also says she is 'not as bad as some others', is 'able to say no' if offered a cigarette, and 'isn't bothered if people ask her not to smoke'. All this *might* be seen to suggest that Mary is not 'positioned' by these languages, but is calling – almost at random, and certainly without adherence – on a range of discursive resources, and it does not matter to her that they might be seen as incoherent and contradictory. But Gillies does not go this way; instead, she takes from Mary a passing reference to a 'gradual brainwashing thing' to reassert that Mary has absorbed, and been constructed as victim by, a discourse of 'lack of control over herself' (74). This allows Gillies to go to examples of health education literature in which, she argues, there is a 'prevalence of a discourse of addiction' (81), and even beyond that to much wider 'concepts of self-control and restraint' (82) within which the discourse of addiction then finds a home. Mary's *references* to addiction thus become *symptoms of discourses located by other means*. But we do not know, and apparently do not need to know, if Mary has ever encountered – let alone absorbed – any of these wider discourses. This brings into focus what it means to identify a 'discourse'. What standards of evidence are required to 'name' something as a coherent, effective discourse? And what standards then apply to knowledge about people's encounters with those, sufficient to count as having been 'positioned' by them? That, of course, is among the tasks that audience research has set itself.

Willig's own essay presents some outcomes of a larger project on the discourses of safe sex. Drawing upon interviews with heterosexual men and women, she identifies a series of discursive frames which they use to explain how they make or perhaps would make decisions about 'safety'. These include: marital safety ('I wouldn't be with him/her if I didn't trust them'); trust ('it would be very hurtful to suggest I don't trust her'); and problems of interrupting a romantic encounter at a critical moment. She also identifies the devices that people use to distinguish 'innocent victims' of STDs from other people.

Willig opens by counterposing a discourse analytic approach to conventional social cognition approaches, concluding with these comments: 'Social cognition models have received limited empirical support. They can account for up to 50 per cent of the variance in declared intentions to adopt health behaviours but only control up to 20 per cent of variance in actual behaviour' (112). This is an apt and perfectly valid criticism of social cognition approaches, and it references the long tradition of research into the gaps between people's declared attitudes and their behaviour. What is striking is the *absence of any wish to mount equivalent tests of a discourse approach*. Why? After all, in theory, discourse theory has a distinction quite closely matching that between attitudes and actions. In the book's introduction, Willig distinguishes two regions of discourse work: the investigation of discursive *practices* and of discursive *resources*.[6] Discursive practices are the 'local' communicative regimes which individuals and groups use in ordinary communication. Discursive resources, on the other hand, are more widely distributed. Because of this, they are more obviously researchers' constructs, but still make strong claims on reality in that we try to understand local discursive practices through them.

There is nothing wrong with this double articulation, providing it remains double, and thus open to tests. But in Willig's research the distinction collapses. Having discovered that her respondents use these explanatory frames, she concludes that they are 'predominantly disempowered' by them:

> The marital discourse positioned spouses as safe by definition, which meant that talk about sexual safety constituted a challenge to the nature of the relationship itself. Those who position themselves within this discourse are required to take sexual risks with their partner in order to negotiate a trusting relationship. (118)

First there is that slippage between apparent *choice* ('position themselves') and apparent *domination* ('positioned'). But then there is the fact is that this argument elides the very distinction which Willig insisted on earlier in relation to social cognition approaches: between intention and action; between talk and behaviour. In the absence of other kinds of testing investigation, we simply do not know how far, or for whom, this kind of talk might be disempowering. One could well imagine a process of *management* if someone was nervous, in which another discourse – say, about contraception – could allow trust to be made compatible with safety. In other words, Willig is assuming a complete congruence between her interviewees' 'local' talk (discursive practice) and a wider discourse. I wonder what 'proportion of variance' she sees herself as explaining . . .

The final essay raises a different dimension of my problems with discourse analysis. David Harper presents some selected aspects of his larger doctoral study on the discursive processes involved in establishing and then evaluating drug therapies of mental illness. It is important to note in this case that we have here only a very small part of a larger study. Harper bases his investigation on interviews with a mix of psychiatric professionals and users of their services. He first lists a range of explanations offered by professionals to account for failures of drug regimes, and identifies within the talk that proposes these a body of 'symptom-talk' which thereby engenders a structured distinction between 'surface' phenomena and 'underlying' pathology. Everything thereafter turns on one medium-sized quotation from a consultant psychiatrist, 'Dr Lloyd'.

Lloyd appears to offer several distinct explanations why a drug regime failed to alter the belief systems of a psychotic patient. Harper teases out these explanations, showing how they in turn reference 'sociological, behavioural, cognitive, personality and biological psychiatry', all the time surrounded by 'fluid' cautions and qualifications (134). As an explanation this fails, he argues, because nothing could refute it. But it does work to sustain Lloyd's expertise: 'The extract warrants the continued use of medication here despite there being no change in psychotic symptoms' (136). The remainder of the essay moves between drawing out implications for courses of action that could be adopted by various interest groups, and a self-reflexive angst over claiming his account as 'true', and thus empiricist.

My concerns are partly theoretical, partly tactical, but driven by one question: why should we trust Harper's 'reading' of Lloyd's account? Theoretically, his cautions against 'truth' largely let him off the hook, and the essay format colludes with this. We have no grounds for determining what will *count* as a completed analysis. One of the features of expertise is that not everything that is believed or known can be said explicitly at one point. So, what else indeed did Lloyd say in the interview? The use of that single quoted paragraph may have denied him reasonable space to make sense. What could have made his account less 'fluid'? This points up a problem for *us* as analysts: what can we responsibly do, in setting up and carrying out interviews and in analysing and presenting them, that will make our accounts of them fair, and will enable readers to assess them?

I have tried to delineate a number of issues with discourse analysis that emerge through the practices of these writers. They can be summarised as follows:

1. The *problem of the unity and coherence of the 'research object'*, leading on to (a) the problem of *readers' genres*, and (b) implicit claims of *cumulative influence*.
2. Presumptions about *persuasiveness* and associated *concepts of power*.
3. Issues of *investigative completeness and testability*, leading on to
   (a) researchers' responsibility for their claims' implications, and
   (b) *visibly trustworthy* methods of analysis.

CHALLENGING THE 'POWER' OF DISCOURSE

How might we go about remedying these problems? There is first, I think, a question of attitudes. The simple excitement that many discourse theorists have felt at the emergence of their field, thence its tendency to intellectual imperialism, need now to be tempered. Discourse theory does not explain the world, it helps us to understand *parts* of it. And it is the relation between those parts and the rest that is at stake here. It will mean, therefore, being a bit more modest and sensible than has always been the case. Take this opening sentence: 'Language organised into discourses (what some contributors here call inter-pretative repertoires) has an immense power to shape the way that people, including psychologists, experience and behave in the world' (Burman and Parker 1993: 1). Really? Immense power over which people? When and where, precisely? Under what circumstances? With what determinable and checkable outcomes? Researchers should back off from this kind of talk, and take some responsibility for spelling out how such claims might be tested. To challenge this kind of talk is not to attempt to rubbish all the work that has gone on under such inflated circumstances. It is to ask that discourse researchers – as indeed any other kind of qualitative researcher – consider why anyone should *trust* them. Why should any reader *trust* their selection of materials for analysis, their mode of analysis, and the ways in which they draw conclusions from those? The notion of 'trustworthiness' is, for me, the qualitative researcher's equivalent of quantitative researchers' 'triad' of validity, reliability and generalisability.

But to avoid 'trustworthiness' becoming simply a rhetorical claim, we require a set of distinct principles, properly following which will enhance the strength that discourse work can claim. Each of the following is intended to be an answer to the problems I have enunciated above.

1. The Defensible Corpus

In all kinds of quantitative research, the issue of the reliable sample is a first con-sideration. In qualitative research the principles cannot be anything like the same, but that does not excuse us from having good grounds for our selections. I propose to call the bounded group of items a qualitative researcher studies her/his 'corpus', in order to mark this off from the quantitative researcher's 'sample'. I would argue that a corpus should be subject to various tests which amount to measures of the trustworthiness of the analysis. In selecting a corpus for analysis, I propose that *to the extent that there are defensible grounds for its selection*, this alone *adds to the stature of the analysis*. So what are such defensible grounds?

Suppose a discourse researcher chooses to study a TV interview with a famous person (there are a number of examples of such analyses). On convenience grounds, this is attractive. The materials are nicely bounded, were produced and distributed independently of the analyst, and were (presumably) seen by a large number of people. But choice for convenience alone must increase the provisionality of any claims.

Take an interestingly complicated example: Abigail Locke and Derek Edwards (2003) analysed the Grand Jury cross-examination of Bill Clinton during the 'Lewinsky Affair'. They are particularly interested in the ways in which Clinton defended his own position by attributing emotional insecurity to Lewinsky. This apportioned some of the blame, and thereby exonerated himself. It might seem that the focal, indeed televised, nature of the cross-examination guarantees the value of this corpus. And indeed at one level it surely does. But at another, it remains problematic because they impose their own framework of relevance on it. Most of the essay is a close analysis of particular attributions, but here is how they close their account:

> Lewinsky's disposition towards irrationality and heightened
> emotions . . . provided the basis for various alternative accounts he was
> able to offer, of key and controversial events and readings of events.
> Rather than exploiting a young and vulnerable White House intern, and
> persuading her to lie under oath, he was helping and counselling an
> emotionally vulnerable friend with whom he had responsibly ended
> some regrettably 'inappropriate contact' . . . Clinton's accounts of
> interactions with Lewinsky worked to soften or rebut any notions of
> perjury and exploitation. (2003: 253–4)

This notion of the 'work' Clinton's talk achieved, made visible by their alternative account of what *might* have been said instead, raises their description to the level of significance. But it does so at a price. Missing is any sense of the *questions* asked, and of this being a Grand Jury investigation. Here was a piece of theatre, where *both* attackers and defenders shared an interest – in not harming the *status of the Presidency per se*. Clinton's line of defence, I would argue, is made possible by the inquisition's institutional context. Whether they or I am right or wrong depends upon a wider contextual knowledge – and that is just my point.

If there is independent evidence of the cultural importance of a corpus – which needs to identify *to whom* and *under what circumstances* it was important – to that extent the analyst has two advantages: s/he will already have a sense, from knowledge of the nature of the people concerned, of what aspects may be most relevant to attend to; and s/he will have the strongest grounds for the relevance of the outcomes of the analysis.

2. The Defensible Method

Qualitative (therefore including discourse) methods always suffer from the difficulty that they are harder for other analysts to check. Many things contribute to this. Pressures of time, the virtual disappearance of the monograph, increasing disciplinary specialisation – all contribute to a tendency to produce smaller, more enclosed pieces of research. Journals impose tight word limits, and that restricts how far authors can make plain their methods of using their materials. (Actually, there are solutions – web journals need not restrain length, and can include subjunctive pages, and it is not inconceivable for an author to point in any publication to a personal webspace which could display more fully the elaborated methods of analysis.) This pulls us in two directions. In one direction, with a very small corpus, it is possible to show more detail of the materials, and to show the methods of analysis in action, but it carries the higher risk of 'privileged choice' – that is, favouring cases which suit a conclusion reached on other grounds. In the other direction a larger corpus is harder to display, and therefore the methods used to examine it tend to greater opacity. My argument is this: the conveniently small corpus is at great risk of never being more than illustrative. In the act of becoming more than this, it inevitably grows. We have to face and find solutions to the problems of managing (both analytically and presentationally) large bodies of discursive materials.

Consider a possible study. From time to time, in any culture, certain expressions rise up (often, interestingly, out of fictional contexts) to encapsulate attitudes and relationships.[7] Some examples: 'Gizza job' (out of *Boys from the Black Stuff*); 'Loadsamoney!' (from Harry Enfield's popular Thatcherite); 'You might very well think that, I couldn't possibly comment' (from Ian Richardson's rising politician Francis Urquhart in *House of Cards*); 'We wantses it, my preciousssss' (Gollum in *The Lord of the Rings*). These have the great virtue that we know – we will have chosen them for consideration – because they have such high salience. And a great deal can be said, discursively, about these, in all their minimalism. Their very pithiness itself is in fact an important consideration. But an analysis of any such epithets that did not tackle the *variety of contexts of use* would not pass beyond the illustrative. We learn much more if we can also consider *who* uses them *in what ways*, and *with*

what evaluative accents – indeed, with what bodily expressions they were associated (by turns, mock head-butt; loud money-brandishing; suave pseudo-
diffidence; ingratiating sneakiness).[8] Such a broader analysis could disclose
how apt such an expression is to incorporation into wider discursive constructions and debates, and that is precisely the point. But then, from having begun
with some of the smallest and most enclosed corpuses conceivable, in order to
achieve significance we have to expand them greatly. We are forced back to tack-
ling the problems of the 'inconvenient' corpus! How do we manage the analysis of a large set of materials, and then present them satisfactorily?

Of course, particular fields within discourse research have strict and shared
procedures for presenting samples of talk, particularly transcription rules.
These mainly govern the stages prior to analysis.

3. Taking Responsibility for Implied Claims

It is arguable (I would argue it) that all analyses of texts and discourses will
inevitably make some substantive claims about things beyond themselves. Most
typically, these are claims about reception.[9] Who are the 'people' who will
receive the discursively organised 'messages' that the analyst has disclosed, and
what is the possible impact of these? 'People' here needs to be in quote-marks,
since – again, perhaps inevitably – our analyses use 'figures of the audience'. We
do not name actual people (individuals or groups) but more likely *kinds* of
people. The moment we move beyond the loosest and least satisfactory use of
terms like 'the audience' or 'the spectator', we begin to impute characteristics
to them. The difficulty is that these imputations are simultaneously pseudo-
empirical, and theoretically charged. Here is an example to explain what I mean.

Michael Stubbs (1996) has recently proffered a new way of doing discourse
analysis, which exploits the power of modern computers to permit the comparison of grammatical forms with vast data sets and thus to disclose patterns
and regularities, and he offers interesting examples of what the method can
achieve. In one chapter, he explores and compares two final messages from
Robert Baden-Powell, one to the Scouts, the other to the Guides. Drawing on
a corpus analysis of the two messages, he has valuable things to say about the
ways in which the grammar of the two letters embodies, among other things,
sexist ideas about the separate roles of men and women (and the ways in which
these can be embedded in, for instance, talk about 'happiness', which might at
first sight appear gender-neutral). But then he has this to say about how the
Guides might have responded to the inherent sexism of Baden-Powell's
message to them:

> They express, quite explicitly, the view that women and men have very
> different places in the world, and many aspects of these views would

now appear deeply objectionable, or perhaps just ridiculous, to many people. Their tone strikes us, over fifty years on, as patronizing and naïve. And there is no reason to suppose that Girl Guides down the years have passively absorbed BP's message. They may have actively contested it, given it subversive readings, laughed at or just ignored it. There is no direct way to investigate this, although one indication is that the Guides text has long been out of print. (1996: 84)

Notice in here two linked tendencies. First, the salient feature is gender. That may sound unproblematic, until we consider that it is also *only* gender. This is not middle-class girls and boys in the UK in early twentieth-century conditions, in the sphere of leisure relations; it is just 'girls' and 'boys'. And the address of the messages is thus presumed to be 'about' gender as such. That might not matter in itself, since Stubbs might argue that his gender-analysis could be extended and supplemented by attention to class (for instance, what vocabularies are assumed? What modes of 'official speech' are used, and so on?), except that the *theoretical stance* of this argument has already taken us further. Secondly, what we see here strongly recalls Stuart Hall's encoding/decoding model. It begins by measuring the corpus against our concerns. So, first we determine that the messages are 'sexist'. That already carries an implication. If a reader *were to* have a *passive* encounter with these messages, they might well be 'inscribed' into a damaging self-definition. Of course, if they 'actively' resisted or negotiated or mocked, that safely distances them. It is curious how this model of activity/passivity, despite frequent critiques, persistently inheres in models of this kind.

I would argue the case differently. In the range of options open to middle-class women at that time, Baden-Powell's communication could well have counted as a *radical* one. Here they were, being addressed in their own right. They had a role, and one demanding conscious attention and work – all contributing to a feeling that this was a *positive* rather than a demeaning message. And from other historical researches we know that women could actively collaborate in promulgating (what we might see as) 'sexist' definitions of themselves (see, for instance, *Women in the Third Reich*). Stubbs's analysis is thus compromised by his model.

These, then, are my proposals for reforming the use of discourse analysis within cultural studies. It should come as no surprise to realise that in essence I am arguing that discourse work needs always to be conducted within an explicit recognition that talk of all kinds arises within the circuit of culture. The recognition of that circuit, embracing history, production practices, textual form, reception and recirculation is one of the great achievements of cultural studies.[10] None of this means that only projects which achieve all the above are worth doing. Rather, I am arguing for being honest about limits and boundaries.

Discourse work, like any other worthwhile research, is strong to the extent that it recognises its inevitable inclusion of implicative claims, which it cannot itself test. It must therefore acknowledge the *provisional* nature of its findings but try to articulate what might take matters further.

A VERY BRIEF EXAMPLE

Although this example from work I have been personally involved in is very brief, you will be able to see, I hope, how it follows the principles I have laid out. I would want to stress that this is *one way*, but only one among many, to observe these.

The *Lord of the Rings* international audience project was precisely designed to test some of the kinds of claims that circulate in both academic and public spheres, about how audiences might relate to, and be affected by, a film such as this: an enormously successful fantasy trilogy, based upon a very English story, trumpeting its New Zealand production and settings, and yet made with Hollywood studio money. From the outset, then, it had a serious ambition to contribute to our knowledge of cross-cultural film reception. Among our several means of gathering materials, we used a questionnaire whose results were fed into a searchable database. The questionnaire combined quantitative aspects (multiple-choice response and self-allocation scales, plus demographic information) with qualitative ones (free-text opportunities to explain the quantitative responses, along with questions about particular aspects of the film). In all, just under 25,000 completed responses were received, in fourteen languages. In terms of *scale* of corpus, this was going to be complex to handle. In terms of *questions*, we simply could not assume in advance what the film would mean to different people.

I use one key investigation I undertook, to illustrate how we tried to secure trustworthiness. A sequence of quantitative searches led us to identify a separation. Within the world set, we found that while the most *common* descriptor for the film was 'epic', the one chosen by those most *committed* to the film was 'spiritual journey'. These were among twelve options we had offered audiences (with the further possibility to nominate their own) to characterise their overall sense of the story. A further set of quantitative explorations, using twelve countries with the highest overall rates of responses, found a complex patterning. An inverse relationship emerged between the strength of separation between common and committed responses, and the proportion of repeat-readers of the books in the country. Indeed, in five countries with low proportions of repeat-readers, the 'spiritual journey'/'epic' vanished. We therefore wanted to know (1) what these terms meant generally within the world set, and (2) how the separation of common vs committed choices worked within each country.

The database allowed us to take random samples, and to gather together their answers to our first free-text question: 'what did you think of the film?'. This had come immediately after we had asked people to tell us how much, on a five-point scale, they had enjoyed the film. Those grouped answers, gathered in this fashion, now constituted our corpuses: 100 each from the world set of those who had nominated 'epic', or 'spiritual journey' (but excluding each other so as to minimise overlap) among their up-to-three terms to describe the story; then, fifty for twelve countries each from each of the most common choices and most committed choices (again, excluding each other). Each corpus included examples ranging from one-word expressions of pleasure ('wow!', 'fantastic', and so on) to quite elaborated explanations of why and how people had enjoyed the film.

If you would like to see the procedures in detail, they are available online.[11] In brief, the analysis involved:

- a close reading of the two world sets, from which a coding scheme was developed that could encompass everything said;
- producing formal definitions of the – in the end – ten codings;
- the systematic application of these, ensuring they covered everything;
- a first-level analysis of the codings to disclose similarities and differences both in frequencies, and in kinds of mention;
- from these, an examination of how, within each corpus, elements were linked and moves made between kinds of talk, with the aim of disclosing discursive connectors.

From these, a portrait of the typical elements was constructed and then tested against the most explicit and elaborated examples. This stepped analysis was then repeated for the two sets from each of the twelve countries, in order to produce a portrait of their culture-specific patternings of choices.

If you would like to see the outcomes in detail, they are published in the main book from the project.[12] What I believe we were able to achieve through this means was a trustworthy account of two things:

1. the different core meanings of *The Lord of the Rings* for those whose encounter with it was based deeply in the books, and their history;
2. the ways in which these core meanings were altered by the local circumstances of the book/film's history and reception in some very different country-contexts.

Although doing this was undoubtedly tough, I believe that this carefully ramified set of stages and procedures increases the trust that can be placed in our findings. It also had the effect of revealing to us things that completely surprised us. All this allowed us to go back to ask what could make sense of the peculiarities in responses in each country, and so not overlook what discourse analysis can easily suppose or take for granted.

SUMMARY: KEY POINTS

- The chapter traces the rise and spread of discourse theory and analysis, a multi-faceted development and one of the fastest growing areas of cultural theory and methodology.
- It examines the ways it contains within many of its formulations complex claims about the responses of those on the receiving end of discursive forms and communications. The problems inherent in this are traced to the ways in which many formulations of 'discourse' presume on particular models of 'cultural power', which are in themselves antipathetic to the very notion of audience research.
- The essay explores in detail a number of cases where such formulations are at work, within examples of discourse analyses of specific kinds of cultural materials, and it explains why they may be problematic.
- It offers as a way forward a series of methodological tests which can be applied to cases of discourse analysis, which could reduce the subjectivity and strengthen the trustworthiness of discourse analytic claims, and make them more open to empirical testing by reception research.
- The essay very briefly introduces materials derived from the international *Lord of the Rings* audience research project, within which discourse analytic methods were used to examine responses to the film adaptation of Tolkien's books.

FURTHER READING

Discourse analysis is recognised as a wide-ranging set of approaches, deriving from competing paradigms and models. A very good survey of the main approaches, at both theoretical and applied levels, is the pair of volumes edited by Margaret Wetherell et al. (2001). A range of journals carry important exemplars of the various kinds of work undertaken under the banner of discourse analysis, notably *Text*, *Discourse and Society* and *Critical Discourse Studies*. These journals also contain important debates between practitioners within the various major 'schools' of language and discourse work. A range of audience researches have at various points claimed to use discourse analytic methods, not always very systematically. Although written before the expression 'discourse analysis' became popularised, Ien Ang (1985) remains an important example of the critical examination of language to reveal social and cultural understandings. Martin Barker and Kate Brooks (1997) examine various approaches, and outline a set of procedures of an approach compatible with cultural studies' general audience research practices.

NOTES

1. See, as examples, Norman Fairclough (1992); Stef Slembrouck (2005); and Wetherell et al. (2005).
2. Recently I have encountered two interesting variants. 'Positioning analysis', associated in particular with the work of Michael Bamberg, claims to find a mid-way between conversation analysis (CA) and critical discourse analysis (CDA). I do not yet feel confident enough to comment on this. See, for instance, Korobov and Bamberg (2004).
3. It is necessary to say something about the relations of this critique to the long-running, and perhaps inevitably unfinished debate between two traditions of work on talk: conversation analysis, and critical discourse analysis. In a series of often tetchy exchanges, scholars in the two camps have rehearsed arguments against each others' approaches. It might appear at a quick glance that my argument sides me with the CA camp. That would not be right at all. I am very largely persuaded by the critique of CA offered by, for instance, Michael Billig. In an exchange in *Discourse and Society* (Billig and Schlegoff (1999)), Billig argues that while CA presents itself as strictly empirical, concerned only with looking and seeing what are the organising characteristics of 'ordinary conversations', in fact it is heavily based upon a 'foundational rhetoric' which among other things presumes a working distinction between 'ordinary conversations' and 'official or institutional talk' – the former being presumed to be equal and participative, and thus not inflected by power-relations until specifically proved otherwise by formal qualities (such as imbalances in turn-taking). Emanuel Schlegoff's cross response to this critique badly misses the point, I think, because Schlegoff simply cannot accommodate the idea that research such as his *necessarily involves theoretical commitments*. But the problem is that my acceptance of Billig's critique hits a limit when he himself stops just there, with that acknowledgement of theory-tasks ('CDA aims to make explicit such tasks, in order to enable a theoretically based choice between available rhetorics and attendings/disattendings' (575)). And it is clear that it is the question of 'power' that is the heartland of the Billig/Schlegoff disagreement. What Billig does not go on to do is

to consider how those commitments, and the findings which they thus prompt, might be *tested*. Without that, in the end, the CA/CDA choice is purely one of political preference.

4. I cannot in the space I have give as full an account of this book as it deserves. A much longer critical review of it is contained in Terry Threadgold's (2003) essay.

5. In fact I have chosen not to explore one essay (by Joan Pujol). This is because the issues it raises are rather different, and would concern the sheer untraversable distance between her weighty theoretical framework deriving from Derrida and Ricoeur, and some hardly digested fragments of empirical material.

6. This distinction is derived from Edwards and Potter (1992). In another essay, Willig has explored this distinction further. See her essay with Gillies, (Gillies and Willig 1997).

7. See Eric Partridge (1986) for a fascinating collection of such catchphrases.

8. I have recently been using the marvellous online database LexisNexis to explore the evolution of references to 'Gollum' before, during and after the appearance of the films of *The Lord of the Rings*. Methods of both analysis and presentation have posed real challenges. It remains to be seen, by others, how successful I have been.

9. See, for instance, my *IRIS* essay (Barker 1998), and *From Antz to Titanic*(2000).

10. For a clear statement of the nature and importance of this circuit, see Paul du Gay et al. (1997).

11. Go to www.users.mib.aber.ac.uk (Cross-Cultural Pleasures).

12. Martin Barker and Ernest Mathijs (2007).

Linking with the Past

CHAPTER 9

Engaging with Memory

Emily Keightley

Memory has enjoyed a well charted resurgence in the postwar period in cultural production, social life and academic study (see Huyssen 2000; Misztal 2003; Radstone 2000). The social dislocations that occurred in the aftermath of the world wars, and the radical trauma of the Holocaust, threw into sharp relief issues of remembrance and commemoration (Wolf 2004; Margalit 2002). In more recent years, a growing disillusionment with the rhetoric of progress which has been so central to modernity has required a reconsideration of pasts that had been hurriedly discarded. At this historical juncture memory is becoming an increasingly key feature of popular culture, from the booming heritage industry to the Radio Four 'Memory Experience' series in 2006. Unsurprisingly, memory as both a subject and as a mode of investigation is becoming increasingly common in the field of cultural studies.

In contemporary academia the resurgence of memory is not so much contested in terms of its occurrence but in terms of its implications for the construction of individual and collective temporal identities and historically rooted cultures. This would at first seem a non-sequitur, how can a boom in popular memory result in anything other than an enhancement of historicity and increasingly democratised relationship towards studying history? However, the positioning of memory and history in a hierarchical relationship has contributed to the insidious construction of memory as a vernacular impersonation of professional historiography (Weissberg 1999: 11–12), with the verifiable, document-led reconstructions of professional history being set against subjective fantasies of experience lost to time.

This chapter is part of a growing body of work that seeks to resist this valuation and emphasise the importance of memory as a topic of research and a mode of investigation by considering memory on its own terms, rather than via the epistemological criteria born of elitist academic history and by the more generalised influence of empiricism in the social sciences. Here, memory will be considered as a vital resource for cultural studies. Its unique provisions in the task of interrogating contemporary culture as a site of struggle, pleasure and agency will be identified. This will firstly involve considering the nature of contemporary memory and its importance in relation to the broader interests of cultural studies. The potential ways of situating memory and utilising it in empirical cultural studies research will be outlined and examined using relevant studies in the area.

MAKING THE CASE FOR MEMORY

In commonsense parlance, memory is considered an individual faculty. Our memories are often talked about as stores, or repositories of accounts of the past that we call up when we desire, or sometimes involuntarily in response to a contemporary trigger. The intense particularity of our most painful and pleasurable memories seems to deny the need to look beyond the individual in order to make sense of the experience. If this was the case, cultural studies would find memory's texts and narratives little use. But remembering is a process that exceeds the psychology of the individual. It speaks to more than personal experience, implicating the everyday operations of social and cultural relationships which are performed in the creation of memory narratives and embodied in the resulting cultural texts. It is necessary to consider the commonalities and collective trends in memory, the features of their communication and representation, and their ritualised performances, all of which suggest that memory is more than an expression of individual consciousness, and is both socially and culturally constructed.

In terms of the social nature of memory, it is Maurice Halbwachs's pioneering work that emphasises the collective role of remembering and the individisibility of remembering from its social context. Memory was not merely the recall of the past as it was experienced; Halbwachs (1995: 44) states that an individual's memory is the 'intersection of collective influences' from that of the conventions of the family to the norms of the culture to which the individual belongs. The relationship between memory and social environment is not a one-way flow: although what is remembered is dictated by the groups in which we participate, remembering also has a social function in the present. By remembering according to particular social conventions, those conventions are constantly being affirmed and re-constructed. Remembering aids the organisation of social and cultural life by constantly endowing us with a meaningful communicative currency out of which we can build social relationships, group affiliations and consensus. Remembering can never be performed outside of a social context. The remembering agent is always the occupant of a particular social position or role, necessarily shaping their ideas and knowledge about the past. Although social affiliations may be multiple, the action of remembering extends beyond the individual and enters a web of social communication and knowledge, acting on, as well as through, the social world.

This functional relationship does not provide a full account of memory in contemporary life. In order for memory to exist and have any role in lived experience it must be represented and communicated. Terdiman (1993: 8) goes as far as to suggest that all memory is representation in the sense that in order to be recognised as memory, it has to be re-constructed as a representation from the narrated anecdote to the public portrait. Memories are texts with narrative codes and representational conventions; they have omissions and reinterpretations, polysemic readings and intense personal resonances. It is this turn towards the representational nature of memory which ultimately makes memory an intimate concern for cultural studies, as memory is the mode by which we represent our experiences to ourselves in all its particular and general dimensions. We have therefore to move away from the functionality of Halbwachs's model to allow for a more contingent notion of memory that can incorporate our multiple social positionings, some of which may conflict with each other. The memory text is a construction created in what Radstone (2000: 18) calls the 'liminal space' between public and private pasts and as a result should always be considered as a mediation between the two.

It is however simplistic and misleading to suggest that personal experience is merely recalled through the prism of public structures of power and representational conventions. Remembering as a form of generating temporal representation involves a reciprocal relationship between the individual and the collective in the generation of mnemonic texts. Memories are constructed by the multiple positionings of the remembering subject but also, in the communicative act, perform those positions and in doing so help to reconcile them. Alternatively memory can be an act of resistance, actively rejecting the collective or cultural codes with which it is shot through, repositioning the subject in new coordinates of time and space and meaning. What is clear from this conceptualisation is that the meanings of memories are always provisional.

Seeing memory as a representation necessarily problematises any simple relationship between a memory and the experience to which it refers. History's benchmarks of enduring truths and measurable veracity will inevitably be failed by memory, but rather than compromising the value of memory, this raises questions over the utility of these criteria as a way of judging memory at all. This is not to suggest their rejection is enough to validate memory as an object and mode of research. The difficulty in conceiving of memory as ultimately constructed can result in a polarisation of meaning: either memory is conceived of as meaning-less if measured by traditional historiographical standards, or, a relativistic standpoint is adopted where all memories are equally valid and valuable as representations of experience. This raises important ethical and political questions as representations of the past do clearly have a transactional value in the present. For example, the ways in which the Holocaust is remembered both privately and publicly have enduring repercussions for our understanding of it in the present. Memory narratives which seek to deny its existence or attenuate its severity must be adjudged politically dangerous and ethically unsound.

These political and ethical criteria provide us with a starting point from which to take our bearings for the assessment of memory. Like other forms of representation, we can recognise an intimate relation between memory and lived experience, but rather than seeking to measure this in terms of an objective, verifiable truth-for-all-time, we can consider the transactional potential of memory, and its capacity for transformation in the present and future. Memories can be assessed in pejorative ways, as for instance when a lost past is mourned without taking bearings for the present and future, when a memory denies the experience of others or when it supports conservative or regressive action in the present. Positive valuations of memory can be made where the dialogic relation between past and present is being maintained as the present and future are not isolated from the act of remembrance, where remembering is creative and the past is being used as a resource in the service of progressive aims, or where the remembering act is characterised by empathy as a recognition of the experience of others.

Jameson's (1991) postmodern account of memory privileges the former valuation of memory in contemporary life. In a world of surface style and pastiche, he claims the dialogic relationship between temporal fields has been curtailed. Historicity becomes impossible and cultural amnesia inevitable. In this dystopian account we have abandoned our memories in favour of a simulated version. In stark contrast is Lipsitz's (1991, 1994) recognition of the potential for social and cultural memory to be articulated in and through mediated texts and technologies. Both of these accounts are feasible as the resources are available in contemporary society both for the articulation of memory, and for its abandonment. It is these alternatives that make the study of memory so important for cultural studies. The theoretical possibilities available for historical engagement in contemporary life have been claimed, but it is for cultural studies to investigate the everyday mnemonic activities which are performed under these conditions and the temporal moorings that they provide for those who engage in them.

To operationalise this evaluative framework, we must also modify our understanding of truth and authenticity in terms of what memory can provide. The truth to which traditional historiography makes a claim is an enduring one, fixed through time. Memory's claims to truth are fleeting, transient and contingent, where the meanings of memories are valid only for the dialogic moment of remembrance. As time moves on, so does memory; it takes on new forms, builds different narratives and makes new connections between past, present and future.

Understanding memory as a constructed representation always implicates the conditions of their creation and performance. For cultural studies this involves considering how ideology and power relationships have formed particular memories and how they operate in their service. The conditions of the original experience, the role of the memory in the present and the conditions under which it is remembered are all important sites for investigation. For example, Hobsbawm and Ranger (1984) investigated the invention of particular traditions and their hegemonic utility. However, ideological structures cannot simply be taken to determine memory and its meaning. The imposition of hegemonic frameworks of remembering is undeniable, but the temporal environment is always one with marginal space accounts of the past with the potential for alternative memory to be forged and practised. Conflicting and competing memories are formed and re-formed in the public and private domain, for affective pleasure and active resistance. Memory is always contingent and encoded into the fabric of our material and imaginative world in complex and ambivalent ways.

So as a resource for cultural studies, memory allows us to centralise everyday temporality as it speaks to the vernacular untidiness of lived practices of remembering that conventional historiography aims to smooth away. The study of remembering embraces the vicissitudes and silences of history and explores the relations of power involved in its construction. But memory is more than an alternative history, it is also about the marginalised present. It concerns the power structures that impact on the ways in which we are able to draw on our own pasts in the interests of our present and futures. It is concerned not only with past experience but also with the resources we have for renewal and resistance and how this is enacted in the most private moments of reflection, in the routine actions of social life and in public cultural space. The private and public dimensions of remembering as a representational practice and memory as representation of temporalised experience can be made explicit, and the oscillations between them rendered visible, allowing the individual, the social and the cultural to be seen in their mutualities. The particular and the general are brought to bear, not by the exclusion of one to illuminate the other, but in twin focus. Memory is central to understanding cultural life, not because it *is* the past, but because it is the modality of our relation to it (Terdiman 1993: 7).

WORKING WITH MEMORY

Remembering is an act that takes many forms and so it should come as no surprise that its study is equally diverse, ranging from the investigation of memories of particular incidents, activities or periods of time (Hirsch and Spitzer 2003; Kuhn 2002a), the investigation of the use of memories by specific social groups, peoples or individuals (see Burlein 1999; Lipsitz 1994), to more generalised assessments of the potential for memory in contemporary societies (see Huyssen 2000; Hoskins 2001). There are, however, two key dimensions to the investigation of memory as a cultural form. Firstly, memory as a research method involves eliciting memories in oral or written form about a topic of interest to the researcher such as a given event or period of time. The key feature of this mode of research is that the process of generating empirical data always involves the generation of narratives which then form the basis of the analytical process. Secondly, there is the investigation of memory as an object of research. This might involve memory as a generalised activity, memory as it is enacted by a specific group or individual or memories of a specific event, place or period. Here, memory is often but not always the method of generating data. Historical memory documents can be used, such as an autobiography or a family album. The main concern is how memory is enacted and how it operates in everyday life as a specific mode of temporal engagement.

It is important to stress that although I am going to discuss the two approaches separately, they are not mutually exclusive modes of study. In fact in cultural studies, one will never appear without a consideration of the other. It is a matter of where the focus or specific interest of the study lies. For the purposes of this part of the chapter, the distinction is a useful heuristic tool. In the discussion of existing cultural memory studies, these two dimensions will be brought together and their various combinations will be highlighted.

MEMORY AS A METHOD

Memory as a method of research involves using remembering in order to generate data which can then be examined through various modes of analysis. This use of memory is not specific to cultural studies, nor has it emerged in a disciplinary vacuum. Psychoanalysis draws heavily on the elicitation of memory as a therapeutic tool, using memory as a mode of accessing the features of an individual's formative experiences. In social and cultural history, memory has been used to great effect in the gathering of data to formulate alternative histories or to uncover marginalised accounts of particular events or periods of time (Leydesdorff 1999) despite its rather low ranking on the scale of traditional historiographical credibility. The motivation for using memory as a way of generating data in all of these instances is in large part due to the striking and vivid detail that memory narratives provide. This has led to a general preference for qualitative modes of elicitation using oral unstructured interview formats and, for some participants, written accounts.

As a result studies of memory have been drawn into the debate over the epistemological validity of qualitative methods (see Hammersley 1996 for an overview) and the veracity of remembered accounts. For cultural studies, this is familiar territory and the premises of the positivist argument can be largely rejected by such moves as challenging the historiographical hierarchies of 'evidence'. However questions of validity should not be completely cast aside. Although the constructedness of memory can be embraced, completely fabricated memories are as problematic for cultural studies as for conventional history, for to make any claim regarding the impact of past or present power relationships on remembered experience would then become tenuous. Methodological strategies such as triangulation (which will be considered in more detail later) can be employed when using memory to ensure that the epistemological challenges memory poses are met.

An early use of memory in cultural studies was conducted during the 1980s by Richard Johnson and the Birmingham Popular Memory Group (part of the Centre for Contemporary Studies) using everyday memory narratives as a way of constructing a popular socialist memory which prioritised feminist and anti-racist accounts of the past (1982: 214). The elicitation of everyday working-class memory provided unique access to accounts of the past marginalised in conventional history. They situated their work in relation to oral history as a historical method that has failed to account for the plurality and multi-layered nature of everyday memories and in relation to presentist accounts of cultural memory such as Hobsbawm and Ranger's top-down model of invented tradition (see Misztal 2003: 61–7 for an overview of the Popular Memory Group's work). This use of memory illustrates that remembering can be used as a method to achieve broadly historical aims, both by formulating historicised cultural theory which posits dominant memories as contestable by vernacular memory, and through the related activity of generating these alternative or democratised narratives of the past.

The key distinction between the use of memory in cultural studies and more conventional oral history is not always easy to make. Their elicitation of memories which are used as primary data is the same: it is the choice of memories that are used, the ways that they are framed and treatment of that data which makes the key difference. Cultural studies has an explicit concern with power manifested in class, gender and ethnic relationships. This shapes the respondents who are chosen and the dimensions of the narrative which are prioritised in analysis along with the analytical framework itself. Cultural studies uses memory narratives to excavate these particular social relations where oral history may stop short of this kind of deconstruction and treat the narrative simply as an alternative account of events. In the recounting of experiences, sense-making structures that we employ to make meaning from our everyday lives are made visible, providing new perspectives on events and periods of time. The process of retelling opens up to scrutiny the process of sense-making and allows an examination of how experience and the sense we make of it is inflected with the social and cultural structures of daily life, past and present.

Distinctively, cultural uses of memory as a mode of generating data are concerned with the form as well as manifest content of memory. Memory can be analysed as a specific mode of discourse which bears the hallmarks of its social and cultural production as much as they are constituted in the memories' content. Attention to the words chosen in the construction of memories, metonymy, pauses and laughter are all considered in the ways that they contribute to the construction of temporal meaning. Rather than being treated as a transparent documentary data, 'each testimony must be considered as a text to be analysed on several levels' and must 'be understood hermeneutically' (Jedlowski 2001: 31–2). The concern with the way meaning is constructed is also a specifically reflexive one as the circumstances of memory elicitation in the research process are considered as constitutive elements in the narrative construction of the memory in the same way that the broader social and cultural conditions under which the memory is constructed are considered. It is in this sense that where memory is used as a method in cultural studies, it must also be considered as an object of study. Memory is never used in a transparent manner and is always reflexively considered as a construction. The memory as a text, as well as the information it provides, must always be subject to scrutiny.

MEMORY IN ACTION: THE MEMORY–WORK METHOD

Memory work is a method developed in Germany in the 1980s by Frigga Haug and others and was used in Haug's work on female sexualisation (1987). The intention of the method was to use memory to bridge the gap between theoretical accounts of women's experience and experience as it is lived, in order to make sense of the ways in which women become part of, and act in, society (Onyx and Small 2001: 773). In Haug's project, researchers' own memories were generated on particular topics pertinent to female sexualisation and were then used as data in order to investigate the processes by which women become sexually socialised. The memories of each of the group members were the empirical element of the research.

The method itself is a collective process involving a group of researchers. The process of research involves three key steps or phases (Onyx and Small 2001). Firstly the group selects a stimulus phrase or topic and each member writes a memory relating to that stimulus. The memories were written 'from the standpoint of others' in order to make the processes of sexualisation strange or to denaturalise thoughts, feelings and experiences, preventing the desire to defend one's memories or justify particular experiences (Haug 1987: 58). The memories are constructed to communicate only the nature of the experiences, excluding any value judgements or interpretations, with the maximum detail possible. In the second phase the written memories are then deconstructed by the group. This may involve looking for similar features between memory-narratives in order to generate themes and identify recurring commonalities in the form or content of the experiences. Particular discursive constructs such as metaphors or clichés are identified which may allude to underlying meanings of the experience and its relation to the rememberer. Highlighting notable absences in the narrative is crucial as it may reveal those aspects of experience that are undesirable or socially unacceptable (Crawford et al. 1992: 49–50). This analysis illuminates the way experience is constructed according to particular norms and conventions of (in this case) gendered experience and how we make sense of that experience within the confines of those structures. The final step in memory work is one of further theorisation. The written memory and the discussion of it is connected and situated in relation to academic theory and is used to contribute to wider discussions in a relevant area of study. This can be performed collectively, but is most frequently in the process of writing up the memory work on an individual basis (Onyx and Small 2001: 777).

The key advantage of this kind of memory method is that it speaks to some of the key epistemological concerns of cultural studies more broadly. Primarily, in common with feminist work like Haug's, using memory as a method has permitted a blurring of the traditional hierarchy of researcher and researched. Where scientific positivism has polarised the expert and the layperson, with the expert inhabiting a privileged position in the construction of knowledge, this method centralises lived experience as an important source of knowledge about, and agency within, the social world. As Haug suggests, this use of memory serves as a refusal 'to understand ourselves simply as a bundle of reactions to all powerful structures . . . we search instead for possible indications of how we have participated in our own past experience' (1987: 35).

It is clear from Haug's work that memory can be used to investigate cultural phenomena beyond memory. In Haug's own work, the processes of female sexualisation are the central concern of the investigation. Aside from the intricate level of detail it provides, using memory is particularly fruitful as it allows the processes of sexualisation to be considered in a way that respects the historical nature of the process under investigation. In the writing and collective discussion of the memory, experience is made external to the rememberer and is recontextualised. Through this process, the historical specificity of the memory is made reflexively explicit as are the socio-cultural forces which structure both the experience and its reconstruction.

Memory work also highlights another provision of memory as mediating the general and the particular. Memories are at once intensely private and seemingly unique, and inextricably shot through with the social conditions of their production, as is true of lived experience. Memories, which are experience reconstructed or literally *re*presented, provide a representation of that relationship and so the raw materials with which to unpick one from the other, or at the least identify their points of connection and divergence. In Haug's case, this is done by finding the resonances of gendered social relations in the stories of the individual. In this sense, using memory can help to illuminate both the specificity and the collective nature of experience.

Using memory in this way is not without its problems. Crawford et al. (1992) directly address positivistic concerns with notions of truth and accuracy of the memory narratives which form the empirical base of memory work by suggesting that the point of investigation in memory work is the process of construction that is constituted in the narratives, not the accuracy of the account as a representation of the past. This, whilst true, does obscure the fact that completely fabricated memories are problematic as they can compromise the commitment to investigating lived experience. In other applications of memory as a way of generating data, this may become even more problematic if the memories elicited are being used to make sense of a particular historical event or period. In this case, triangulation with other forms of data such as documentary evidence or other narrative accounts would be the most methodologically sound way of ensuring the validity of the data without compromising the emphasis which is placed on vernacular accounts as a legitimate source of knowledge.

In memory work, the memories elicited are of a written kind. For many researchers this will not be the case as many uses of memory as a method involve the oral elicitation of a layperson's memories, similarly to the oral history interview. This raises methodological questions not addressed in Haug's memory-work method, not least how the data should be approached once gathered. In oral history, a written summary or synopsis of the key points covered in the interview may be sufficient but for a cultural analysis which seeks to take into account the memory narrative as discourse and attend to the content, a full transcript of the memory narrative must be made on which further analysis can be performed, as was seen in the memory-work method. However, for many research projects the time, space and resources for collective analytical processes may not be available, in which case the processes of identifying themes and features of the narratives and identifying the role of social conventions and hegemonic norms in their discursive construction and manifest content must be undertaken systematically by the individual researcher.

For those not working as a research group or collective, memory narratives will be collected from those external to the project, raising the issue of unequal relations between researcher and researched. This can be addressed in both the data gathering and analytical stages of a study using memory. Qualitative interviewing as a method allows the research participant to guide the data generation process to a considerable degree, allowing them to communicate those memories which they feel are relevant, rather than those demanded by the interviewer. The analysis of data in this situation will inevitably bear the hallmarks of the researcher and their particular evaluation of the participant's memories. This does not mean that researchers have *carte blanche* to impose their own interpretations and valuations of the memory narratives, rather that researchers have an obligation to be reflexive about their own role in both the elicitation of the narratives and in their subsequent interpretation in order to maintain the democratic and egalitarian position of the researcher and participant to the greatest extent possible.

MEMORY AS THE OBJECT OF RESEARCH

The investigation of cultural memory as an object of study rests on the shared assumption that memory is a key site through which the lived experience of time can be examined. The investigation of memory as a key feature of social experience can take several forms. In the first instance, memory can be studied as discourse. As in all analyses of representations of the past generated by memory methods, this centres on a concern with memory as narrative. The codes, conventions and norms of representing the past as a memory can be examined, and in so doing the routine ways that we make sense of experience can be investigated. This investigation may centre on how particular social factors such as gender, ethnicity, age or class are enacted through and encoded into memory acts or texts.

Another dimension of studying memory as a mode of action or engagement is an examination of its performance, ranging from the private time and space devoted to the construction and viewing of the family album to the public space allocated to physical memorials and their ritualised usages. Considering the form and performance of memory, at individual and collective levels, allows an assessment of the imaginative role of memory in everyday public and private life. The form and location of memory in everyday life intimately connects to the possibilities it has for us in engaging with our own historicity and fostering a temporally sensitive consciousness, and so the investigation of memory as a research subject is always concerned with what memory provides for us in our contemporary lives.

Memory can be investigated in several different ways. Andrew Hoskins, for example, considers the changing role of memory in a media-saturated everyday life in a largely theoretical way. The broad cultural and societal temporal shifts are considered, and from this he extrapolates the potential there is for remembering in contemporary society and the forms that this might take under intensely mediated conditions. Alternatively, physical embodiments or representations of memory, past or present, might be used in order to illuminate the ways in which memory and time itself are constructed in both public and private domains. Pierre Nora's vast study of French *lieux de memorire*, focusing on those sites 'where [cultural] memory crystallises and secretes itself' (1989: 7) from the archive to the commemorative ritual, is an extensive example of how this might be achieved.

Memory can also be studied using an empirical approach that emphasises the lived experience of memory as a mode of temporal consciousness and action rather than attending only to the textual forms that memory may take. This might involve utilising memory as a method of generating memory narratives which can then be examined in order to illuminate the role of memory in the contemporary life of a given individual, group or population. The sites and texts of memory are not examined in terms of their inherent textual historical potential, but in terms of the ways in which these potentialities are actually performed in everyday engagements with them. When examined from this perspective, sites of memory which have been alleged to curtail historical engagement, such as those emerging from the heritage industry, may be used in ways that draw on alternative frameworks of temporal understanding, opening up new possibilities for the making of temporal meaning. Human subjects do not approach sites and texts of memory empty-handed, and in examining contemporary memory it is crucial to understand what it is that people do with the temporal resources of modernity rather than assuming that they are at the mercy of them.

STUDYING MEMORY IN PRACTICE: HOW WOMEN REMEMBER

My own research has been concerned with the investigation of memory as it is enacted in everyday life: the actions and performances it involves, the texts which are used, and the social and imaginative currency memory has in the life-cycle. Underlying this research is a commitment to the idea that memory is, on both an individual and collective level, one of the key ways in which we make sense of our experience and make sense of ourselves as temporal beings. The only way that this can be examined is by talking about everyday remembering with the individuals who enact it. The method therefore is based on qualitative interviewing in a manner similar to that of oral history with the exception that a lot of the discussion involves a reflection on how the past is remembered in the present, rather than an elicitation of accounts of the past itself.

In a cultural study of this kind, other methodological commitments must be upheld. The socio–cultural and historical conditions of the individual rememberer must be considered in the analytical process and are therefore crucial in the earlier stages of participant recruitment. A completely random sample of participants would require incredibly extensive and diverse investigation of the social vectors constituted in each participant. This is beyond the capacity of many smaller research projects and therefore the study of a particular group of people may be necessary. This was the approach chosen in my own study. It resulted in the specific consideration of women's experiences and enactments of memory. It is important to note that this form of selectivity should not presume the selected group's homogeneity; rather, the study must respect the diversity of experience within that group. In my own study this was achieved by including women of different ages and various ethnic backgrounds.

In respecting the specificity of experiences of remembering as well as commonalities between women, the data and ensuing analysis does not lend itself to extrapolation to wider populations. Rather than being an empirical study which seeks to construct ideas about the influences of social variables through the analytical process and apply them to a wider population, this study seeks to understand how social variables such as gender, age and ethnicity converge in specific and plural ways for a particular individual and impact on their specific uses and enactments of memory. So, rather than moving from the particular and applying it to the general, this study begins with the general. It then moves on to examine this in its particular manifestations.

In order to achieve data that could demonstrate how people engage with memory in their everyday lives, it was of utmost importance that the elicitation of accounts of remembering was participant-led. Nineteen in-depth interviews were conducted with a range of participants and were unstructured in format. Key themes were introduced such as photographs, music, family, and history, but the participant was able to determine the specific areas of discussion that were pertinent to their own experience of remembering. The interviews were transcribed and then subjected to a process of analysis.

The analytical process is much more difficult to formulate here than in the structured step-by-step processes of the memory-work method. The transcripts were read and key themes identified. These included materials of memory, familial memory, imagination, bodily sensations, and arenas of memory and mediated memory. The transcripts were broken down into the initial themes and then reconsidered, generating new thematic structures until a satisfactory series of commonalities and differences could be identified between the transcripts. In tandem with the thematising of the transcripts, the transcripts were also read intuitively. Segments of transcript that appeared out of place, unusual or unexplainable were identified and set aside. This often involved the striking or incongruous use of language or intensely emotional episodes or anecdotes. The themes were then worked up analytically, drawing out through the process of writing the relationship between the individual women, their socio-cultural and historical position and their enactments of memory. The intuitively identified anomalies were deconstructed individually and read against the background of the patterned usages of memory identified through the thematic analysis.

There are of course considerations and limitations when examining the lived experience of memory in this way. As with the memory-work method, the qualitative mode of enquiry is labour-intensive, particularly in the analytical process. Annette Kuhn has utilised information technology to go some way in countering this by using a qualitative data analysis software package to manage and in part analyse the interview data which she generated in her study of cinema and cultural memory (2002a: 240–54). Where larger numbers of transcripts are generated, this is a particularly useful methodological tool, although a note of caution must be sounded. Even the most sophisticated data analysis software will not be able to match the researcher's own eye in picking out the smallest details and the most unusual connections and relationships in data. It is therefore appropriate to consider software of this kind as an aid to the analytical process rather than a substitute for it.

Another cause for concern in an analytical process of this kind is one that is faced by grounded theory more generally, namely that the 'truth' the researcher produces through the interpretative process of analysis is one that is verifiable. Pidgeon (1996) identifies two general responses to this concern. In some cases the research participants will be part of the analytical process and the researcher may share her/his analysis with the participants who are then invited to comment. The rationale is that if the analysis is acceptable and recognisable to the participant, then greater confidence can be held in the interpretations that have been made. The problem is that the interpretative process may draw on complex theory or be written in inaccessible academic prose making it difficult for the participant to assess the analysis. In addition, this approach relies on the assumption that the researcher must be wrong if the participants do not like their interpretation, which is a dangerous step in the direction of unqualified relativism. Alternatively, the researcher can make sure that the data is presented in such a way that other specialists reading the work can assess how the researcher arrived at the conclusions and the extent to which they seem reasonable given the data with which the researcher was working. This is why many studies of cultural memory, including Annette Kuhn's, Frigga Haug's and my own, all include extensive transcripts or memory-narrative excerpts to show the data on which the analysis is based.

It is important to consider carefully any other key areas which the study seeks to illuminate alongside memory as this will have a considerable influence on the methodological choices that are made. For example, my own research is centred squarely on how memory is enacted and used in everyday life and it is made manageable by considering only a particular kind of person and social circumstances. An alternative way of limiting the study would be to focus on people's memories of a particular event or period, as Kuhn does in her study. This would raise some different, but no less important issues surrounding the establishment of empirical validity. In the latter case, some account of the event or period would be necessary alongside the participants' elicited accounts as the event or period must be considered historically in its own right. In my study it was necessary to investigate theoretically the notion of gender which formed a key analytical dimension of the research. The relationship between the participants' accounts and some sense of a verifiable historical reality becomes more pertinent and must be established. This may necessitate the inclusion of other sorts of data in the process of analysis.

Kuhn does this in a very comprehensive way by using a questionnaire to gain a broader sense of how cinema-going in the early to mid-twentieth century is remembered, and by performing a historical enquiry into cinema-going based on published and unpublished documents including periodicals from the period, statistical data and archival materials (2002a: 240–54). She uses these to contextualise her informants' narratives and uses a process of triangulation in order to identify concurrences and vicissitudes in the data collections. It is important to note that this does not involve the construction of a hierarchy of data where the participants' accounts are deferred to historical documentary 'evidence'; rather, it means that where divergences occur, reasonable explanations must be sought whilst bearing in mind that multiple accounts of the same period of event are not only possible but inevitable. The challenge for the researcher is to make sense of any divergences or differences that are encountered (see Deacon et al. 2007 for further discussion of triangulation in the social sciences). Whilst Kuhn's study is limited in the account it can provide of the multiple everyday uses of memory as the study focuses on memories of a particular activity, the benefit of her use of multiple forms of data is that she is able to retain the strikingly vivid detail of the participants' narratives whilst incorporating a broader generalisability with regard to the historical experience of cinema-going.

CONCLUSION: THE FUTURE OF CULTURAL MEMORY STUDIES

This chapter has sought to distinguish between the use of memory as a method and the study of memory as an object of research. What has become clear over the course of the chapter is that these two dimensions of study are inextricable from one another in cultural studies despite the fact that they are separated elsewhere, such as in oral history. The reflexive deployment of memory means that it can never be used in a transparent manner, and where it is used as a mode of gathering data, it must be subjected to analytical investigation. The methods and approaches to memory in cultural studies can be blended according to the aims of the study in question. The diversity of their employment is as broad as the field of cultural studies itself.

There are, however, some important defining features of doing empirical studies of cultural memory. First is the commitment to bring everyday enactments and vernacular sites of memory to the fore and to investigate these in a way that does not construct them as the poor relation of historical documentary evidence. In particular, using memory as a method is an epistemological statement of the relevance of the everyday in social-scientific work. A second feature is that memory, like experience, is always seen as the nexus of the social and the individual; the particular and the general are seen in their mutual interrelationships and not at the expense of one another. It is in this sense that the study of cultural memory is seen as a way of prising open the relationship between public structures, forces and relationships and private lives as they are lived. As Annette Kuhn suggests, memory stories, in both their content and form, 'betray a collective imagination as well as embodying truths of a more personal salience' (2002a: 11).

This leads on to a third feature: the way memories are understood as data. Studies of cultural memory always analyse the discursive form of memories as well as their manifest content. The discourse of memory, whether linguistic, visual or physical, is always constructed and choices were always made in that process. It is the responsibility of the researcher to identify those choices and make sense of why they were made under particular social, historical and spatial conditions.

Memory studies is not a singular key that will unlock all of the secrets of the form and meaning of contemporary or historical culture. There are limitations, both in terms of pitfalls in methodology which we have considered in the case studies, but also more generally in terms of the contributions it makes to the field of cultural studies. In respecting the inestimable importance of everyday life and participants' autonomy in the research process, it is easy to slip into an assumption that all vernacular memory is a utopian articulation of temporal consciousness, brimming with historical potential and transactional value. As with most assumptions and totalising claims, this is rarely the case; memory is a complex engagement with the past with the potential to be both a utopian space of free expression and truth, or a dystopian nightmare of denial, partiality and longing (Radstone 2000: 5). It is the challenge of empirical cultural studies to make sense of the mediation between these two possibilities as they are enacted everyday in people's lives.

It is also the responsibility of empirical cultural studies to recognise that the study of the particular and specific performances of remembering can only take us so far in this project. The qualitative methods so frequently used to capture the minutiae of everyday remembering and to deal adequately with the complex relationships between the social and the individual manifested in memories mean that many studies of cultural memory are not generalisable and reveal only a limited or partial picture of contemporary memory. It is here that the more general theorising of temporality in late modernity of the kind that theorists such as Andrew Hoskins and Andreas Huyssen engage in has a crucial role, as it enables temporal consciousness and historical engagement to be conceived on a much broader collective level. Theorising of this kind enables the impact that more generalised shifts in the conditions of late modernity might have on the resources at our disposal for performing memory in everyday life to be assessed in holistic ways that studies so close to everyday activities cannot possibly hope to attain.

If cultural memory studies are to continue developing and flourishing, it is also important to consider the relationship of cultural memory studies to other forms of cultural enquiry, particularly cultural history with which it is so intimately connected. As I hope this chapter has demonstrated, memory and history should not be considered as completely separate activities, nor should one be valued higher than the other. As distinct modes of enquiry, they have different benchmarks of validity, but this does not mean that these are irreconcilable, as Annette Kuhn's work shows. Memory and history clearly have points of intersection in terms of how they can illuminate one another. Memory is a method by which historical data can be brought to life and fruitfully contextualised with depth, detail and alternative perspectives, while historical enquiry can help make sense of the changing role of memory over historical time.

SUMMARY: KEY POINTS

- The chapter explains and outlines why memory is vitally important to cultural studies research. This importance is centred on the need to reconcile the seemingly paradoxical coexistence of accelerating contemporary experience and a popular boom in vernacular forms of memory.
- Memory is addressed both as a method for investigating cultural phenomena and as a topic for cultural investigation in its own right. In both of these senses, memory is considered as a mode of temporal consciousness which generates meaning that is ultimately contingent on past, present and future, rather than a faculty which provides a transparent window on the past.
- Memory is considered as a method of investigation in cultural research and is applied using a case study. Memory is also considered as a topic of concern for cultural studies and is illustrated using a case study.

- Memory is considered in a holistic sense, not just as an individual faculty but as socially and culturally constructed and communicated. The relationship between the individual and the collective in representing the past is positioned as reciprocal, mutually interdependent and constantly negotiated.

FURTHER READING

Memory has been dealt with in a rather disparate manner across the social sciences and humanities. Recently, assessments of and investigations using memory have begun to coalesce into a coherent field of enquiry which is coming to be known as 'memory studies'. This coalescence is reflected and advanced by the establishment of a journal of the same name in 2008. Radstone (2000) offers a useful overview of the use of memory in the humanities and the social sciences. Historical and cultural studies concerning temporality in modernity and postmodernity have paid considerable critical attention to memory. Jameson (1991) suggests that memory has been fatally compromised by the imperatives of postmodernity whilst Huyssen (1995) provides a more hopeful assessment of contemporary memory in his study of contemporary incarnations of time and history, as does Samuel (1994). The marginal status of memory in studies of modernity is considered in Pickering and Keightley (2006) with particular attention to the concept of nostalgia. Sociological studies of memory have emphasised the collective nature of remembering. The sociological study of memory has been led by Halbwachs (1926/1995). Olick and Robbins (1998) provide a good overview of studies in this area, and more recently Wertsch (2002) provides a comprehensive assessment of collective memory and its relationship to history. Feminist work has looked at the role of memory in the construction of gendered identities. Haug (1987) considers how memory can be used as a research tool to excavate the processes of identity construction whilst Kuhn (2002a, 2002b and, with McAllister, 2006) considers the ways in which media are involved in memory. Cultural accounts of the mediation of memory include Lipsitz's (1990) consideration of American popular culture and collective memory and Keightley and Pickering's (2006) assessment of the mnemonic potential of photography and phonography. Cultural accounts of memory are increasing to match the previous dominance of social accounts. Bal, Crewe and Spitzer (1999) offer a fascinating edited collection which foregrounds the reciprocal relationship between past and present.

CHAPTER 10

Engaging with History

Michael Pickering

Engaging with history is a popular experience. It is popular in the sense that it is widespread and has huge appeal. It involves a variety of activities that include visiting museums and heritage sites, watching history programmes on television, collecting antiques and compiling a family history. Over the past thirty years, the development of popular interest in the past, in these and many other ways, has grown up alongside the development in academic life of a sceptical questioning of the value of historical enquiry and a drastic suspicion about the very grounds on which history is represented. There is a tremendous irony in this, and not a little pathos, though saying that should not be taken as a plea to desist from questioning how the past is reconstructed or how historical knowledge is constituted in the public domain. Historical representations should always be subject to question, for political and ethical as well as epistemological reasons. The study of history is nothing without contestation and debate, the advancement of alternative sources and alternative interpretations, or critical assessment of the grounds on which it is based in any particular case. This is quite different to dismissing such study or rejecting the value of thinking about the past both in itself and in its relations with the present and the future.

Both popular culture and academic enquiry become etiolated without such thinking. Some of the most important work in cultural studies has been informed by thinking in historical terms, whether this has been manifest in tracing the lineaments of social criticism, the realisation of popular resistance and creativity in the past, the long-term linkages between media development, democracy and structures of power, the recurrent waves of social fears and anxieties among the middle classes, or the bearings that imperial social relations have had on the development of national identity. The necessary corollary of this is that cultural studies is weakened when it abandons such thinking, when it becomes fixated with stridently immediate concerns and insistently new

issues, in a faddishness and obsession with trend-spotting that runs the danger of mimicking what it attempts to track. The implication then seems to be that the past is over and done, severed of any connection with what is happening now. When 'now' becomes regnant, in any intellectual field, it ceases to command any viable resources for temporal reflexivity and is condemned to repeat the past. The vitality of cultural studies depends, in one key dimension of its development, on keeping the diverse interactions between 'then' and 'now' in continual and active view of each other.

This final chapter builds on the previous one by approaching history as both topic and tool. It conceives of history as a broad set of resources for studying everyday cultures in the past and as a broad set of techniques and strategies for thinking about historical experience and representation in the present. The two-way focus this involves is intended to address the ways in which history shapes and informs current cultural practices and formations, and the ways in which history is only accessible to us analytically through our cultural participations and understandings in the present. Its purpose is to suggest that engaging with history within cultural studies has two major strands: doing cultural history in a way that is informed by general theoretical and hermeneutical issues, including those informing cultural studies; and developing critical analysis of contemporary uses and manifestations of the past in contemporary culture, including media representations of the past and versions of the past in the vernacular traditions and conventions of everyday life. It may seem to some that only the second strand belongs properly in the domain of cultural studies, but my argument is that both strands are stronger for being intertwined. My own work has always moved between social and cultural history on the one hand, and media and cultural studies on the other, with the historical and contemporary forms of analysis informing and enriching each other. I cannot think of either without the other, or can do so only temporarily, when caught up in the coils of a particular task, so bringing cultural history and contemporary media/cultural studies into a closer intellectual relationship seems to me vital in developing a broad understanding of long-term cultural processes, the dynamics of cultural traditions, patterns of continuity along with structures of emergence and social change, over the whole modern period.

There are various methods you can adopt for engaging with the past through either of these strands, both in themselves and in the ways they relate to each other. There are also two particular pitfalls of interpretation and analysis which may arise through work in either strand. The first of these falls prey to an excessive insistence on historical difference. It is of course vital that this insistence is made, but not to the extent that what is specific to a particular period, its prevalent social conditions and lived qualities of experience and consciousness, is seen as wholly confined to that period. This is the pitfall of relativist particularism, and its weakness lies in being unable to negotiate historical continuities. The second pitfall is a reversal of the first. Absolutist presentism sees the past entirely through the lens of a current outlook and perspective. Its weakness lies in being unable to negotiate both historical continuities and historical change. It fails to register historical difference in anything other than the most superficial way and so is radically deficient in temporal reflexivity. This is to pose both pitfalls in the starkest and most extreme manner so that their less obvious manifestations can be readily identified and measured against them. The chapter will discuss what they involve in greater detail so that you can beware of them in your own work. Finally, I want to highlight the importance of two interdependent ways of engaging with the past.

When we embark on any historical research, the different methods we may pursue in building up evidence, putting it together into some reasonably coherent manner and making analytical sense of it all, are all time-consuming, involving many hours in the archives, for example, or days in the field interviewing informants in an oral history project. At first what you are studying historically may seem quite foreign, but gradually, as a result of these painstaking activities, you develop an understanding of what particular forms of past experience may have involved, and of how the evidence you have to hand in some way speaks to that experience. You may seem at times only to be hitting on the obvious, and at others to be struggling to grasp the historical sense of what you are studying, to get past what seems alien. In contrast to these times, there are moments of insight when you see the evidence anew, or realise that the evidence you are gathering reveals the character of historical experience in a radically different way. This can fire your imagination and make you feel that the meaning of the evidence is revealed in ways not possible before this point was reached. It seems that you have at last intensively recognised something you were searching for. These moments are unpredictable, and they depend on the long hours when you are studiously acquiring evidence and knowledge of your particular research topic. They are the basis for the moment when you reach a newly experienced depth of engagement with the evidence, which may involve deriving a contrary meaning to that which the evidence seems to assert. Such moments are not possible without the platform of knowledge you have laboriously assembled, whether through secondary or primary sources, but when they arrive they seem to give historical research its whole point and value. They illuminate understanding of the research material in both backwards and forwards directions.

REOPENING DIALOGUE

Working across the borderlands between history and cultural studies can be a frustrating experience. Many historians are hostile to cultural studies, and

many cultural studies scholars appear oblivious of the value of historical practice, historical understanding and historical perspectives on what they study.
This has led to history being sidelined in cultural studies for the past quarter
century. With their size presumably being a measure of their intended com-
prehensiveness, we may take two major collections of cultural studies as indicative of this. Toby Miller's (2001) blockbuster anthology, *Companion to Cultural
Studies*, omits history from the mix even though it runs to nearly 600 pages. An
earlier, equally gargantuan volume of proceedings from the 1990 Cultural
Studies conference in Urbana, Illinois, contained just one contribution from a
historian, Carolyn Steedman, who expressed uncertainty and doubt about why
cultural studies should want history at all:

> Will there be any room for detailed historical work; or are students of
> cultural studies bound to rely on grand schematic and secondary
> sweeps through time? Will there be any room for the historical case-
> study in its pedagogy? What good is it all to you, anyway? Perhaps no
> good at all . . . (Grossberg et al. 1992: 621)

This rather disillusioned answer to her own questions was made because the
dialogue that existed between historical practice and cultural studies in its early
formation had broken down.

There were various reasons for this, but the clash of approaches represented
by Edward Thompson's (1978) *The Poverty of Theory* and Richard Johnson's
(1978) neo-Althusserian critique of 'socialist-humanist history' contributed
much to the impasse, while later debates between historians and advocates of
poststructuralism served only to deepen it. Within cultural studies, as Tara
Brabazon (2005: 53) has put it, the historical clock stopped while the sociological and semiological watches 'continued to be wound, scrutinised and
updated'. The result has been debilitating on both sides, but particularly for
cultural studies, where one of its leading lights in the 1980s, mixing preten-
tiousness and absurdity in high degree, could write: 'We're on the road to
nowhere. All of us. There's nowhere else but here for us. No other time but
now' (Hebdige 1988: 239).

One of the sources of frustration in this impasse has been the failure of historians and cultural studies practitioners to learn from each other. The former
stand potentially to gain a firmer understanding of the need to conceptualise key
categories, to theorise major findings, and to develop an analytical framework
for the presentation of their evidence rather than supposing that such evidence
will speak for itself. The latter stand potentially to gain a firmer understanding
of the need to relate concepts, argument and theory to empirical evidence as a
means of validation and verification, to bring different sources and contrary evidence into confrontation, and perhaps most importantly of all, to develop a

sense of long-term continuities as well as of short-term changes. Ideologically, certain continuities are imagined or mythical, as in many nationalist histories, but these are quite different to similarities of response to, say, new forms of social encounter and relationship, or new media of communication and interchange, that can be traced across the past century and more. Exploring the past for a sense of connections of this kind enables us to draw creatively and reflexively on what the past has bequeathed, to discover what was different then and learn from that difference while also adapting and taking forward what can be gleaned across successive waves of social and cultural change. Close attention to contemporary issues, problems and struggles is not incompatible with historical awareness and imagination. They may productively inform each other.

Here is an example. In the early 1990s, an African-American man called Tyrone Brown was given a life sentence when he tested positive for marijuana. This was in violation of his ten-year probation for stealing two dollars from a man in Dallas. In changing the original sentence, the white judge commented: 'Good luck, Mr Brown', and the court-appointed defence lawyer failed to object. Tyrone Brown served seventeen years in prison before gaining his release. In reporting this long-overdue event, Dan Glaister wrote:

> The case became notorious after it emerged how lenient the same judge was with a well-connected white man who was given probation for murder. He repeatedly breached probation, including by using cocaine, but Judge Dean sent him to a private treatment centre rather than jail and gave him 'postcard' probation whereby he wrote to the court once a year. (*The Guardian*, 19 March 2007)

The gross disparity of treatment in these two cases may seem unusual, the fortuitous outcome of a racially biased judge, but it needs to be understood as a historical strand extending back across a long and troubled record of unequal penal treatment and racially structured discourse. This has recently been traced by Carol Stabile through its particular manifestation in US crime news. Both quantitatively and qualitatively, the contrasting media coverage given to black and white victims of crime in US culture has always been enormous. It extends back to the initial stages of North American press history in the early nineteenth century. Various white crimes, including even the horrific practice of lynching, have not only been ignored, dismissed or played down, but the far higher rate of white crime more generally has also been overlooked in favour of the exaggeration of black crime. The conventional emphasis in the narratives of US crime news has long been on the production of white fear. In this, the lines between victims, victimisers and protectors have been strictly regularised and patrolled, with blacks rarely assigned the status of victims but instead usually construed as innately criminal.

This is the enduring pattern of media reporting and representation historically analysed by Stabile. She also attends to the ways in which it intersected with gender ideology, for this added considerably to the white supremacist injustices suffered by African Americans, all the way from Jacksonian times to the contemporary period.[1] In the nineteenth century a mixture of gender ideology and racism underpinned the pathological othering of black women as including 'abnormal strength, aggressive sexuality, and manifestations of dysfunctional maternalism' (Stabile 2006: 5). Especially after the abolition of slavery and the introduction of post-bellum Jim Crow legislation, black masculinity became coded as inherently criminal because fears of race-mixing and miscegenation led to the ideological construction of a threatening, atavistic black menace forever poised to wreak havoc in heartland America, especially in relation to white womanhood (Tolnay and Beck 1995: 254). This stereotype swung to the opposite pole from pious Uncle Tomism and the stereotype of the happy-go-lucky darky. In the late nineteenth-, early twentieth-century period, it provided legitimation for intensified oppression and violence against African-American men. The forms these took were in some ways specific to that time, but long threads of continuity can clearly be traced from such stereotypical race/gender representations to what a Los Angeles police sergeant in the 1990s described as a white female highway patrol officer's 'fear of a Mandingo sexual encounter'.[2] It was this which offered the pretext for the beating and arrest of black motorist Rodney King, in a now notorious case that, following the acquittal of three police officers involved in the assault on King, led to the most serious urban disturbance and violence in the United States since the 1965 Watts uprising.

Stabile shows how, more than any other ethnic group – such as the Irish or the Chinese – over the course of US history, African Americans were depicted as criminals and villains in the discourse of crime news and reportage. The great value of her study lies in its demonstration of how a historical perspective can reveal the establishment, development and persistence of journalistic discourse over a long period of time. Such discourse has of course not been completely unchanging, but as Stabile notes, crime stories, 'more than other kinds of stories, conform to very traditional and rigid sets of criteria, perhaps because ideologies governing deviance are very slow to change' (2006: 9). By tracing how the racist construction of social deviance in the United States has developed such enduring and rigid criteria, Stabile raises awareness of the need to shift what she calls the logic of racialised androcentrism, which is the central theme of her book.

As this example suggests, the gulf that developed between history and cultural studies in the 1980s and 1990s was perhaps more evident in Britain, for over the past fifteen years or so, in the United States and elsewhere, important historical work has been done that has clearly been influenced by cultural studies. Stabile's

White Victims, Black Villains is just one recent example. The kind of detailed case study somewhat forlornly called for by Steedman is certainly in evidence, and is part of the general shift from social to cultural history in which reflexive attention to questions of sources and practices is much more to the fore. This is, of course, true of Steedman's own work, and it is not hard to find other instances of historical work, including some in Britain, that is informed by cultural studies and postcolonial studies, though never in hock to them. This is clearly the case with Catherine Hall's (2002) *Civilising Subjects*, the central project of which is to reconstruct the connected histories of colonisers and colonised in the British empire, and to analyse the unequal structures of power that affected both colony and metropole. The mutually constitutive relation between colonial periphery and imperial centre has been a key theme in both imperialist history and post-colonial studies since the late 1980s, but Catherine Hall is the first to explore this relation in such depth and detail. The importance of the book lies also in the time-span covered, for the period from 1830 to 1867 on which she concentrates saw a considerable shift in race-thinking in Britain, a hardening of attitude and disposition towards black people that marked the demise of abolitionism and the development of a new form of racism whose shadow has stretched across the intervening time between then and now.

Hall's approach to studying the relations of centre and periphery in empire is to examine the historical cross-over between Birmingham and Jamaica. In her introduction she explains how this approach had its origins in her own biography – in her Baptist family background, her marriage to Stuart Hall, whose own family background was in Jamaica, and their time living in Birmingham, where Stuart became director of the Centre for Contemporary Cultural Studies (now regrettably axed by the university in which it was housed). The book is an extended case study of these two places, exploring in particular the role of Birmingham's nonconformists in Jamaican affairs. As a result of her two-way attention, Hall is able to show how imperial culture was woven into the social life of Birmingham, and how race was lived at this local level during the second quarter of the nineteenth century. The activities of nonconformist missionaries were especially important in informing questions of race and empire in the town, and these are central to Hall's analysis. Throughout the book she is sharply attentive to the cross-overs between the different position-alities of gender and social class as well as ethnicity. Divisions between people and nations were extensively reworked through the discourses associated with these categories. They contributed enormously to how the English saw the rest of the world and how their own identities were formed. What emerged was a new grammar of difference that we have slowly been learning to unspeak in our own late-modern historical period.

The lives of those who forged the links between Birmingham and Jamaica form many of the strands in Hall's narrative, and are in part what makes the book so fascinating as we follow the interwoven currents of self-steered biographies and broader historical processes. The life of one man in particular, Edward John Eyre, recurs at different points, and is rightly central, for he was responsible for the brutal reprisals following the Morant Bay rebellion in 1865. Once the book is finished and closed, what remains is a profound sense of how the lives of particular individuals were deeply implicated in the sweeping historical canvas in which they were situated, and through which their subjectivities were formed. We are reminded of how the stories of lives are subject to the tides of hope and disillusionment, as is the stuff of history itself, but the achievement of the book rests as well in the ways it affirms the agency of colonised black people, their independence of thought and action, and resistance to being remade according to the lights of the variety of people involved in their colonisation.

Dismissing examples like this as historical writing that has no place in cultural studies work is not only to miss the purpose of interrogating connectedness across time in relation to the temporal specificities of the past, but also to fail in registering the value of past histories in present debates about identity, nation, ethnicity, cultural encounter and interaction. As well as being conditioned by prevailing structures of power, these are products of historical processes which ensure that continuities remain while also being part of social change. Methodologically, the politics of representation have always to be historicised, and not least in order to disrupt the ways in which such forms of representation as racial or gender stereotypes are naturalised or considered only as a matter of cognitive operation. Of course, the benefit of bringing historical case studies onto the stage of contemporary values and understandings does not rest there. Another example of such benefits lies in the power of the past to shock us into relativised awareness of what we may have come to accept as commonplace or taken-for-granted.

For example, today vast amounts of money are spent annually on advertising, people are bombarded with advertisements on a routine basis, and children take up advertising slogans as they once used to take up skipping rhymes in the playground. Our everyday lives are so permeated by advertising that few of us seek to question or challenge it. It seems an inevitable feature of our social experience, continually eroding the bonds of solidarity by bolstering the individualism of consumer culture. An appropriate historical perspective can dispel this assumption by showing us that, in both Europe and America, advertising only achieved significant ascendancy in the early twentieth century. More importantly, it has not always been accorded blanket acceptance as part of the fabric of everyday experience. In an important recent account, Inger Stole (2006) reminds us of how modern advertising in the USA met with fierce political opposition in the 1930s. A militant consumer movement in that decade condemned advertising for undermining people's ability to make informed and judicious choices in the market. Developing against a background that had seen the growth of a powerful corporate culture, it sought to transform advertising into a source of genuine product information. The hope was that advertising could be made to serve as an honest guide rather than seducing, manipulating and deceiving its public. When the movement became perceived as a major threat to advertising, the industry retaliated, using its leverage over the media to gain favourable treatment. The struggle was lost in 1938 with the passing of the Wheeler-Lea Amendment to the Federal Trade Commission Act, after which consumer activism was automatically the target for right-wing political attacks, but Stole argues that its importance remains undiminished by the intervening seventy years, for what consumer activists of the 1930s clearly understood is what has subsequently been forgotten.

This is that in a democratic society the place and purpose of advertising should be determined by the citizenry. Advertising becomes a pernicious influence for democracy when the media develop an economic dependence on advertising revenue. The defeat of the consumer activist movement in the 1930s meant that, contrary to its own democratic interests, advertising became naturalised in the United States, an unassailable cultural element of day-to-day experience. Stole tells an instructive story, not least because demands for advertising reform and regulative control over the advertising industry have never again been on the political agenda in North America. It is not simply a matter of lamenting a missed opportunity that could have brought about significant change in the influence and role of advertising in American popular culture, lamentable though that is. More significantly, by reminding us that pervasive advertising was not always sanctioned and accepted as an ineradicable feature of everyday culture, Stole demonstrates how the attempt to transform advertising content and practice in the 1930s continues to provide an example of what might still be done if, as she puts it, we can 'connect a past struggle with modern concerns and possibilities' (Stole 2006: xv). This would show that the struggle is not to be relegated to an unrecoverable past. It would show that it is not even over.

EXTENDING DIALOGUE

At the start of this chapter I warned against the methodological pitfall of using present values and standards to assess past practices and institutions. Avoiding and detecting this has long been a shibboleth among professional historians, and while some now find it too cut-and-dried, it continues to be applied, as for instance in John MacKenzie's indictment of the modern critique of Orientalism for having 'committed that most fundamental of historical sins, the reading back of contemporary attitudes and prejudices into historical periods'

(MacKenzie 1995: 214). Basing your whole methodological approach to studying and representing the past solely in this way is obviously able to achieve little
beyond the reinforcement of contemporary attitudes and prejudices and so
impoverish historical understanding, but at the same time it would be foolish
to believe that contemporary attitudes and prejudices can be utterly suspended
or considered to have no bearing at all on historical study and representation.
Empiricism of that kind exists at the opposite pole from the subjectivist
insistence on the unknowability of the past that is commonly struck today. Both
of these positions miss what is most valuable about engaging with history,
which is to bring its irrevocable otherness into encounter with the present in
order that we may better understand how things have changed and how we have
arrived historically within the present, how people in the past have responded
to historical processes in their own time, how historical difference can inform
the sense we have of our own historicity, and also how despite changed conditions and circumstances certain continuities endure across time.

   There is nothing value-free or disinterested in this, for historical analysis is
inevitably informed by contemporary assumptions and prejudices, values and
beliefs, but analysis is weak when it fails to challenge its own starting points and
initiating means of approach, and arrive at a different place from where it
began. That is why this chapter advocates bringing historical and cultural
analysis into conjunction. The principle underlying this is that these forms of
analysis are not necessarily at cross purposes but can be made to complement
each other even if, and perhaps especially if, they challenge each other and make
us rethink what the evidence can tell us and how we can understand it on the
one hand, and on the other how our concepts and theories are relative and have
limits in how they can be applied or what they can explain.

   This is quite different to saying that we can only understand the past
through contemporary perspectives. We cannot successfully oppose historical
objectivism simply by reversing it, which is the postmodernist strategy.
Ironically, such a move endorses the relentless presentism of history represented on television when its aim is to maximise audience levels and satisfy
advertisers, for then the emphasis falls on populist appeal rather than on engaging with the challenge of historical difference. It is vital that we insist on that
challenge in the interests of a broader and more complex account, not in the
interests of elevating academic historiography over and above popular
accounts, but in order to show that historical method is not simply driven by
contemporary concerns or imperatives. Yet that is only one step, and it is vital
we move beyond it. We do not do that by retreating into professional history as
the only abiding way of engaging with the past, or by using academically
accredited forms of history as a way of policing film or television versions of
history for their accuracy or veracity, for in thinking historically we need to
engage as well with popular experiences of pastness and understand how they

are constructed and negotiated. In this section I want to highlight two ways of beginning this task before returning to some of the methodological issues attendant on engaging with history.

According to a well-known saying, news is the first draft of history, one that is necessarily constructed in the heat of the moment, driven by the deadline, and subject to the editorial and institutional demands of the newspaper or broadcasting channel for which it is produced. The news is history written in a hurry. It is also produced without the benefit of hindsight. This is only an initial recognition, and we do not move much beyond it even when their conditions of production are taken into account in using news sources as one amongst others that are drawn on in compiling data for a historical study of a particular event, theme or period in the past. It is important that we also analyse the ways in which a topic, person, group or nation has been constructed and represented in news narratives and accounts in the past. Analysing the constitutive discourse in which such narratives and accounts are realised can show us how the meanings of history's first drafts have been negotiated for readers or viewers. So, for example, in a recent co-written textbook on methods in media and cultural analysis, I took two newspaper accounts of significant historical events and examined them in order to understand how the meaning and significance of those events was constructed immediately after their occurrence, in the heat of the historical moment.

The first of these involved an assassination attempt on the Iraqi premier, General Abdul Karim Kassem, as it was reported on the front page of the *Daily Mail* for 8 October 1959. The analysis of this attended closely to the key themes and linguistic structure of the report, along with all the various component parts of the story, and as a result was able to show that even the smallest syntactical devices can contribute significantly to the meaning of the story as it was constructed at the time. In this case the use of inverted commas around certain words cast doubt on the veracity of the claims contained in these words.[3] Following this event, claims had been made inside Iraq that the assassination attempt was the result of a traitorous conspiracy, and that Kassem had been central to the liberation of the country. These claims were challenged, perhaps even falsified, by the inverted commas placed around the key words cited in the report: 'conspiracy' and liberated'. Other words used in the subheadings of the report were not framed by inverted commas, and this seemed to create the opposite effect of credibility for warnings about 'serious trouble', 'dangerous forces', and 'seething unrest'. The truth value of these descriptive phrases was certainly far higher than that associated with the claims of political conspiracy and national liberation. The presence or absence of inverted commas not only provided important cues to the reader about the meanings to be taken from the story, but also reinforced the key Orientalist thread running through the story, which is that Iraq at that time was in a volatile and highly unstable state and that the main cause of this was a tyrannical leader. Plus ça change. The story as a whole in its first drafting of history can be seen to have many contemporary resonances in the way events and conditions in Iraq and the Middle East are reported. Among other things, its connectedness with the present is revealed in the name of one of the men involved in the attempted assassination – one Saddam Hussein.

The same lexical markers were used in the *Daily Mirror's* front-page reporting of the shooting of a student by National Guardsmen at Kent State University in Ohio in May 1970 (see edition for 5 May 1970). The banner headline for this story was 'Death of a "Campus Bum"'. Analysis of this story was primarily designed to unpack the relationship between the news text and its accompanying photograph of the dead student. What this revealed was that the story used, in a highly sarcastic way, President Nixon's reference to student protesters as 'bums' who should remember that that they are 'the luckiest people in the world', for one of these 'lucky people' lay dead on the ground in the photo-image that dominated the front page of the newspaper. The use of inverted commas in the lead headline set off the key interpretive line taken throughout the report, with the negative associations that still accrued to the epithet 'bum', as these had been acquired in relation to such figures as unemployed hoboes and railroad tramps in the economic depression of the 1930s, being turned against Nixon's response to student protests against the war in Vietnam and Cambodia. The tragic deaths of the students at Kent State University have subsequently become etched in collective memory in the United States. Despite this it has always been denied that there was any order given to commence the shootings. They were accidental, the unfortunate result of panic among the assembled troops. Although eight guardsmen were indicted, no one has ever been prosecuted.[4]

These cases are intended here simply as illustrations of what can be done in the interrogation of sources and how these seem to have provided key lines of interpretation in public understanding and collective memory. There is, of course, much else involved in such interrogation and the kinds of textual analysis involved are themselves subject to certain methodological limitations that need to be taken into account and compensated for by other accompanying methods and attendant processes of contextualisation.[5] Close readings of news as historical sources can nevertheless prove very revealing even if they are just one part of an overall approach, not only for their temporally immediate treatment of a historical event, but also because they afford an opportunity to assess changes and continuities in both broadsheet and tabloid journalism. Change in journalistic discourse is not as rapid as is often thought. The conventions of such discourse take time to become conventional. The textual codes and conventions of journalism are the result of a gradual process of development, with change tending to occur slowly and over time, and the continuities remaining far more apparent. This is, of course, in direct contrast to journalism's more usual pattern, with each day's news bringing a fresh tide of stories and continually erasing those that had broken on the shore of the previous day. It is a pattern of eternal evanescence, and historical knowledge is our only significant counter to it.

This kind of work can be extended to other sources such as newspaper photographs and documentary footage, drawing on other analytical tools from semiotics and film studies. A fine example is Patrizia Di Bello's analysis of two nineteenth-century images of the same subject: one is a wood engraving of Queen Victoria and Princess Beatrice, published on the front cover of the *Lady's Newspaper and Pictorial Times* on 14 March 1863, and the photographic carte-de-visite that was almost certainly its original, taken by Chèmar Freres in Brussels. In both images Princess Beatrice is seated on her mother's knee. One of the Queen's arms encircles her daughter's waist and clutches the girl's dress with her hand. The Queen's other hand touches her daughter's as they both look down at an oval framed photograph. The picture is that of Prince Albert, who died in 1861. The image is remarkable for its intensely private moment produced for public consumption, its strategy of public appearance as popular representation, and its manifestation of an emergent celebrity culture. The royals' downward gaze towards the photograph of a dead husband and father was matched by the downward gaze of Her Majesty's subjects, the ordinary readers of an illustrated magazine, viewing this performance of private mourning via a public mode of looking.

Di Bello shows how both moments complement each other compositionally through a series of interrelated curves which encompass the oval frame of the photograph, the hands of the child holding it, the hands of the Queen holding her daughter, the shapes of the Queen's headdress and the princess's headband, the rounds of their eyelids as they look downwards at the photograph, the slopes of their arms, shoulders and dresses, and beyond the image itself, the hands of the viewer (also female) holding the magazine which has used the image on its front page as a major selling point.

What unites this series is touch just as much as sight: the hands touching the photograph, the mother's hand touching her daughter's, and the reader's touching the physical artifact that reproduces the image. This physical condition of engagement with photographs is often overlooked, but the engagement is always as much tactile as visual and, unlike a painting, the photograph's availability to being handled is vital in its role as a vehicle of interpersonal remembering. Di Bello reminds us that in this instance it is a gendered touch that is involved. She relates this to the qualities of affective power that became associated with women's touch in the nineteenth century. Such power was held to be transformative, personalising increasingly factory-made products valued by price into signs of security, gentility and care valued by use. In this the Queen is shown as exemplary – 'not only of widowhood or motherhood, but also of feminine ways of looking at photographic images: closely, with a gaze defined by her gender and by her touch rather than by the realism of the image or by the value of the photographer' (Di Bello 2005: 10). Suggestively, Di Bello develops out of this the sense of 'specifically feminine ways of using mechanically produced and reproduced images'. Working through them was a tactile female gaze quite different to the distancing, mastering effect of the male gaze. The dynamics of vision and touch involved in this produced sentimental meanings, sensations, fantasies and pleasures that were constructed as feminine, 'and thoroughly modern' (2005: 15).

Historians have for a long time treated photographic images in a highly naïve way, assuming them to provide transparent windows into past scenes and events, so merely including them with little explanatory comment as illustrations in written accounts. Work on the realist visual image in film and media studies has begun to help historians move beyond this limited conception of such images. It is certainly now rather uncommon to find a historian approaching past photographs without some awareness of the need to understand how they mediate whatever it is they depict. This brings me to the second approach to popular engagements with the past which I want to outline, for it may include not only sources such as newspaper stories or photographic images but also fictional treatments of past personages, events and periods. Engaging with history here means examining media representations of the past, and while these may involve historical sources, attention generally moves in either one of two ways.

One approach to such research involves focusing on how media representations of the past, in say historical costume drama or Hollywood films, construct mythical notions of national lineage, foster conservative forms of social nostalgia, or encourage a particular view of history such as one based on an individualist interpretation of past changes and developments. The research is intended to reach a critical outcome since it is usually based on political opposition to the limitations of the material or the motivations underlying it. Another approach is to concentrate equally if not more on how people take up, assimilate and derive meaning and value from media representations of the past without any prior assumption that these representations will have a reactionary or diminishing effect. Much important work has followed the first approach, as for instance in exploring whether media versions of past events and episodes side with the structurally powerful or those in social locations habitual to exploitation, subjugation or oppression. The second approach may yield data that confirms such divisions, but it is open to what it may find, and so may discover forms of group-based resistance or lines of popular interpretation that run across the ideological grain of the media products consumed, as, for instance, with women's consumption of historical romance, vernacular parodies of media forms and figures, or the uses made of popular music from the past among particular social groups.

Oral histories of particular social groups, or of historical themes such as childhood or sex education, have often been associated with popular radicalism and applied more to subordinated or marginalised social groups either because these have been written out of history in the upper case, or hidden from it because of its assumptions of what is historically of significance and value. This has opened up history considerably and to some extent democratised it, producing many valuable accounts that would otherwise have gone unmade and unheard, but oral history is certainly not confined to any particular research objectives and can be very widely adopted. One particular line of research using oral history techniques is to investigate media consumption among previous generations using key social categories such as gender, ethnicity and social class as the main differentiating variables in the fieldwork.[6] All such work of course draws on people's store of memory and skills in recalling and narrating the past. They are closely related to the forms of research discussed in the previous chapter in that they either intersect with them or valuably complement them. Together they can form a considerable battery of research approaches and techniques for building up knowledge of how both media and vernacular representations of the past constitute cultural resources and public repertoires for engaging with history, not least because this kind of knowledge cannot be derived from official archives or is only available in certain limited forms through, say, county record offices or libraries where media documents and past media output may be stored.

A good deal of the work on film and television history is based on analysis of the texts that are involved. There are various methods that have been drawn on in this, such as those taken from structuralism, semiotics or approaches to the study of discourse, but the work itself has in many ways been impelled by the imperatively felt need to critique the object of study, and so dispel the negative psychological and social consequences of 'master narratives' or 'dominant ideologies' that the analysis was designed to expose. Such critique has often been valuable and incisive, especially when revealing the support for the ideological status quo contingent upon the present-centredness of historical media representations, but too often it has assumed these negative consequences on the basis of textual analysis unaccompanied by any other sustained research techniques. It has also been part of the legacy of melancholia involved in twentieth-century mass culture criticism. Questions of objectivity, authenticity, authority lay just beneath the surface, if not fully in view. These presupposed a clear demarcation between professional and popular histories. This has itself now become regarded with suspicion, partly because professional historians do not and cannot occupy a value-neutral or atemporal standpoint, and partly because the best of popular histories, by the way they reconstruct the past or stimulate the historical imagination, belie the case for authentic/inauthentic distinctions between academic and popular forms.

MAINTAINING DIALOGUE

We study the past in a radically altered fashion to the ways in which it was lived, for in looking back we select particular features from the past and subject them to scrutiny from a changed perspective. Our own historicity ensures that we experience and understand the past differently to the way it was historically experienced and understood. But it is also because we are historical that we can appreciate how others in the past have been historically formed and conditioned, and so gain some measure of the historical character of their experience, mentality and identity, with the scope of that measure marking out and giving identity to the generic distinction between historical experience and historical understanding as well as the inevitable distance between 'then' and 'now'. This distinction explains why over time our ways of engaging with history do not remain the same. Historical accounts and representations are continually subject to challenge and revision because of changes in historicities and historical variations of outlook and perspective. Today no one writes like Gibbon or Macaulay. Today we have a greatly expanded sense of what historical study embraces compared with a century ago, with the recognition that history is ordinary having become widespread. Along with this, research methods for engaging with historical sources and historical representations also change, so that today gaps in what can be gathered from archival repositories may be filled by oral history research or the analysis of photographic images from the past.

When we analyse a cultural text, form or mode of performance and attempt to understand it historically, we may move in two different but complementary ways. We can examine its particular conventions of language, expression and action, its structuring codes and stylistic features, which may be identified readily enough with a particular historical period. We can also attend to historical conditions and circumstances to see how the cultural text, form or mode of performance relates to them. The difficulties of reconciling these two methods are considerable, but the effort at integration is always preferable to its alternatives: ahistorical textualism and factualist objectivism. These alternatives fail to attend either to textual specificities or to historically specific cultural dynamics. They do not deliver any developed sense of the ways in which cultural texts or forms have been put together, experienced and participated in, as well as being actively selected and identified with as appropriate to a particular historical experience.

In historical cultural studies, you need to look at the distinctions and relations between social experience and structures of symbolic exchange without attempting to bring them into any straightforward or fixed correspondence, either at a particular time, or over the course of time as certain forms are adopted, carried forward and temporally revalidated, or subsequently rediscovered and seen in a different light. This is to come again, from a particular angle, at the sense of history as never finished, never over, always in a certain pattern of movement in relation to the present, and always contestable in how it is interpreted and understood. The past is always a produced past and always, historically, in production.

As we try to keep such considerations in mind, we have to strive to reestablish the connections that have become lost, and on the basis of the specific materials we gather and the methods we adopt in order to do this, somehow imagine our way back into the broader pattern of once-lived experience to which they relate. This is central to historical hermeneutics, 'to make one's own what was initially alien' when we first encountered it (Ricoeur 1981: 185). This involves moving with what Hans-Georg Gadamer calls 'effective-historical consciousness', which recognises the contingency of our own cultural and temporal location, and bringing this into confrontation with different historical horizons, always bearing in mind that the horizon is both 'something into which we move and which moves with us' (Gadamer 1996: 304). Yet making your own what is initially alien is not at all straightforward, especially where your own values and principles are involved. These may seem to create difficult, if not insuperable obstacles to negotiating the cultural horizons of the past, and to keeping open the dialogue between past and present that is vital for engaging with history and thinking historically. In drawing towards a conclusion, I want briefly to recount what this involved for me in a research project that has recently come to fruition (Pickering 2008). This project involved trying to make analytical sense of the long cultural tradition in Britain of blackface minstrelsy.

This tradition lasted from the early nineteenth to the late twentieth century, and did so in a sustained though continually modifying process as it adapted to new media and new cultural forms. It involved white people, usually but not invariably men, blacking their faces in grotesque 'nigger' style and wearing costumes supposedly characteristic of the African-American plantation hand or urban dandy. Either as solo acts or more usually in minstrel ensembles, the make-up and costumes served as the vehicle for a distinct form of popular entertainment involving a broad range of acts amongst which comedy and sentimentalism were highlighted. The minstrel show produced and disseminated a variety of racist stereotypes. These were integral to the songs, sketches, jokes and dances which all formed part of blackface acts and shows.

There were various difficulties in trying to develop a historical cultural analysis of this particular cultural form. Most people in cultural studies who study popular music, and even most historians of popular music, choose to focus on the kinds of music they themselves like and find appealing. The opposite was true for me in studying blackface songs and acts. Initially the material felt very alien, and at times quite repellent in its racist representations and values. Overcoming this hurdle was not confined to sitting at my desk and thinking about it, for I had also to handle the embarrassment of talking about my object of research in the many archives and libraries across the country where I gathered my material. This was research that was decidedly uncool. In the book that eventually got written, I doubt whether I ever fully overcame its alien qualities for me. I certainly have not made this entertainment form 'my own', but it does, I think, represent the outcome of trying to understand the popular attraction and appeal of blackface minstrelsy across the different generations who participated in it as a cultural tradition. Minstrel acts and shows were patronised by men, women and children of all social classes. Analysing what they took from it had to account for its appeal across particular cultural dispositions, sensibilities and outlooks, how it fed into and influenced historically developing forms of racism, social evolutionism and imperialist values, and how in Britain it developed its own distinctive features that were part of a broader popular culture and, in a number of significant ways, at variance with the minstrel show's North American counterpart. But most of all, researching and writing the book involved not falling prey to the temptation of smug condemnation.

Such condemnation had been my starting point, and it was this that made the cultural form so alien. It took some while to accept that little was to be gained by seeing it entirely through my own values, never mind my own preferences and tastes. I could not wish these away, nor would I have wanted to. The research was hardly intended to produce an endorsement, much less a vindication of the blackface phenomenon. So I had to find a way of working with my own values while also seeking to develop a historical understanding of British minstrelsy's huge popular appeal. The task was to explain why there was an abiding need for such a demeaning form of popular music and entertainment, based as it was on a hugely derogatory, generalised view of black people and black cultural achievements. It was only gradually that I began to appreciate British minstrelsy as a multi-faceted musical and theatrical enterprise that could not be reduced to any single or unitary meaning. Its racism was central, and this at times appeared to be the source for such a meaning, but it became clear that minstrelsy would not have maintained such long-lasting popularity if all it had served was a deep-seated belief in white racial superiority. Along with its racist stereotyping, its historical significance derived from the cultural permit it gave to otherwise unavailable versions of licence, display and release. Beginning to understand it in that way was a breakthrough. It meant arriving at one of the points mentioned in the preface to this chapter where what is being studied becomes illuminated in quite a different way to how I first understood it, enabling me to take the analysis forward and considerably expand its scope.

Negotiating the problem of cross-historical response could therefore only be managed by learning the trick of avoiding both present-centred anachronism and its antithesis, the convenient distancing across time of relativist particularism. These are two sides of the same coin, for they entail a view of the past as chronically different or chronically the same as our own historical world. My own affiliations and values had to be the starting-point for the research, but could not be entirely bound by them because this would mean that the research would simply have ended up confirming them. This would have entailed failing to engage with some of the key issues in the circuit of historical hermeneutics. These include trying to avoid the twin pitfalls of anachronism and relativism, both of which undermine the task of historical understanding. The point of developing such an understanding of blackface minstrelsy in Britain – and in the process trying to explain its wide and lasting appeal in musical and theatrical forms which were based on that appeal – is to comprehensively establish the case for such forms never being repeated or, when they do seem to be appearing once again, of having to hand ways of resisting and countering them. In the end that may be its only lasting value. The real benefit of hindsight lies in not repeating the past.

KEY POINTS: SUMMARY

- The chapter argues that engaging with history should be a key aspect of doing cultural studies, and vice versa.
- One of the benefits of this would be the avoidance of myopic forms of presentism and particularism.
- Two broad approaches to realigning history and cultural studies were advocated: first, through bringing historical awareness more fully into the analysis of contemporary cultural forms and practices; and second, through applying cultural analysis of various kinds to media representations of history, including news for its first drafts of history.
- Such alignment would also be facilitated by the closer engagement of professional historians with popular experiences of the past and audience negotiations of media representations of the past.
- The relationship between contemporary values and researching the past was outlined; how such values methodologically affect historical practice was discussed via a specific example.
- While it is always wise to think critically about the grounds on which any form of historical analysis or representation is made, it is also wise always to historicise.

FURTHER READING

There are few books that deal with relations between history and cultural studies, but see Steinberg (1996); Pickering (1997); Brabazon (2005). I have tried to employ a historical approach in reconceiving stereotyping theory: see Pickering (2001). Work on media representations of history is steadily growing and the following are representative recent examples of this branch of study: Landy (2001); Edgerton and Rollins (2001); Roberts and Taylor (2001); Higson (2001, 2003); Edensor (2002: ch. 5 on the film *Braveheart*); Gillett (2003); Voigts-Virchow (2004); Rosenstone (2006); and *European Journal of Cultural Studies*, 10: 1, February 2007: special issue on Televising History. Some titles relating to historical hermeneutics include Palmer (1969); Heidegger (1973); Ricoeur (1981, 2004b); Warnke (1987); Gadamer (1996); Pickering (1999, 2004). On cultural history, see Chartier (1988); Hunt (1989); Burke (1997). Jordanova (2000) and Black and MacRaild (2000) provide useful introductions to historical method; Munslow (2003) surveys new approaches to history, and Steedman (1992, 2001, 2005) offers valuable reflections on historical research and writing.

NOTES

1. Stabile (2006: 1) opens her account with the case of Jeremy Strohmeyer, an eighteen-year-old white man who in 1997 raped and strangled a seven-year-old African-American girl in a women's bathroom. Needless to say, the murderer in this case did not become the subject of 'endless debate about a potentially violent and psychotic white culture'.
2. This was a reference to the 1975 film *Mandingo* in which a black slave burns down a plantation and escapes with a southern blonde bombshell (Stabile 2006: 169).
3. These are sometimes referred to as 'scare quotes' in order to deter readers from naïve assumptions about their meaning. Cultural studies writings are knowingly replete with them.
4. In the light of history, as the saying has it, the *Daily Mirror's* sceptical reporting of the event and Nixon's scant regard for dissent and freedom of expression appears to have been vindicated, for there has recently been discovered in a Yale University archive a thirty-seven-year-old audio recording of the command to fire. The recording was made by a student who placed a reel-to-reel tape recorder on the windowsill of his dorm room overlooking the protests (see *The Guardian*, 2 May 2007).
5. See Deacon et al. 2007: 170–92, 215–25 for further detail associated with the analysis of these two historical texts and an outline of the limitations of this form of analysis.

6. On the BSc in Media and Communication Studies in the Department of Social Sciences at Loughborough University, we annually engage students in a research project of this kind (see Deacon et al. 2007: ch. 12 for a detailed guide to what is involved in this project).

Bibliography

Abolafia, M. (1996) *Making Markets: Opportunism and Restraint on Wall Street*, Cambridge, MA: Harvard University Press.

Alasuutari, P. (1995) *Researching Culture: Qualitative Method and Cultural Studies*, London: Sage.

Alasuutari, P. (1999) 'Introduction: Three Phases of Reception Studies', in P. Alasuutari (ed.), *Rethinking the Media Audience: The New Agenda*, London: Sage.

Ang, I. (1985) *Watching Dallas: Soap Opera and the Melodramatic Imagination*, London: Methuen.

Ang, I. (1996) 'Culture and Communication: Towards an Ethnographic Critique of Media Consumption in the Transnational Media System', in J. Storey (ed.), *What is Cultural Studies? A Reader*, London: Arnold.

Angrosino, M. V. (2002) *Doing Cultural Anthropology: Projects for Ethnographic Data Collection*, Prospect Heights: Waveland Press.

Appadurai, A. (1996) *Modernity at Large*, Minneapolis: University of Minnesota Press.

Attwood, F. (2002) 'Reading Porn: The Paradigm Shift in Pornography Research', *Sexualities* 5: 1, 91–119.

Bagdikian, B. (2004) *The Media Monopoly*, Boston: Beacon Press.

Bal, M., Crewe, J. and Spitzer, L. (eds) (1999) *Acts of Memory: Cultural Recall in the Present*, Hanover, NH: Dartmouth College.

Banks, M. (2001) *Visual Methods in Social Research*, London: Sage.

Barbash, I. and Taylor, L. (1997) *Cross-Cultural Filmmaking: A Handbook for Making Documentary and Ethnographic Films and Video*, London: University of California Press.

Barker, C. and Galasiński, D. (2001) *Cultural Studies and Discourse Analysis: A Dialogue on Language and Identity*, London: Sage.

Barker, M. (1998) 'Film Audience Research: Making A Virtue Out Of Necessity, *IRIS (French/American Film Journal)* 26, 131–48.

Barker, M. (2003) 'Assessing the "Quality" in Qualitative Research: The Case of Text-Audience Relations', *European Journal of Communication* 18: 3, 315–35.

Barker, M. (with Austin, T.) (2000) *From Antz to Titanic: Reinventing Film Analysis*, London: Pluto Press.

Barker, M. and Brooks, K. (1998) *Knowing Audiences: Judge Dredd, its Friends, Fans and Foes*, Luton: University of Luton Press.

Barker, M. and Mathijs, E. (eds) (2007) *Watching the Lord of the Rings: Tolkien's World Audiences*, New York: Peter Lang.

Barthes, R. (1972) *Mythologies*, London: Cape.

Baym, N. (2003) 'Tune into Tomorrow' in Nightingale, V. and Ross, K. (eds), *Critical Readings: Media and Audiences*, Maidenhead and New York: Open University Press, pp. 236–51.

Beauvoir, S. de (1984) *The Second Sex*, Harmondsworth: Penguin.

Becker, H. S. and Geer, B. (1972) 'Participant Observation and Interviewing: A Comparison', in Manis, J. G. and Meltzer, B. N. (eds), *Symbolic Interaction: A Reader in Social Psychology*, Boston: Allyn and Bacon, pp. 102–12.

Belenky, M., Clinchy, B., Goldberger, N. and Tarule, J. (1986) *Women's Ways of Knowing*, New York: Basic Books.

Bennett, T. (1992) 'Putting Policy into Cultural Studies', in Grossberg, L., Nelson, C. and Treichler, P. (eds), *Cultural Studies*, London and New York: Routledge, pp. 23–37.

Berger, A. (1997) *Narratives in Popular Culture, Media and Everyday Life*, London: Sage.

Berger, J. (1992) *About Looking*, New York: Vintage.

Berlant, L. (2000) 'The Subject of True Feeling: Pain, Privacy and Politics', in Ahmed, S., Kilby, J., Lury, C., McNeil, M. and Skeggs, B., *Transformations: Thinking Through Feminism*, London: Routledge.

Bernard, R. H. (2002) *Research Methods in Anthropology: Qualitative and Quantitative Methods*, Walnut Creek: AltaMira Press.

Bertaux, D. (1981) *Biography and Society*, London: Sage.

Biella, P., Changon, N. and Seaman, G. (1997) *Yanomamö Interactive: The Ax Fight* (book and CD ROM), Wadsworth: Thompson Learning.

Billig, M. and Schlegoff, E. A. (1999) 'Critical Discourse Analysis and Conversation Analysis: An Exchange', *Discourse and Society* 10: 4, 543–82.

Bird, E. S. (2003) 'News We Can Use: an Audience Perspective on the Tabloidisation of News in the United States', in Nightingale, V. and Ross, K. (eds), *Critical Readings: Media and Audiences*, Maidenhead and New York: Open University Press, pp. 65–86.

Black, J. and MacRaild, D. (2000) *Studying History*, Basingstoke and London: Macmillan.

Bloor, M., Frankland, J., Thomas, M. and Robson, K. (2001) *Focus Groups in Social Research*, London: Sage.

Bloustein, G. (2003) *Girlmaking: A Cross-Cultural Ethnography on the Process of Growing Up Female*, New York: Berghahn Books.

Bly, R. (1991) *Iron John*, Shaftesbury: Element.

Born, G. (2004) *Uncertain Vision: Birt, Dyke and the Reinvention of the BBC*, London: Secker and Warburg.

Brabazon, T. (2005) *From Revolution to Revelation: Generation X, Popular Memory and Cultural Studies*, Aldershot, UK and Burlington, VT: Ashgate.

Bruner, E. (1986) 'Experience and its Expressions', in Turner, V. and Brunner, E. (eds), *The Anthropology of Experience*, Urbana: University of Illinois Press.

Bryman, A. (1992) *Quantity and Quality in Social Research*, London: Routledge.

Bryman, A. (2006) 'Paradigm Peace and the Implications for Quality', *International Journal of Social Research Methodology* 9: 2, 111–26.

Bryman, A. and Cramer, D. (2005) *Quantitative Data Analysis with SPSS 12 and 13: A Guide for Social Scientists*, Hove: Routledge.

Burgelin, O. (1968) 'Structural Analysis of Mass Communications', in McQuail, D. (ed.), *Sociology of Mass Communications*, Harmondsworth: Penguin.

Burke, P. (1997) *Varieties of Cultural History*, Oxford: Polity.

Burlein, A. (1999) 'Countermemory on the Right: The Case of Focus on the Family', in Bal, M., Crewe, J. and Spitzer, L. (eds), *Acts of Memory: Cultural Recall in the Present*, Hanover, NH and London: University Press of New England.

Burman, E. and Parker, I. (1993) *Discourse Analytic Research: Repertoires and Readings of Texts in Action*, London: Routledge.

Burton, F. and Carlen, P. (1979) *Official Discourse: Discourse Analysis, Government Publications, Ideology and the State*, London: Routledge.

Cardozo, H. (1937) *March of a Nation*, London: The Right Book Club.

Carey, J. (1985) *Communication as Culture: Essays on Media and Society*, Boston: Unwin Hyman.

Caygill, H. (1998) *Walter Benjamin: The Colour of Experience*, London and New York: Routledge.

Cesar, J. (1992) *Walter Benjamin on Experience and History*, San Francisco: Mellen Research University Press.

Chamberlayne, P., Bornat, J. and Wengraf, T. (2000) *The Turn to Biographical Methods in the Social Sciences*, London: Routledge.

Chaplin, E. (1994) *Sociology and Visual Representations*, London: Routledge.

Chartier, R. (1988) *Cultural History*, Cambridge: Cambridge University Press.

Christopherson, S. and Storper, M. (1986) 'The City as Studio, the World as Back Lot: The Impact of Vertical Disintegration on the Location of the Motion Picture Industry', in *Environment and Planning D: Society and Space*, vol. 4.

Clifford, J. and Marcus, G. E. (1986) *Writing Culture*, Berkeley, Los Angeles and London: University of California Press.

Collini, S. (1999) *English Pasts: Essays in History and Culture*, Oxford and New York: Oxford University Press.

Collins, C. (1996) 'To Concede or Contest?', in Barker, C. and Kennedy, P. (eds), *To Make Another World: Studies in Protest and Collective Action*, Aldershot, UK: Avebury.

Coolidge, F. (2006) *Statistics: A Gentle Introduction*, London: Sage.

Cook, J. and Fonow, M. (1986) 'Knowledge and Women's Interests: Issues of Epistemology and Methodology in Feminist Sociological Research', *Sociological Inquiry* 56: 4, 2–29.

Coover, R. (2003) *Cultures in Webs* CD ROM, Watertown: Eastgate Systems.

Cowlishaw, G. (2007) 'Changing our minds', PDF available at http://www.hss.uts.edu.au/conferences/ethnography/gillian-cowlishaw-intro.pdf (accessed 22 May 2007).

Crawford, J., Kippax, S., Onyx, J., Gault, U. and Benton, P. (1992) *Emotion and Gender: Constructing Meaning from Memory*, London: Sage.

Crawford, P. I. and Postma, M. (eds) (2006) *Reflecting Visual Ethnography*, Leiden and Højberg: CNWS Publications and Intervention Press.

Critcher, C. (2003) *Moral Panics and the Media*, Buckingham: Open University Press.

Crotty, M. (1998) *Foundations of Social Research: Meaning and Perspective in the Research Process*, St Leonards, NSW: Sage.

Curran, J. (1978) 'Advertising and the Press', in Curran, J. (ed.), *The British Press: A Manifesto*, London: MacMillan.

Curran, J. and Seaton, J. (2003) *Power Without Responsibility*, London: Routledge.

Czarniawska, B. (2004) *Narratives in Social Science Research*, London: Sage.

D'Acci, J. (1994) *Defining Women*, Chapel Hill: University of North Carolina.

Davies, M. M. (2004) 'Micky and Mr Gumpy: the Global and the Universal in Children's Media', *European Journal of Cultural Studies* 7: 4, 425–40.

Davis, A. (2002) *Public Relations Democracy: Public Relations, Politics and the Mass Media in Britain*, Manchester: Manchester University Press.

Davis, A. (2007) *The Mediation of Power: A Critical Introduction*, London: Routledge.

Deacon, D., Bryman, A. and Fenton, N. (1998) 'Collision or Collusion: A Discussion and Case Study of the Unplanned Triangulation of Quantitative and Qualitative Research Methods', *International Journal of Social Research Methodology* 1: 1, 47–63.

Deacon, D. and Golding, P. (1994) *Taxation and Representation*, London: John Libbey Press.

Deacon, D., Pickering, M., Golding, P. and Murdock, G. (2007) *Researching Communications: A Practical Guide to Methods in Media and Cultural Analysis*, London: Hodder Arnold.

Desjarlais, R. (2003) *Sensory Biographies: Lives and Death among Nepal's Yolmo Buddhists*, London: University of California Press.

Dewey, J. (1980) *Art as Experience*, New York: Perigee (first published 1934).

Di Bello, P. (2005) 'Vision and Touch: Photography and Women's Popular Culture in the Nineteenth Century', in Toulmin, V. and Popple, S. (eds), *Visual Delights Two: Exhibition and Reception*, Eastleigh, UK: John Libbey.

Downing, J. (1984) *Radical Media*, Boston: South End Press.

Doyle, G. (2002) *Media Ownership: The Economics and Politics of Convergence and Concentration in the UK and European Media*, London: Sage.

Drackle, D. (2004) 'Introduction', in Edgar, I., *Guide to Imagework: Imagination-based Research Methods*, London and New York: Routledge.

Du Gay, P. (ed.) (1997) *Production of Culture/Cultures of Production*, London: Sage/Open University Press.

Du Gay, P., Hall, S., James, L., Mackay, H. and Negus, K. (1997) *Doing Cultural Studies: The Story of the Sony Walkman*, London: Sage/Open University Press.

During, S. (2005) *Cultural Studies: A Critical Introduction*, Abingdon: Routledge.

Dyer, R. (1982) *Only Entertainment*, London: Routledge.

Eco, U. (1992) (with Rorty, R., Culler, J. and Brooke-Rose, C., ed. Collini, S.) *Interpretation and Overinterpretation*, Cambridge: Cambridge University Press.

Edensor, T. (2002) *National Identity, Popular Culture and Everyday Life*, Oxford and New York: Berg.

Edgar, I. (2004) *Guide to Imagework: Imagination-based Research Methods*, London and New York: Routledge.

Edgerton, G. R. and Rollins, P. C. (eds) (2001) *Television Histories*, Lexington: University Press of Kentucky.

Edwards, D. and Potter, J. (1992) *Discursive Psychology*, London: Sage.

Ericson, R. V., Baranek, P. M. and Chan, J. B. L. (1989) *Negotiating Control: A Study of News Sources*, Milton Keynes: Open University Press.

Eskin, B. (2002) *A Life in Pieces*, London: Aurum Press.

Evans, J. and Hall, S. (1999) 'What is Visual Culture', in Evans, J. and Hall, S. (eds), *Visual Culture: The Reader*, London: Sage and the Open University.

Ewick, P. and Silbey, S. (1995) 'Subversive Stories and Hegemonic Tales: Toward a Sociology of Narrative', *Law and Society Review* 29: 2, 197–226.

Fairclough, N. (1992) *Discourse and Social Change*, Cambridge: Polity Press.

Fairclough, N. (1995) *Media Discourse*, London: Arnold.

Feld, S. (2003) 'Introduction', in Feld, S. (ed.), *Cine-Ethnography Jean Rouch*, Minneapolis and London: University of Minnesota Press.

Ferguson, M. and Golding, P. (eds) (1997) *Cultural Studies in Question*, London, New York and New Delhi: Sage.

Fielding, J. and Gilbert, N. (2006) *Understanding Social Statistics*, London: Sage.

Fiske, J. (1996) 'British Cultural Studies and Television', in Storey, J. (ed.), *What is Cultural Studies? A Reader*, London: Arnold.

Fiske, J. and Hartley, J. (1978) *Reading Television*, London: Methuen.

Foucault, M. (1975) *Discipline and Punish: The Birth of the Prison*, London: Penguin.

Fraser, N. (1995) 'From Redistribution to Recognition? Dilemmas of Justice in a "Post Socialist" Age', *New Left Review* 212, 68–93.

Frith, S. (1983) *Sound Effects: Youth, Leisure and the Politics of Rock*, London: Constable.

Gadamer, H.-G. (1996) *Truth and Method*, London: Sheed and Ward.

Gans, H. J. (1979) *Deciding What's News: A Study of CBS Evening News, NBC Nightly News, Newsweek and Time*, New York: Pantheon.

Garnham, N. (1990) *Capitalism and Communication: Global Culture and the Economics of Information*, London: Sage.

Geertz, C. (1983) *Local Knowledge*, London: Fontana Press.

Geertz, C. (1986) 'Making Experience, Authoring Selves', in Turner, V. and Bruner, E. (eds), *The Anthropology of Experience*, Urbana: University of Illinois Press.

Geraghty, C. (1991) *Women and Soap Opera: A Study of Prime Time Soaps*, London: Polity.

Gergen, K. J. and Gergen, M. M. (1986) 'Narrative Form and the Construction of Psychological Science', in Sarbin, T. R., *Narrative Psychology: The Storied Nature of Human Conduct*, New York: Praegar.

Geurts, K. L. (2002) *Culture and the Senses: Bodily Ways of Knowing in an African Community*, Berkeley, Los Angeles, London: University of California Press.

Gillett, P. (2003) *The British Working Class in Film*, Manchester and New York: Manchester University Press.

Gillies, V. and Willig, C. (1997) ' "You Get the Nicotine and That In Your Blood": Constructions of Addiction and Control in Women's Accounts of Cigarette Smoking', *Journal of Community and Applied Social Psychology* 7: 285–301

Gilligan, C. (1982) *In a Different Voice*, Cambridge, MA: Harvard University Press.

Gitlin, T. (1978) 'Media Sociology: the Dominant Paradigm', *Theory and Society* 6, 205–53.

Gitlin, T. (1994) *Inside Prime Time*, London: Routledge.

Glaser, B. and Strauss, A. (1968) *The Discovery of Grounded Theory*, London: Weidenfeld and Nicolson.

Glasgow University Media Group (1976) *Bad News*, London: Routledge.

Glasgow University Media Group (1980) *More Bad News*, London: Routledge.

Goffman, E. (1959) *The Presentation of Self in Everyday Life*, Harmondsworth: Allen Lane.

Goffman, E. (1971) *Relations in Public: Micro-Studies of the Public Order*, New York: Basic Books.

Goffman, E. (1976) *Interaction Ritual: Essays on Face-to-Face Behavior*, New York: Doubleday.

Goldman, R. (1992) *Reading Ads Socially*, London: Routledge.

Grasseni, C. (2004) 'Video and Ethnographic Knowledge: Skilled Vision and the Practice of Breeding', in Pink, S., Kürti, L. and Afonso, A. I. (eds), *Working Images*, London: Routledge.

Gray, A. (1997) 'Learning from Experience: Cultural Studies and Feminism', in McGuigan, J. (ed.), *Cultural Methodologies*, London, Thousand Oaks, New Delhi: Sage.

Gray, A. (1999) 'Audience and Reception Research in Retrospect: The Troubles with Audiences', in Alasuutari, P. (ed.), *Rethinking the Media Audience: The New Agenda*, London: Sage.

Gray, A. (2002) *Research Practice for Cultural Studies: Ethnographic Methods and Lived Cultures*, London: Sage.

Grimshaw, A. (2001) *The Ethnographer's Eye*, Cambridge: Cambridge University Press.

Grimshaw, A. and A. Ravetz (2004) *Visualizing Anthropology*, Bristol: Intellect.

Gross, A. S. and Hoffman, M. J. (2004) 'Memory, Authority and Identity: Holocaust Studies in Light of the Wilkomirski Debate', *Biography* 27, 1: 25–47.

Grossberg, L., Nelson, C. and Treichler, P. (eds) (1992) *Cultural Studies*, New York and London: Routledge.

Guba, E. and Lincoln, Y. (1982) 'Epistemological and Methodological Bases of Naturalistic Inquiry', *Educational Communication and Technology Journal* 30: 4, 233–52.

Hacking, I. (1994) 'Memero-politics, Trauma and the Soul', *History of the Human Sciences* 7: 2, 29–52.

Hacking, I. (1995) *Rewriting the Soul: Multiple Personality and the Sciences of Memory*, Princeton: Princeton University Press.

Halbwachs, M. (1995) *On Collective Memory*, Chicago and London: University of Chicago Press (first published 1926).

Halford, S. and Knowles, C. (eds) (2005) 'More Than Words: Some Reflections on Working Visually', themed issue of *Sociological Research Online* 10: 1, available at http://www.socresonline.org.uk/10/1/knowleshalford.html.

Hall, C. (2002) *Civilising Subjects: Metropole and Colony in the English Imagination 1830–1867*, Cambridge: Polity.

Hall, S. (1973) *Encoding and Decoding in Media Discourse*, Stencilled Paper no. 7, CCCS, Birmingham: University of Birmingham.

Hall, S. (1973/1993) 'Encoding and Decoding in Television Discourse', in S. During (ed.), *The Cultural Studies Reader*, London: Routledge.

Hall, S. (1980) 'Introduction to Media Research at the Centre', in Hall, S., Hobson, D., Lowe, A. and Willis, P. (eds), *Culture, Media, Language*, London: Routledge.

Hall, S. (2001) 'Foucault: Power, Knowledge and Discourse', in Wetherell, M. et al. (eds), *Discourse Theory and Practice: A Reader*, London: Sage.

Hall, S., Critcher, C., Jefferson, T., Clarke, J. and Roberts, B. (1978) *Policing the Crisis: Mugging, the State, and Law and Order*, London: Macmillan.

Hammersley, M. (1996) 'The Relationship between Qualitative and Quantitative Research: Paradigm Loyalty versus Methodological Eclecticism' in Richardson, J. (ed.), *Handbook of Qualitative Research Methods of Psychology and the Social Sciences*, Leicester: BPS Books, pp. 159–74.

Hansen, A. (1998) 'Media Audiences: Focus Group Interviewing', in Hansen, A. et al. (eds), *Mass Communication Research Methods*, Basingstoke: Macmillan.

Hansen, A., Cottle, S., Negrine, R. and Newbold, C. (1998) *Mass Communication Research Methods*, London: Macmillan.

Haraway, D. (1991) *Simians, Cyborgs and Women: The Reinvention of Nature*, London: Free Association Books.

Haraway, D. (1997) *Modest_Witness@Second_Millenium. FemaleMan©_Meets_OncoMouse™*, New York: Routledge.

Harding, S. (1987) 'Is There a Feminist Method?' in Harding, S. (ed.), *Feminism and Methodology*, Bloomington: Indiana University Press, pp. 1–14.

Harding, S. (ed.) (1987) *Feminism and Methodology*, Bloomington: Indiana University Press.

Harding, S. (1993) 'Rethinking Standpoint Epistemology', in Alcoff, L. and Potter, E. (eds), *Feminist Epistemologies*, New York and London: Routledge.

Hardy, B. (1975) *Tellers and Listeners: The Narrative Imagination*, London: The Athlone Press.

Hartley, J. (1982) *Understanding News*, London: Methuen.

Hartley, J. (1996) *Popular Reality: Journalism, Modernity, Popular Culture*, London: Arnold.

Hartley, J. (2003) *A Short History of Cultural Studies*, London: Sage.

Haug, F. et al. (1987) *Female Sexualisation: A Collective Work of Memory*, London: Verso.

Heap, N., Thomas, R., Einon, G., Mason, R. and MacKay, H. (eds) (1995) *Information, Technology and Society*, London: Sage/Open University Press.

Heath, Stephen (1982) *The Sexual Fix*, Basingstoke: Palgrave.

Hebdige, D. (1979) *Subculture: The Meaning of Style*, London: Sage.

Hebdige, D. (1988) *Hiding in the Light*, London and New York: Comedia.

Heidegger, M. (1973) *Being and Time*, Oxford: Blackwell.

Heider, K. (1976) *Ethnographic Film*, Austin: University of Texas Press.

Herbst, S. (1998) *Reading Public Opinion: Political Actors View the Democratic Process*, Chicago: University of Chicago Press.

Herman, E. and Chomsky, N. (2002) *Manufacturing Consent*, New York: Pantheon.

Herman, E. and McChesney, R. (1997) *The Global Media: The New Missionaries of Global Capitalism*, London: Cassell.

Higson, A. (2001) 'Heritage Cinema and Television', in Morley, D. and Robins, K. (eds), *British Cultural Studies*, Oxford and New York: Oxford University Press.

Higson, A. (2003) *English Heritage, English Cinema*, Oxford and New York: Oxford University Press.

Hilliard, C. (2006) *To Exercise Our Talents*, Cambridge, MA and London: Harvard University Press.

Hills, M. (2002) *Fan Cultures*, London: Routledge.

Hirsch, M. and Spitzer, L. (2003) ' "We Would Never Have Come Without You": Generations of Nostalgia', in Hodgkin, K. and Radstone, S. (eds), *Contested Pasts: The Politics of Memory*, London: Routledge.

Hobsbawm, E. and Ranger, E. (1984) *The Invention of Tradition*, Cambridge: Cambridge University Press.

Hobson, D. (1982) *Crossroads: The Drama of a Soap Opera*, London: Methuen.

Holmes, O. W. (1861) 'Sun Painting and Sun Sculpture', *Atlantic Monthly*, July, pp. 14–15.

Hornsby-Smith, M. (1993) 'Gaining Access', in Gilbert, N. (ed.), *Researching Social Life*, London: Sage.

Hoskins, A. (2001) 'Mediating Time: The Temporal Mix of Television', *Time and Society* 10: 2, 213–33.

Howarth, D. (1998) 'Discourse Theory and Political Analysis', in Elinor, S. and Tanenbaum, E., *Research Strategies in the Social Sciences: A Guide to New Approaches*, Oxford: Oxford University Press, pp. 268–93.

Howe, R. (1988) 'Against the Quantitative-Qualitative Incompatibility Thesis, or Dogmas Die Hard', *Educational Researcher* 17: 8, 16.

Howes, D. (2005) *Empire of the Senses: The Sensory Cultures Reader*, Oxford: Berg.

Hubbard, G., Cook, A., Tester, S. and Downs, M. (2003) *Sexual Expression in Institutional Care Settings: An Interactive Multi-media CD ROM*, Stirling: University of Stirling, Department of Applied Social Science.

Hughes, D. (1995) 'The Construction of Knowledge, Objectivity and Dominance', *Women's Studies International Forum* 18: 4, 395–406.

Hunt, L. (1989) *The New Cultural History*, Berkeley: University of California Press.

Huyssen, A. (1995) *Twilight Memories: Marking Time in a Culture of Amnesia*, New York and London: Routledge.

Huyssen, A. (2000) 'Present Pasts: Media, Politics, Amnesia', *Public Culture* 12: 1, 21–38.

Inglis, F. (1993) *Cultural Studies*, Oxford: Blackwell.

Jagger, A. (1983) *Feminist Politics and Human Nature*, Brighton: Harvester.

Jameson, F. (1991) *Postmodernism, or, the Cultural Logic of State Capitalism*, London: Verso.

Jay, M. (2005) *Songs of Experience*, Berkeley, Los Angeles and London: University of California Press.

Jedlowski, P. (2001) 'Memory and Sociology: Themes and Issues', *Time and Society* 10: 1, 29–44.

Jenkins, Henry (1993) *Textual Poachers: Television Fans and Participatory Culture*, London and New York: Methuen.

Jenkins, Henry (2003) 'Interactive Audiences?', in Nightingale, V. and Ross, K. (eds), *Critical Readings: Media and Audiences*, Maidenhead: Open University Press, pp. 279–95.

Jenkins, Henry (2006) *Convergence Culture: Where Old and New Media Collide*, New York and London: New York University Press.

Johnson, H. (1996) 'What is Cultural Studies Anyway?', in J. Storey (ed.), *What is Cultural Studies? A Reader*, London: Arnold.

Johnson, R. (1978) 'Thompson, Genovese, and Socialist-Humanism', *History Workshop Journal* 6, Autumn, 79–100.

Johnson, R. et al. (1982) *Making Histories: Studies in History-Writing and Politics*, Minneapolis: University of Minnesota Press.

Jordanova, L. (2000) *History in Practice*, London: Arnold.

Katz, J. and T. J. Csordas (2003) 'Phenomenological Ethnography in Sociology and Anthropology', *Ethnography* 4, 275–88.

Kearney, C. (2003) *The Monkey's Mask*, Stoke on Trent, UK and Sterling, USA: Trentham Books.

Kearney, R. (2002) *On Stories*, London: Routledge.

Kearney, R. (2004) *On Paul Ricoeur: The Owl of Minerva*, Aldershot, UK and Burlington, VT: Ashgate.

Keightley, E. and Pickering, M. (2006) 'For the Record: Popular Music and Photography as Technologies of Memory', *European Journal of Cultural Studies* 9: 2, 149–65.

Kirkpatrick, J. (2003) *Transports of Delight: The Ricksha Arts of Bangladesh*, Bloomington and Indianapolis: Indiana University Press.

Kitzinger, J. (1994) 'The Methodology of Focus Groups: The Importance of Interaction between Research Participants', *Sociology of Health and Illness* 16: 1, 103–21.

Knapp, S. and Michaels, W. B. (1985) 'Pragmatism and Literary Theory III: A Reply to Richard Rorty, What is Pragmatism?', *Critical Inquiry* 1, 466–73.

Knorr Cetina, K. and Bruegger, U. (2002) 'Global Microstructures: the Virtual Societies of Financial Markets' in *American Journal of Sociology* 107: 4, 905–50.

Knowles, C. and Sweetman, P. (eds) (2004) *Picturing the Social Landscape*, London: Routledge.

Korobov, N. and Bamberg, M. (2004) 'Positioning a "Mature" Self in Interactive Practices: How Adolescent Males Negotiate "Physical Attraction" in Group Talk', *British Journal of Developmental Psychology* 22, 471–92.

Korobov, N. and Bamberg, M. (2006) '"*Strip Poker! They Don't Show Nothing!*": Positioning Identities in Adolescent Male Talk about a Television Game Show', in De Fina, A., Bamberg, M. and Schiffrin, D. (eds), *Talk and Identity in Narratives and Discourse*, Amsterdam: John Benjamins Publishing.

Kress, G. and Trew, T. (1978) 'Ideological Dimensions of Discourse, or: "How the *Sunday Times* Got *its* Message Across"', *Sociological Review* 26, 755–76.

Krippendorff, K. (2004) *Content Analysis: An Introduction to its Methodology*, 2nd edn, Beverley Hills, London, New Delhi: Sage.

Kruks, S. (2001) *Retrieving Experience: Subjectivity and Recognition in Feminist Politics*, Ithaca, NY: Cornell University Press.

Kuhn, A. (2002a) *Everyday Magic: Cinema and Cultural Memory*, London and New York: I. B. Tauris.

Kuhn, A. (2002b) *Family Secrets: Acts of Memory and Imagination*, London: Verso.

Kuhn, A. and McAllister, K. (eds) (2006) *Locating Memory: Photographic Acts*, Oxford and New York: Berghahn Books.

Kvale, S. (1996) *Interviews: An Introduction to Qualitative Research Interviewing*, London: Sage.

Lacey, N. (2000) *Narrative and Genre: Key Concepts in Media Studies*, London: Palgrave.

Landy, M. (ed.) (2001) *The Historical Film*, London: The Athlone Press.

Lanzmann, C. (1995) 'The Obscenity of Understanding: an Evening with Claude Lanzmann', in C. Caruth (ed.), *Trauma: Explorations in Memory*, Baltimore: Johns Hopkins Press.

Lappin, E. (1999) 'The Man with Two Heads', *Granta* 66: 9–65.

Lather, P. (1988) 'Feminist Perspective on Empowering Research Methodologies', *Women's Studies International Forum* 11: 6, 569–81.

Lawler, S. (1999) 'Getting Out and Getting Away: Women's Narratives of Class Mobility', *Feminist Review* 63, 3–24.

Lawler, S. (2000) *Mothering the Self: Mothers, Daughters, Subjects*, London: Routledge.

Lawler, S. (2008) *Identity: Sociological Perspectives*, Cambridge: Polity.

Leydesdorff, S. (1999) 'Gender and the Categories of Experienced History', *Gender and History* 11 (3): 597–611.

Lévy, Pierre (1997) *Collective Intelligence: Mankind's Emerging World in Cyberspace*, Cambridge, MA: Perseus Books, pp. 13–19.

Lewis, J. (1997) 'What Counts in Cultural Studies', *Media, Culture and Society* 19, 83–97.

Lindlof, T. R. and Taylor, B. C. (2002) *Qualitative Communication Research Methods*, London: Sage.

Lipsitz, G. (1991) *Time Passages: Collective Memory and American Popular Culture*, Minneapolis: University of Minnesota Press.

Lipsitz, G. (1994) *Dangerous Crossroads: Popular Music, Postmodernism and the Poetics of Place*, London: Verso.

Lister, M. and Wells, L. (2000) 'Seeing Beyond Belief: Cultural Studies as an Approach to Analysing the Visual', in Leeuwen, van T. and Jewitt, C. (eds), *The Handbook of Visual Analysis*, London: Sage.

Lister, R. (2003) *Citizenship: Feminist Perspectives*, Basingstoke: Palgrave Macmillan.

Livingstone, S. and Lunt, P. (1994) *Talk on Television: Audience Participation and Public Debate*, London: Routledge.

Livingstone, S., Wober, M. and Lunt, P. (1994) 'Studio Audience Discussion Programmes: An Analysis of Viewers' Preferences and Involvement', *European Journal of Communication* 9: 4, 355–80.

Locke, A. and Edwards, D. (2003) 'Bill and Monica: Memory, Emotion and Normativity in Clinton's Grand Jury Testimony', *British Journal of Social Psychology* 42, 239–56.

Loizos, P. (1993) *Innovation in Ethnographic Film*, Manchester: Manchester University Press.

Lundy, P. and McGovern, M. (2006) 'Participation, truth and partiality: participatory action research, community-based truth-telling and post-conflict transition in Northern Ireland, *Sociology* 40: 1, 71–88.

Lury, C. (1996) *Consumer Culture*, Cambridge: Polity.

MacDougall, D. (1997) 'The Visual in Anthropology', in Banks, M. and Morphy, H. (eds), *Rethinking Visual Anthropology*, London: New Haven Press.

MacDougall, D. (1998) *Transcultural Cinema*, Princeton: Princeton University Press.

MacDougall, D. (2005) *The Corporeal Image*, Princeton: Princeton University Press.

MacKenzie, J. M. (1995) *Orientalism: History, Theory and the Arts*, Manchester and New York: Manchester University Press.

Maechler, S. (2001) *The Wilkormiski Affair: A Study in Biographical Truth*, London: Picador.

Magee, B. (2003) *Clouds of Glory: A Hoxton Childhood*, London: Jonathan Cape.

Malnar, J. and Vodvarka, F. (2004) *Sensory Design*, Minneapolis, MI: University of Minnesota Press.

Manis, J. G. and Meltzer, B. N. (eds) (1972) *Symbolic Interaction: A Reader in Social Psychology*, Boston: Allyn and Bacon, Inc.

Mannheim, K. (1956) *Essays on the Sociology of Culture*, London: Routledge.

Marcus, G. and Fischer, M. (1986) *Anthropology as Cultural Critique*, Chicago and London: University of Chicago Press.

Margalit, A. (2002) *The Ethics of Memory*, Cambridge, MA and London: Harvard University Press.

Martinez, A. (ed.) (2000) *Taller de las cuatro estaciones*, Madrid: Alas de Colibri Ediciones.

Marvasti, A. B. (2004) *Qualitative Research in Sociology: An Introduction*, London: Sage.

McGuigan, J. (ed.) (1997) *Cultural Methodologies*, London: Sage.

McGuigan, J. (2006) 'The Politics of Cultural Studies and Cool Capitalism', *Cultural Politics* 2 (2): 137–58.

McLennan, G. (1995) 'Feminism, Epistemology and Postmodernism', *Sociology* 29: 3, 391–409.

McQuail, D. (1987) *Mass Communication Theory*, 2nd edn, London: Sage.

McRobbie, A. (1996) 'All the World's a Stage, Screen or Magazine: When Culture is the Logic of Late Capitalism', *Media, Culture and Society* 18 (2): 335–42.

McRobbie, A. (1997) 'The Es and the Anti-Es: New Questions for Feminism and Cultural Studies', in Ferguson, M. and Golding, P. (eds), *Cultural Studies in Question*, London: Sage.

Mead, M. (1975/1995) 'Visual Anthropology in a Discipline of Words', in Hockings, P. (ed.), *Principles of Visual Anthropology*, The Hague: Mouton.

Merton, R. K. and Kendall, P. L. (1946) 'The Focused Interview', *American Journal of Sociology* 51, 541–57, re-printed in Fielding, N. (2003) *Interviewing*, vol. 1, London: Sage.

Meyer, A. (2007) *The Child at Risk: Paedophiles, Media Responses and Public Opinion*, Manchester: Manchester University Press.

Miles, M. (1983) 'Towards a Methodology for Feminist Research', in Bowles, G. and Duelli, R. Klein (eds), *Theories of Women's Studies*, London: Routledge.

Miller, D., Kitzenger, J., Williams, K. and Beharrell, P. (1998) *The Circuits of Mass Communication*, London: Sage.

Miller, R. L. (1999) *Researching Life Stories and Family Histories*, London: Sage.

Miller, T. (ed.) (2001) *A Companion to Cultural Studies*, Malden, MA and Oxford: Blackwell.

Misztal, B. (2003) *Theories of Social Remembering*, Maidenhead and Philadelphia: Open University Press.

Mitchell, D. (1999) *Ghostwritten*, London: Hodder and Stoughton.

Mohanty, C. T. (1987) 'Feminist Encounters: Locating the Politics of Experience', *Copyright* 1, Fall, 30–44.

Morgan, D. L. (2003) 'Focus Groups', in N. Fielding (ed.), *Interviewing*, vol. 1, London: Sage.

Moriarty, E. (2005) 'Telling Identity Stories: The Routinisation of Racialisation of Irishness', *Sociological Research Online* 10, 13.

Morley, D. (1992) *Television, Audiences and Cultural Studies*, London: Routledge.

Morrison, D. (1998) *The Search for a Method: Focus Groups and the Development of Mass Communications Research*, Luton: John Libbey Media/ULP.

Munslow, A. (2003) *The New History*, Harlow: Longman.

Murdock, G. (1997). 'Thin Descriptions: Questions of Method in Cultural Analysis', in McGuigan, J. (ed.), *Cultural Methodologies*, London: Sage.

Murdock, G. and Pink, S. (2005) 'Ethnography Bytes Back: Digitalising Visual Anthropology', in *Media International Australia*, no. 116, pp. 10–23.

Murray, R. (1989) 'Fordism and Post-Fordism' and 'Benetton Britain', in Hall, S. and Jacques, M. (eds), *New Times: The Changing Face of Politics in the 1990s*, London: Lawrence and Wishart.

Nash, C. (ed.) (1990) *Narrative in Culture: The Uses of Storytelling in the Sciences, Philosophy and Literature*, London: Routledge.

Negus, K. (1992) *Producing Pop: Culture and Conflict in the Popular Music Industry*, London: Arnold.

Negus, K. (1999) *Music Genres and Corporate Cultures*, London: Routledge.

Negus, K. and Pickering, M. (2004) *Creativity, Communication and Cultural Value*, London, Thousand Oaks, New Delhi: Sage.

Nightingale, V. (1982) 'Images of Foreigners: The British Report', in Halloran, J. D. (ed.), *Young Viewers and Their Images of Foreigners*, Munich: Stiftung Prix Jeunesse, pp. 59–106.

Nightingale, V. (1983) 'International Imagery: a Study of British Children's Explanations of Other Countries', in *Media International Australia*, no. 28, May 1983, pp. 23–35.

Nightingale, V. (1992) 'Contesting Domestic Territory: Watching Rugby League on Television', in Albert Moran (ed.), *Stay Tuned: An Australian Broadcasting Reader*, Sydney: Allen and Unwin, pp. 156–66.

Nightingale, V. (1996) *Studying Audiences: The Shock of the Real*, London and New York: Routledge.

Nightingale, V. (1997) 'Ad-sick, Love-sick, Home-sick', in Dever, M. (ed.), *Australia and Asia: Cultural Transactions*, Richmond, Surrey: Curzon Press, pp. 122–42.

Nora, Pierre (1989) 'Between Memory and History: Les Lieux de Mémoire', *Representations* 26: 7–25.

Oakley, A. (1998) 'Gender, Methodology and People's Ways of Knowing: Some Problems with Feminism and the Paradigm Debate in Social Science', *Sociology* 32, 707–31.

Oakley, A. (1999) 'Paradigm Wars: Some Thoughts on a Personal and Public Trajectory', *International Journal of Social Research Methodology* 2: 3, 247–54.

Olick, J. K. and Robbins, J. (1998) 'Social Memory Studies: From "Collective Memory" to the Historical Sociology of Mnemonic Practices', *Annual Review of Sociology* 24, 105–40.

Onyx, J. and Small, J. (2001) 'Memory-Work: The Method', *Qualitative Enquiry* 7 (6): 773–86.

Pallasmaa, J. (1999/2005) 'Lived Space: Embodied Experience and Sensory Thought', in *Encounters: Architectural Essays*, Hämeenlinna, Finland: Rakennustieto Oy.

Palmer, R. (1969) *Hermeneutics*, Evanston, IL: Northwestern University Press.

Parkins, W. (2004) 'Out of Time: Fast Subjects and Slow Living', in *Time and Society* 13: 2/3, 363–82.

Partridge, Eric, *A Dictionary of Catchphrases: British and American from the Sixteenth Century to the Present Day*, London: Routledge 1986.

Peacock, A (1986) *Report of the Committee on Financing the BBC*, London: HMSO.

Philo, G. (1990) *Seeing and Believing: The Influence of Television*, London: Routledge.

Philo, G. (1999) *Message Received: Glasgow Media Group Research 1993–1998*, Harlow: Longman.

Pickering, M. (1997) *History, Experience and Cultural Studies*, Basingstoke and London: Macmillan.

Pickering, M. (1999) 'History as Horizon: Gadamer, Tradition and Critique', *Rethinking History* 3: 2, 177–95.

Pickering, M. (2001) *Stereotyping: The Politics of Representation*, Basingstoke and New York: Palgrave Macmillan.

Pickering, M. (2004) 'Experience as Horizon: Koselleck, Expectation and Historical Time', *Cultural Studies* 18: 2/3, 271–89.

Pickering, M. (2008) *Blackface Minstrelsy in Britain*, Aldershot, UK and Burlington, VT: Ashgate.

Pickering, M. and Keightley, E. (2006) 'The Modalities of Nostalgia', in *Current Sociology* 54 (6): 919–41.

Pidgeon, N. (1996) 'Grounded Theory: Theoretical Background', in Richardson, J. T. E. (ed.), *Handbook of Qualitative Research Methods*, Leicester: BPS Books.

Pini, M. and Walkerdine, V. (2005) 'Girls on film: video-diaries as "auto-ethnographies"', www.women.it/cyberarchive/files/Pini.htm (accessed on 12 May 2007).

Pink, S. (2004) *Home Truths*, Oxford: Berg.

Pink, S. (2006) *The Future of Visual Anthropology*, Oxford: Routledge.

Pink, S. (2007) *Doing Visual Ethnography*, London: Sage.

Pink, S. (forthcoming) 'Walking with video', *Visual Studies* 22: 3.

Pink, S., Kurti, L. and Afonso, A. I. (eds) (2004) *Working Images*, London: Routledge.

Pink, S. and A. Martinez Perez, M. (2006) 'A fitting "social model": culturally locating telemadre.com', in *Home Cultures* 3: 1, 63–86.

Platt, J. (2002) 'The History of the Interview', in Gubrium, J. F. and Holstein, J. A. (eds), *Handbook of Interview Research: Context and Method*, London: Sage.

Plummer, K. (2001) *Documents of Life 2*, London: Sage.

Pole, C. (ed.) (2004) *Seeing is Believing? Approaches to Visual Research*, Studies in Qualitative Methodology, vol. 7, Elsevier Science.

Potter, J. and Wetherell, M. (1987) *Discourse and Social Psychology: Beyond Attitudes and Behaviour*, London: Sage.

Prager, J. (2000) *Presenting the Past: Psychoanalysis and the Sociology of Misremembering*, Cambridge, MA: Harvard University Press.

Probyn, E. (1993) *Sexing the Self: Gendered Positions in Cultural Studies*, London and New York: Routledge.

Radstone, S. (2000) 'Working with Memory: An Introduction', in Radstone, S. (ed.), *Memory and Methodology*, Oxford and New York: Berg.

Reinharz, S. (1984) *On Becoming a Social Scientist*, New Jersey: Transaction Books.

Reinharz, S. (1992) *Feminist Methods in Social Research*, New York: Oxford University Press.

Ricoeur, P. (1980) 'Narrative and time', *Critical Inquiry* 7: 1, 169–90.

Ricoeur, P. (1981) *Hermeneutics and the Human Sciences*, Cambridge: Cambridge University Press.

Ricoeur, P. (1991) 'Life in Quest of Narrative', in Wood, D. (ed.), *On Paul Ricoeur: Narrative and Interpretation*, London: Routledge.

Ricoeur, P. (2004a) 'Existence and Hermeneutics', in Ricoeur, P., *The Conflict of Interpretations: Essays in Hermeneutics*, London: Continuum.

Ricoeur, P. (2004b) *Memory, History, Forgetting*, Chicago and London: University of Chicago Press.

Roberts, B. (2001) *Biographical Research*, Maidenhead and New York: Open University Press.

Roberts, G. and Taylor, P. M. (eds) (2001) *The Historian, Television and Television History*, Luton: University of Luton Press.

Rojek, C. (2002) *Stuart Hall*, Cambridge, UK and Malden, MA: Polity.

Rosaldo, R. (1986) 'From the Door of His Tent: The Fieldworker and the Inqvisitor', in Clifford, J. and Marcus, G. E. (eds), *Writing Culture: The Poetics and Politics of Ethnography*, Berkeley and Los Angeles: University of California Press, pp. 77–97.

Roscoe, J., Marshall, H. and Gleeson, K. (1995) 'The Television Audience: A Reconsideration of the Taken-for-Granted Terms "Active", "Social" and "Critical"', *European Journal of Communication* 10: 1, March, 87–108.

Rose, G. (2001) *Visual Methodologies*, London: Sage.

Rosenstone, R. A. (2006) *History on Film/Film on History*, Harlow, London and New York: Pearson Longman.

Ruby, J. (2000) *Picturing Culture: Explorations of Film and Anthropology*, Chicago: University of Chicago Press.

Ruby, J. (2004–6) *Oak Park Stories*, CD ROM series, distributed by Documentary Educational Resources, USA.

Ruby, J. and Chalfen, R. (1974) 'The Teaching of Visual Anthropology at Temple', *The Society for the Anthropology of Visual Communication Newsletter* 5: 3, 5–7.

Said, E. (1979) *Orientalism*, London: Routledge.

Samuel, R. (1994) *Theatres of Memory*, vol. 1: *Past and Present in Contemporary Culture*, London: Verso.

Schiller, H. (1989) *Culture Inc. – The Corporate Takeover of Public Expression*, Oxford: Oxford University Press.

Schlesinger, P. (1987) *Putting Reality Together*, London: Methuen.

Schlesinger, P. and Tumber, H. (1994) *Reporting Crime: The Media Politics of Criminal Justice*, Oxford: Clarendon Press.

Schroder, K. C. (1999) 'The Best of Both Worlds? Media Audience Research between Rival Paradigms', in P. Alasuutari (ed.), *Rethinking the Media Audience: The New Agenda*, London: Sage.

Segal, L. (1987) *Is the Future Female?*, London: Virago.

Shusterman, R. (1992) *Pragmatist Aesthetics*, Oxford, UK and Cambridge, MA: Blackwell.

Simonds, W. (1992) *Women and Self-Help Culture: Reading Between the Lines*, New Brunswick, NJ: Rutgers University Press.

Skeggs, B. (1995) 'Theorising, Ethics and Representation in Feminist Epistemology', in Skeggs, B. (ed.), *Feminist Cultural Theory*, Manchester: Manchester University Press.

Smith, J. (1983) 'Quantitative Versus Qualitative Research: An Attempt to Clarify the Issue, *Educational Researcher* 12: 3, 6–13.

Sofaer, J. (2007) 'Introduction: Materiality and Identities', in Sofaer, J. (ed.), *Material Identities*, Oxford: Blackwell.

Solow, R. (1988) 'Comments from inside economics', in Klamer, A. et al. (eds), *The Consequences of Economic Rhetoric*, Cambridge: Cambridge University Press.

Somers, M. R. and Gibson, G. D. (1994) 'Reclaiming the Epistemological "Other": Narrative and the Social Constitution of Identity', in Calhoun, C. (ed.), *Social Theory and the Politics of Identity*, Cambridge, MA: Blackwell.

Stabile, C. A. (2006) *White Victims, Black Villains*, New York and London: Routledge.

Stanley, L. (1992) *The Auto/biographical I*, Manchester: Manchester University Press.

Stanley, L. and Wise, S. (1983) *Breaking Out: Feminist Consciousness and Feminist Research*, London: Routledge.

Steedman, C. (1989) *Landscape for a Good Woman: A Story of Two Lives*, London: Virago.

Steedman, C. (1992) *Past Tenses*, London: Rivers Oram Press.

Steedman, C. (2001) *Dust*, Manchester: Manchester University Press.

Steedman, C. (2005) 'Archival Methods', in Griffin, G. (ed.), *Research Methods in English Studies*, Edinburgh: Edinburgh University Press.

Stef Slembrouck, 'What is the meaning of discourse analysis', http://bank.rug.ac.be/da/da.htm (accessed on 1 August 2005).

Steinberg, M. P. (1996) 'Cultural History and Cultural Studies', in Nelson, C. and Gaonkar, D. P. (eds), *Disciplinarity and Dissent in Cultural Studies*, New York and London: Routledge.

Steinberg, M. P. (1999) *Fighting Words: Working-Class Formation, Collective Action, and Discourse in Early Nineteenth-Century England*, New York: Cornell University Press.

Steinmetz, G. (ed.) (2005) *The Politics of Method in the Human Sciences: Positivism and Its Epistemological Others*, Durham, NC: Duke University Press.

Stole, I. L. (2006) *Advertising on Trial*, Urbana and Chicago: University of Illinois Press.

Stoller, P. (1992) *The Cinematic Griot: The Cinema of Jean Roach*, Chicago and London: University of Chicago Press.

Stoller, P. (1997) *Sensuous Scholarship*, Philadelphia, PA: University of Pennsylvania Press.

Storey, J. (1996) *Cultural Studies and the Study of Popular Culture: Theories and Methods*, Edinburgh: Edinburgh University Press.

Storey, J. (1999) *Cultural Consumption and Everyday Life*, London: Arnold.

Stubbs, Michael (1996) *Text and Corpus Analysis: Computer Assisted Studies of Language and Culture*, Oxford: Blackwell.

Tagg, John (1988) *The Burden of Representation: Essays on Photographies and Histories*, Basingstoke: Macmillan.

Terdiman, R. (1993) *Present Past: Modernity and the Memory Crisis*, New York: Cornell University Press.

Thornton, S. (1995) *Clubcultures: Music, Media and Subcultural Capital*, Cambridge: Polity Press.

Threadgold, T., 'Cultural Studies, Critical Theory and Critical Discourse Analysis: Histories, Remembering and Futures', *Linguistik online*, 14, 2/03 (accessed on 6 October 2005).

Throop, J. (2003) 'Articulating Experience', *Anthropological Theory*, 3: 2, 219–41.

Tolnay, S. E. and Beck, E. M. (1995) *Festival of Violence: An Analysis of Southern Lynchings, 1882–1930*, Urbana, IL: University of Illinois Press.

Tunstall (1971) *Journalists at Work*, London: Sage.

Turner, V. and Bruner, E. (eds) (1986) *The Anthropology of Experience*, Urbana and Chicago: University of Illinois Press.

Van de Berg, A. (2006) Review of 'The Politics of Method in the Human Sciences: Positivism and Its Epistemological Others', *Canadian Journal of Sociology Online*, May/June, http://www.csjonline.ca/reviews/politicsmethod.html (accessed on 30 January 2007).

Voigts-Virchow, E. (ed.) (2004) *Janespotting and Beyond: British Heritage Retrovisions since the Mid-1990s*, Tübingen: Gunter Narr Verlag.

Walkerdine, Valerie (1990) 'Video replay: families, films and fantasy', in Valerie Walkerdine (ed.), *Schoolgirl Fictions*, London and New York: Verso.

Warnke, G. (1987) *Gadamer: Hermeneutics, Tradition and Reason*, Cambridge: Polity Press.

Weissberg, L. (1999) 'Introduction', in Ben-Amos, D. and Weissberg, L. (eds), *Cultural Memory and the Construction of Identity*, Detroit: Wayne State University Press.

Wertsch, J. V. (2002) *Voices of Collective Remembering*, Cambridge: Cambridge University Press.

Wetherell, M., Taylor, S. and Yates, S. J. (2001) *Discourse Theory and Practice: A Reader*, Milton Keynes: Open University Press.

White, H. (1996) 'Commentary', *History of the Human Sciences* 9: 4, 123–38.

Williamson, J. (1978) *Decoding Advertisements*, London: Marion Boyars.

Willig, Carla (ed.) (1999) *Applied Discourse Analysis: Social and Psychological Interventions*, Buckingham: Open University Press.

Wolf, J. (2004) *Harnessing the Holocaust: The Politics of Memory in France*, Stanford, CA: Stanford University Press.

Wring, D. (2006) 'Focus Group Follies? Qualitative Research and British Labour Party Strategy', *Journal of Political Marketing* 5: 4, 71–97.

Wring, D. (2005) *The Politics of Marketing the Labour Party*, Basingstoke and London: Palgrave Macmillan.

Notes on Contributors

Martin Barker is Professor of Film and Television Studies at the University of Wales, Aberystwyth. He has published thirteen books of research, including (with Roger Sabin) *The Lasting of the Mohicans: History of an American Myth* (University Press of Mississippi, 1996); (edited, with Julian Petley) *Ill Effects: the Media Violence Debate* (Routledge, 1997 and 2001); (with Kate Brooks) *Knowing Audiences: Judge Dredd, its Friends, Fans and Foes* (University of Luton Press, 1998) which presented the findings of an eighteen-month ESRC-funded research project, and (with a contribution from Thomas Austin) *From Antz To Titanic: Reinventing Film Analysis* (Pluto, 2000). In 2001 he published the findings of a second ESRC project on the reception of David Cronenberg's *Crash* in Britain in 1996–7 (*The Crash Controversy: Censorship Campaigns and Film Reception*, Wallflower Press 2001, co-researched and written with Jane Arthurs and Ramaswami Harindranath). His most recent book, *Watching The Lord of the Rings* (co-edited with Ernest Mathijs, Peter Lang, 2007), presents the main findings of the (ESRC-funded) world audience project on the reception of the Jackson/Tolkien movies. He is joint editor of the online journal *Participations*, which is devoted to audience and reception studies.

Dr Aeron Davis is a Senior Lecturer and Director of the MA in Political Communications in the Department of Media and Communications, Goldsmiths College. His research interests include promotional culture, media sociology and news production; public relations, politics and political communications; markets and economic sociology/cultural economy. He has conducted research on communications at Westminster, at the London Stock Exchange, amongst the major political parties and across the trade union movement. He has published on each of these topics in journals and edited collections, and is the author of *Public Relations Democracy* (Manchester University Press, 2002) and *The Mediation of Power* (Routledge, 2007). He is currently researching the influence of media on decision-making in politics and is also working on a book on the rise of promotional culture for Polity Press.

Dr David Deacon is Reader in Media and Politics in the Department of Social Sciences at Loughborough University. He is co-author of *Researching Communications: A Practical Guide to Methods in Media and Cultural Analysis* (2007, with Michael Pickering, Peter Golding and Graham Murdock) and has published widely in the field of media sociology and political communication. Other books include *Taxation and Representation: The Media, Political Communication and the Poll Tax* (1994, with Peter Golding) and *Mediating Social Science* (1998, with Alan Bryman and Natalie Fenton). He is currently completing an investigation of British media reporting of the Spanish Civil War.

Dr Emily Keightley received her doctorate in 2007 from the Department of Social Sciences at Loughborough University, where she was researching media and memory in modernity. Her work to date has been concerned particularly with women's uses of the past and with how women draw on both vernacular and media forms of social remembering and historical reconstruction. Ongoing research will broaden this focus to incorporate the ways in which media and memory are implicated and utilised in men's lives. She has previously written articles on the contrary dimensions of nostalgia in forms of personal and public relations to the past (*Current Sociology*) and photography and phonography as vehicles of memory (*European Journal of Cultural Studies*; *Media History*).

Dr Steph Lawler is Senior Lecturer in Sociology at Newcastle University. Her publications include *Mothering the Self: Mothers, Daughters, Subjects* (Routledge, 2000) and *Identity: Sociological Perspectives* (Polity, 2008).

Dr Anneke Meyer is a Lecturer in Sociology and Cultural Studies at Manchester Metropolitan University. Her research interests also lie in media, social and cultural theory, discourse analysis, governance, childhood, sexuality and parenting. Her publications include *The Child at Risk: Paedophiles, Media Responses and Public Opinion* (Manchester University Press, 2007).

Dr Virginia Nightingale is Associate Professor in the School of Communication Arts at the University of Western Sydney, Australia. Her research interests include media and audience research; the social and cultural implications of media convergence; the emergence of new media forms, such as camera phone images and online image archives; the new audience formations of digital and mobile media cultures; and the audience politics of the media. She is the author of *Studying Audiences: The Shock of the Real* (1996);

Media and Audiences: New Perspectives (2003) and *Critical Readings: Media and Audiences* (2003), both with Karen Ross; and *New Media Worlds: Challenges for Convergence* (2007), an anthology edited with Tim Dwyer.

Michael Pickering is Professor of Media and Cultural Analysis in the Department of Social Sciences at Loughborough University. He has published in the areas of cultural history and the sociology of culture as well as media analysis and theory. His recent books include *History, Experience and Cultural Studies* (1997); *Researching Communications* (1999/2007, with David Deacon, Peter Golding and Graham Murdock); *Stereotyping: The Politics of Representation* (2001); *Creativity, Communication and Cultural Value* (2004, co-written with Keith Negus); and *Beyond a Joke: The Limits of Humour* (2005, co-edited with Sharon Lockyer). He has recently completed a historical study, *Blackface Minstrelsy in Britain*, to be published by Ashgate in 2008.

Dr Sarah Pink is Reader in Social Anthropology in the Department of Social Sciences at Loughborough University. Her research interests are gender, visual and media anthropology, anthropology of the senses and applied anthropology. Her books about visual methodologies include *Doing Visual Ethnography* (2001/2007) and *The Future of Visual Anthropology: Engaging the Senses* (2006). She has used visual methods and media in a number of projects, including the work discussed in her books *Women and Bullfighting* (1997) and *Home Truths* (2004). Her current research is about the development of the Cittàslow (Slow City) movement in Britain.

Index